ADMIRAL
WILLIAM SHEPHERD BENSON
First Chief of Naval Operations

ADMIRAL
WILLIAM SHEPHERD BENSON
First Chief of Naval Operations

MARY KLACHKO
with
DAVID F. TRASK

Foreword by Arleigh A. Burke

NAVAL INSTITUTE PRESS
ANNAPOLIS, MARYLAND

V
63
.B46
K55
1986

Library of Congress Cataloging-in-Publication Data
Klachko, Mary.
   Admiral William Shepherd Benson, first chief of
naval operations.

   Bibliography: p.
   1. Benson, William Shepherd, 1855–1932.
2. Admirals—United States—Biography.
3. United States. Navy—Biography. I. Trask,
David F. II. Title.
V63.B46K55 1986   359′.0092′4 [B]   87-1530
ISBN 0-87021-035-1

Printed in the United States of America

To

My mother, Helena Witrak Klachko,
and
My father, Michael Klachko,

who enlisted in the United States Army and sailed with the first contingent of the American Expeditionary Force on 14 June 1917, recipient of the Mexican Border Service Medal, the World War I Victory Medal with a battle clasp for the Aisne-Marne, and the Purple Heart.

CONTENTS

ILLUSTRATIONS

PREFACE

After World War I, most leading participants in the events of those times published memoirs, but one who did not was Admiral William Shepherd Benson, among the most important naval personages of the day. On 15 May 1915 Benson became the first chief of naval operations of the United States Navy, a post he held until 25 September 1919. On 13 March 1920 he began a tour of duty at the United States Shipping Board, serving as its chairman until 14 June 1921 and thereafter as a commissioner until 9 June 1928.

By relating the story of Admiral Benson's contribution to the United States Navy, this biography fills a gap in naval history. Benson organized the Office of the Chief of Naval Operations, which the secretary of the navy at the time, Josephus Daniels, had strongly opposed, and which the powerful bureau chiefs in the Navy Department greatly resented. Thereafter Benson played a leading role in three exceedingly important events: the naval contributions of the United States to the victory at sea between 1917 and 1919, the negotiation of naval questions at the Paris peace conference in 1919, and the attempt to create a strong American merchant marine after World War I.

I became interested in these questions as I prepared my doctoral dissertation at Columbia University on "Anglo-American Naval Competition, 1918–1922," with Professor William T. R. Fox. My research for the dissertation led me to contact Rear Admiral Ernest M. Eller, USN (Ret.), the director of Naval History, Office of Naval Operations, Department of the Navy. He believed that Admiral Benson's "great services to our country need[ed] recording." I have sought to accomplish this task.

This biography treats seven topics: Admiral Benson as a naval officer; Benson's efforts to develop the Office of Naval Operations and the position of chief of naval operations; the preparation of the United States Navy for service during World War I; the contributions of the United States Navy to the victory of 1918; Benson's role in the development of the navy as an instrument of diplomacy during the Paris peace conference; his efforts to build a powerful merchant marine during the 1920s; and the human side of the man who championed the concept of a "navy second to none."

I would first like to express my appreciation to Admiral E. M. Eller. Without his encouragement, I would not have undertaken the present work. Vice Admiral Edwin B. Hooper, USN (Ret.), who followed Admiral Eller as director of Naval History, shared his predecessor's interest in Benson. I express deep appreciation for his assistance. I am grateful also to Rear Admiral John D. Kane, Admiral Hooper's successor, for his support.

With special gratitude I acknowledge the cooperation of Admiral Benson's children: Mrs. Herman F. Krafft, Commodore Howard H. J. Benson, USN (Ret.), and Rear Admiral Francis Wyse Benson, USN (Ret.). They volunteered helpful insights into the life of their distinguished father that no one else could have provided. I am particularly indebted to Commodore Benson for the privilege of having exclusive use of Admiral Benson's papers in the course of my research and for allowing me to use family photographs. I profoundly regret that neither of Admiral Benson's sons lived to see the publication of this biography. Mrs. Krafft, at the age of 105, remains a strong link to the Benson family memoirs.

I had the good fortune to interview outstanding personalities in both the United States and Great Britain who participated in World War I, as well as people who were associated with important historical actors of those days. Professor Charles Seymour gave me a letter of introduction to Sir William Wiseman, who headed British intelligence in the United States during the war. He in turn introduced me to Sir Arthur Willert and Sir Campbell Stuart, members of the British Mission in the United States during 1917–18. Mrs. Franklin D. Roosevelt provided a letter of introduction to Lord Elibank. On the basis of these contacts, I was able to establish contact with Sir Norman Angell; I. A. D. Bremner, associate editor of the *Shipping World* and the grandson of Sir Archibald Hurd; Admiral of the Fleet Lord A. Ernle Chatfield; Lady Isabella Gamble Geddes, the wife of Ambassador Sir Auckland Geddes; Geoffrey Harmsworth; Commander P. K. Kemp; Lord Killearn; Sir Stephen King-Hall; and Mrs. Wickham Steed. Their conversation, correspondence, and permission to examine private papers were of great benefit.

A number of retired naval officers who were part of the Benson era were most generous. I conferred with and corresponded with Admiral William Veazie Pratt, Admiral Benson's assistant chief of naval operations. Rear Admiral Andrew Francis Carter, Benson's aide, shared his recollections. Rear Admiral Harold C. Train and Captain Richard D. Gatewood, despite ill health, conveyed their impressions of how Benson worked. Rear Admiral Royal E. Ingersoll, who was acquainted with Benson from his youth and had been Benson's chief of naval communications in the Navy Department, kindly conveyed his views of Benson.

Mrs. Theodore Roosevelt, Jr., granted access to her late husband's papers while they were still in her possession at the family's historic estate in Oyster Bay, New York, and she extended enjoyable hospitality. I deeply appreciate the sincere cooperation of Mrs. William S. Sims, who not only granted access to her husband's papers but also speeded their deposit at the Naval Historical Foundation so that I could have quick access to them. I also benefited from an opportunity to interview Mrs. Alice Roosevelt Longworth, "the grand lady of Washington," who related many stories about the personalities of the Benson era.

Many staff members in various depositories and libraries provided assistance over the years. I apologize to those I may neglect to mention.

Dr. Dean C. Allard, head of the navy's Operational Archives Branch in the Naval Historical Center and curator of the General Board Records, was especially helpful, as were members of his staff: Mildred Mayeux, Barbara Gilmore, and Bernard F. Cavalcante, all archivists, and Kathleen M. Lloyd, historian. Harry John at the Federal Records Center in Suitland, Maryland, responded efficiently to requests for personnel records. The former chief of the Manuscript Division, Library of Congress, Dr. John Broderick, lent invaluable support to my investigation of many collections in his charge. I acknowledge also several members of this staff: William H. Mobley, Roger Preston, Russel Smith, Joseph Sullivan, Jr., and Ruth S. Nicolson.

Anthony Nicolosi, then curator of the Naval Historical Collection of the Mahan Library at the U.S. Naval War College in Newport, Rhode Island, granted access to the papers of Admiral William V. Pratt, which are deposited at that institution. Carolyn Jakeman of the Houghton Library, Harvard University, helped me to examine the Walter Hines Page Papers and the William Phillips Journals. Judith Schiff, chief research archivist at the Sterling Library, Yale University, gave able assistance as I consulted the Edward M. House Collection. The staff of Special Collections at Columbia University, and Elizabeth Mason at the Oral History Reseach Office of Columbia University, guided my work at their organizations.

Very important materials were made available in Great Britain because of permission from Her Britannic Majesty's Stationery Office. I warmly acknowledge the support of the British Museum, the Public Record Office, and the Naval Library, Ministry of Defense, all in London. A. J. P. Taylor granted permission to examine the Papers of David Lloyd George and Andrew Bonar Law at the Beaverbrook Library in London. There, Rosemary Brooks, archivist, was most supportive.

Many scholars and fellow researchers showed interest in my work and lent assistance of various kinds. Professor Arthur J. Marder helped arrange a loan of the microfilmed letters and memoirs of Admiral Rosslyn Wemyss, which are located at the University of California at Irvine. Rear Admiral John D. Hayes, USN (Ret.), provided copies of Admiral Benson's letters to Admiral Stephen B. Luce. Colonel Robert D. Heinl, Jr., USMC (Ret.), provided information about Admiral Benson's relations with the Marine Corps. Captain Daniel J. Costello gave me permission to read his doctoral dissertation, "Planning for War: A History of the General Board of the Navy, 1900–1914," and discussed many aspects of the period with me. Dr. Roberto E. Socas allowed me to read his dissertation on "France, Naval Armaments, and Naval Disarmament: 1918–1922." Dr. Thomas Hone made available a section of his study of aviation developments after World War I.

I consulted the works of many scholars, and found the works of the following authorities especially informative: William R. Braisted, Richard D. Challener, George T. Davis, Arthur S. Link, Arthur J. Marder, Elting E. Morison, Stephen Roskill, Harold and Margaret Sprout, Seth P. Tillman, David F. Trask, Archibald D. Turnbull, and Clifford L. Lord.

I am especially indebted to those who read the manuscript: Dr. Dean C. Allard; Admiral Arleigh A. Burke, USN (Ret.); Captain Daniel J. Costello, USN (Ret.); Rear Admiral Robert M. Griffin, USN (Ret.); Vice Admiral Edwin B. Hooper, USN (Ret.); Commander Desmond Thompson, RN (Ret.); Elizabeth Galway Thompson, formerly with the British Navy League; and Eva Piddubcheshen, who also helped to organize material and verify footnotes.

While writing this biography, I encountered serious medical problems. I owe more than I can repay to my physicians, Drs. Murray Rogers and Norman J. Nichols, and my surgeons, Drs. John Vieta and Felician M. Steichen, of Lenox Hill Hospital, New York City, who twice saved my life. My nurse and friend Adelina Granda shortened and brightened the period of my convalescence.

Two loyal friends, the Very Reverend Mother Marie Dolzycka of the Sisters of St. Basil the Great, and Eva Piddubcheshen, shared my joys and sorrows. Such friends are rare; I am truly blessed. Isabel M. Taylor provided beautiful accommodations during my many visits to Washington, D.C.

Finally, I thank my colleague and friend Dr. David F. Trask, chief historian, U.S. Army Center of Military History, who offered useful counsel at several stages in the preparation of this book. Dr. Trask also helped draft the final version, but I alone accept responsibility for its content.

FOREWORD

In this book, Mary Klachko presents an authoritative biography of William Shepherd Benson, the first chief of naval operations. Since I had the good fortune of serving in the same post four decades later, Dr. Klachko's account of Admiral Benson's overall career, and the course he followed in shaping the Office of the Chief of Naval Operations, is of great personal interest. I hope that other readers will share my admiration for Dr. Klachko's fine study of a great naval leader.

Because Admiral Benson did not write his memoirs and has not, until now, been the subject of a biography, his contributions may not have been fully appreciated. For that reason, this volume is especially welcome. One of the many important points made by the author is her contention that Admiral Benson's conceptions of naval policy did not derive from anti-British sentiments, as some authors have stated in the past. Instead, Dr. Klachko argues that the admiral's actions reflected his sturdy American nationalism and dedicated commitment to the well-being of the United States Navy.

When the Congress provided for a chief of naval operations in 1915, many critics considered this decision a step toward the Prussianization of the armed forces, a reference to the undue powers that the German general staff exercised at the time. Among those who held this view in Washington, none was more vociferous than the secretary of the navy, Josephus Daniels of North Carolina. Nevertheless, his selection of Benson, a largely unknown captain, to serve as the first chief of naval operations, assured the development of an institution that won the confidence of the Wilson administration and achieved the broad goals of those seeking to reform the navy's organization. Today it is difficult to dispute the claim that Daniels made a significant contribution to naval reform by placing Benson in the Navy Department when he did.

In 1915, Admiral Benson energetically set himself to the task of determining the responsibilities of his new post and making the exceedingly important decisions that were forced upon him as a consequence of the Great War that had begun in Europe during the previous year. Dr. Klachko has searched diligently for the widely scattered information that allows her to make authoritative interpretations of Benson's contributions to the building of an effective and respected naval organization and to the development of the highest post open to professional naval officers.

All too little is still known about the American merchant marine and its essential role for the nation's security. Dr. Klachko's chronicle of Admiral Benson's long and dedicated service after World War I as a member of the United States Shipping Board constitutes an important contribution to our knowledge of the merchant marine.

Admiral Benson served in the navy during the transition of that service from wood and sail to steel and steam. He knew well the trials of voyages on the old wooden vessels under sail, but he proved fully capable of participating in creating the powerful modern navy that first came into view during the era of World War I. For this reason he deserves an honored place in the pantheon of Americans who have served with great distinction in the nation's sea services.

I congratulate the Naval Institute Press for making this work available and thank the noted historian Dr. David F. Trask for his generous and highly professional contributions in preparing the manuscript for publication. Above all, however, Dr. Klachko deserves our gratitude for telling Admiral Benson's story with a combination of dignity, sympathy, and scholarly fidelity, and for exploring both the personal and professional sides of a memorable sailor. Her volume is a notable addition to the literature on modern naval history.

ARLEIGH A. BURKE
Admiral, U.S. Navy

ADMIRAL
WILLIAM SHEPHERD BENSON
First Chief of Naval Operations

CHAPTER I

TWENTY-EIGHT YEARS IN
THE OLD NAVY
1872–1900

William Shepherd Benson, destined to become the first chief of naval operations, was born into a comfortable Southern family near Macon, Georgia, on 25 September 1855, just six years before the Civil War. His forebears were English in origin, and some were from the North, among them Colonel Thomas Aspinwall, a veteran of the American Revolution who had commanded a fort at Sewell's Point in Massachusetts. Benson's father, Richard Aaron Benson, attended Randolph Macon College. His mother, Catherine Brewer Benson, was the first woman to graduate from Georgia Female College, now Wesleyan Female College of Macon, where her diploma has been preserved since 1888, not only as the initial degree conferred by this institution, but also as the first degree ever granted to a woman by a chartered college.

The Civil War transformed the family's situation. William's father and oldest brother immediately joined the Confederate forces, leaving the rest of the family to cope with growing adversity. In 1864 the family experienced General William T. Sherman's march through Georgia, a visitation, Benson later recalled, that "completely demoralized" his region, turning life into a "struggle for existence." A battle of wits developed between the invaders and the local women, children, and blacks. There were moments "when we hardly knew where the next meal would come from."[1]

Fortunately, William's father returned from the war in good health, and his mother retained her genial disposition and optimistic outlook as the family sought to rebuild. A detachment of Union troops established a headquarters near his grandfather's old colonial home, an event that helped the family to survive the early postwar years. The Bensons had managed to retain some milk cows by driving them into a swamp. Sales of milk to the Yankees permitted purchase of the "absolute necessities of life and some coffee and sugar." Half a century later, Admiral Benson found himself seated next to the Civil War officer James H. Wilson at a banquet. He said: "I remember you, General, more distinctly than you remember me. After you captured Macon, in the spring of 1865, you established your headquarters next to my grandfather's mansion. And there I called on you to get permission to sell milk to your soldiers."[2] It proved difficult to reestablish the Benson plantation, given the promise to award former slaves "forty acres and a mule." Fortunately, the boys rounded up some stray horses and mules, and their father managed to employ a few former slaves. William and his brothers worked the farm. The children did not attend school, because no school was operating in the bleak countryside. Parental tutoring and reading in Richard Benson's library served for education. Five years after the war, the Bensons moved to Macon, where William finally entered Alexander High School.

Less than two years later, when William learned of an opportunity to gain admission to the United States Naval Academy in Annapolis, Maryland, he decided to seek appointment. First, however, he consulted his father, the former rebel, who gave his blessing. Armed with a medical certificate, a school certificate, and a recommendation from his parish pastor, William presented himself for a competitive examination. His principal noted that the candidate had been at school "little more than one year" and that he had studied arithmetic, geography, algebra, Latin, and English grammar. However, "his punctuality and conscientiousness in discharge of school duties have secured the kind esteem of his teachers." The pastor saw William as an individual who was aspiring to "make his mark in the world. . . . No more worthy young man can be found . . . to represent his State . . . at that National Institution."[3]

Benson satisfied his congressman, Thomas J. Speer, who arranged for him to take the entrance examination prerequisite for admission to the Naval Academy, but some time passed before Benson was able to begin his studies. When he presented himself at the Naval Academy, Benson failed tests in mathematics and penmanship. Disappointed but determined, he called on Congressman Speer in Washington, explaining that a lack of formal schooling accounted for his difficulties. He requested reappointment so that he could take another entrance examination in September. Speer proved understanding. "You'll have it, my boy," he told Benson. "I'll appoint you again in the fall, if you think you can pass the examination then." This time Benson passed the entrance examination. Secretary of the Navy George M. Robeson appointed him on 23 September 1872. He was among the first men from the South to enter the Naval Academy after the Civil War.[4]

William Shepherd Benson in Macon, Georgia, 1871.

More vicissitudes lay ahead; Benson failed to pass examinations in algebra and geometry at the end of his first year, and once again he was forced to seek a special dispensation. After resigning on 23 June 1873 to avoid having a record of being "dropped" from the Naval Academy, Benson pleaded his case to the superintendent at Annapolis, Rear Admiral John L. Worden, who suggested that he ask Congressman Speer to reappoint him again. Unfortunately, the Republican Speer had died, and his successor, a Democrat, had "friends of his own to reward." The tireless Benson then decided to appeal to Secretary Robeson, who was vacationing at Rye Beach, New Hampshire. Robeson proved sympathetic. He rescinded Benson's resignation, and on 29 September he

Richard Aaron Benson, Shepherd's father.

allowed the erstwhile cadet to reenter the Naval Academy as a member of the Fourth Class.[5]

Benson thus joined the first group of cadets required to serve four years at the academy and two at sea before receiving a commission. This time he managed to remain in good standing, although he never excelled in the classroom: in June 1877 he finished forty-third in a class

Catherine Elizabeth Benson, Shepherd's mother.

of forty-six. Not lacking spirit, Benson received demerits for infractions such as laughing in ranks, "skylarking" in the corridors, talking in his room after taps, failing to clear his room of disorder before early inspection, playing football in the living quarters, and throwing snowballs in the passageway. He was popular with his fellow cadets, and his reputation for fair play earned him the nickname Judge.

At an infantry drill in the spring of 1876, Benson noticed Mary Augusta Wyse among the spectators. It was a case of love at first sight. Benson wrote later: "I felt that I could not spend life without her, though I did not know who she was, where she came from, or anything at all about her." Benson learned her identity from her escort to the drill, and when he came upon her a few days later as she strolled through the grounds of the academy with a staff member of his acquaintance, Benson seized the opportunity to be introduced to Miss Wyse. A few months later, in September, the couple became engaged. Mary was quite familiar with the military; her father was Colonel Francis O. Wyse, who later attained the rank of general, and her mother, Mary Eliza Pope, was the daughter of Commodore John Pope, U.S. Navy. Three years later, William, who was a Protestant, and Mary, who was Catholic, were married in the drawing room of the Wyse family residence in Deer Park, Maryland, near Washington, D.C. Father Edmund Q. S. Waldron, pastor of the Roman Catholic parish church in Pikesville, Maryland, performed the ceremony on 6 August 1879.

During the two years between his graduation and marriage, Benson began his naval career. His first tour of duty was on the screw sloop *Hartford*. Dissatisfied with his academic standing, Benson took his textbooks to sea as his ship visited Rio de Janeiro and other Latin ports. At the end of this voyage, Lieutenant Commander P. F. Harrington, the commander of the *Hartford*, reported to the secretary of the navy, Richard W. Thompson, that Benson demonstrated "excellent capacity" as well as "general superiority of intelligence and fidelity over any peculiar abilities and advantages." He thought Benson's "habits and moral character . . . without reproach." On New Year's Day, 1879, Benson transferred to the *Essex*, a wooden screw steamer whose commander was Winfield Scott Schley, who later achieved controversial fame during the war with Spain. After further Latin American service, including a visit to the Falkland Islands, Benson went to Annapolis to take the examination for appointment to the rank of midshipman. Schley reported favorably on his service, noting that he had been "attentive to his duty and trustworthy in every particular" and that he was fully qualified for promotion. Successful in the examination, which resulted in his advancement by several numbers in class standing, Benson became a midshipman on 18 June.[6]

Benson's next tour of duty was aboard the ancient frigate *Constitution*, better known as "Old Ironsides," then in service as a training ship for apprentice seamen. At this time Benson had an ugly episode at Panama City, Panama. Sent ashore to find a seaman who had disappeared from the ship, he espied the missing bluejacket in the process of bribing two policemen. When Benson demanded an arrest, a struggle ensued, and the young officer accidentally suffered a wound to the head and a badly ripped uniform from a policeman's sword. All was not lost; the seaman was

The Naval Academy Class of 1879. Benson is the
third from the left in the second row.

apprehended. Later on this voyage Benson contracted typhoid fever, but
he recovered at Norfolk.

At this juncture Benson became a convert to Roman Catholicism,
his wife's faith. As in most things, he arrived at this decision deliberately.
Baptized at St. Ann's Church in New York City in May 1880 and
confirmed later that summer at St. Joseph's Church by John Cardinal
McCloskey in the same city, Benson paid a certain price, because his
mother could not accept his decision. Throughout his life, however,
Benson retained his love and respect for her.

Further service in the *Constitution* occupied Benson's time for a few more
months. On a voyage to Halifax, Nova Scotia, the ship arrived at Bar
Harbor during a beautiful evening. The captain decided to await daylight
before entering the harbor, but by morning a dense fog had developed,
and it endured for a week. During this time the ship almost ran aground
and barely avoided collisions with several vessels. From this experience,
Benson drew a moral that he remembered forty-nine years later: "An
opportunity neglected is an opportunity lost." Further adversity visited
the *Constitution* on its last voyage. A part of the ship's rigging was carried
away off the Virginia Capes, and the ancient *Powhatan* had to tow the
vessel to Newport. The best news for Benson during this period was of
the birth of his only daughter and first child, Mary Augusta, at Deer Park.[7]

On board the USS *Constitution*, 1881. Captain Stephen B. Luce is seated.
Ensign W. S. Benson is second from the left.

In July 1881, Benson reported for duty at the Brooklyn Navy Yard,
where he gained his commission but a negative evaluation. After dem-
onstrating "medium knowledge" in French and Spanish, "above medium knowledge" in navigation, seamanship, and ordnance, and "far
above medium knowledge" in steam engineering, nine years after he
entered the Naval Academy, Benson attained the rank of ensign. As it
happened, Benson's immediate superior at the Navy Yard was none
other than Commander Alfred Thayer Mahan. When the future historian failed to file a report on time, he blamed his subordinate. Mahan's
biographer wrote of this episode: "Young Benson survived Mahan's
damnation with faint praise and went on to become the navy's first
Chief of Naval Operations."[8]
     Another tour of duty at sea followed: Benson served on the screw
gunboat *Yantic*. After participating in exercises off the East Coast, the
Yantic became the first naval vessel to call at Mobile, Alabama, since
the Civil War. While lying at the Brooklyn Navy Yard in 1883, the
Yantic received orders to accompany the *Proteus* in a rescue of the
Greely Arctic expedition. During the rescue, the ice pack crushed the
Proteus, but the *Yantic* saved the boat's crew, and another naval vessel
picked up Greely and five other survivors. Once again Benson earned

commendation at the end of a tour at sea. Commander E. T. Woodward testified to Benson's "ability, habits, and conduct," and Commander George Francis F. Wilde noted his "thoroughly efficient and trustworthy manner."[9]

There followed an interlude ashore. First Benson served on the Naval Advisory Board, helping to supervise the construction of the first protected cruisers built for the Navy—*Chicago, Boston,* and *Atlanta*—and the dispatch vessel *Dolphin,* a type of gunboat intended to transport important papers and personnel. In 1883 Congress authorized funds for this construction, the beginning of the "New Navy" and the regeneration of the sea service after the neglect that followed the Civil War. Very soon, however, Benson moved on to the Branch Hydrographic Office in Baltimore, Maryland, where he conducted a study of coastal areas by mapping the ocean bottom and charting winds, tides, and currents.

Benson's studies in Baltimore prepared him for his next duty at sea, aboard the *Albatross,* the first oceangoing vessel ever built especially to conduct marine research anywhere in the world. This ship belonged to the United States Fish Commission, a civilian agency that conducted research in marine biology for the benefit of the American fishery. The naval personnel who operated the vessels of the Fish Commission usually followed a schedule such as Benson's, which included correcting charts of the Caribbean Sea, making studies of the Gulf Stream, and dredging for biological specimens. When Benson left the ship in November 1887, his superior, Lieutenant Commander Zera L. Tanner, commented perspicaciously on qualities that Benson manifested throughout his naval career: "He is very deliberate in speech and action, but makes very few mistakes; and with his peculiar tact in handling men, usually accomplishes as much or more than many officers whose methods are more vigorous. He has a cool head and good judgment."[10]

Benson now reported to the *Dolphin,* the ship he had helped build four years earlier, to participate in the world cruise of the "White Squadron." Admiral George Dewey later wrote of this adventure: "If, professionally, we had to smile a little when our public exulted over the sending of the White Squadron abroad in order to show our new navy to Europe, we knew that this squadron was only a pioneer of something better to come." After the *Dolphin* reached the West Coast, Benson appeared before an examining board that considered him for promotion, although advancement depended principally on seniority—vacancies generally resulted from retirement, dismissal, or death. His superior, Commander Wilde, testified to Benson's abilities: "I wish to place upon official record, my high appreciation of the character & qualification of Ensign W. S. Benson, U. S. N., now on duty aboard this vessel. His intelligent and zealous performance of duty, as well as his excellent judgement and discretion, merits approbation." Benson proved most proficient in technical developments. On 14 November 1888 he was commissioned lieutenant (junior grade); 28 May was the date of rank. He had been an ensign for seven years, stark testimony to the slowness of promotion during the closing decades of the nineteenth century.[11]

When Benson returned from the world cruise of the White Squadron, he was ordered to the Naval Academy as an instructor in seamanship, naval tactics, and naval architecture, an assignment that must have seemed a considerable vindication for one who had struggled academically as a cadet. This assignment provided Benson an opportunity to become acquainted with his first son, Howard Hartwell James Benson, who was two years old before his father saw him. Benson had been married for more than nine years, but he had spent very little time with his family because of duty at sea. When Benson was at sea, Mrs. Benson returned to Deer Park, but whenever possible she repaired to Atlantic ports where Benson's vessel lay at anchor: Norfolk; New York; Philadelphia; Baltimore; Jamestown, Rhode Island; and Hyannis Port, Massachusetts. Unfortunately, Mrs. Benson destroyed the couple's correspondence after the death of her husband, but his children preserved some letters. They reflect his love for them and his efforts to mold their character, develop their interests, inculcate pride in the navy, and cultivate respect for proper authority.[12]

After an interlude at the Washington Navy Yard, where he received ordnance instruction, Benson once again returned to sea to serve with the United States Coast Survey, a bureau of the Department of the Treasury. He did so as a lieutenant, having been promoted on 27 October 1893, with date of rank from 27 June. Most of this tour was spent along the coast of Mexico and the central American states. On 4 May 1896 Benson took command of the *Endeavor*. Once again he received excellent fitness reports. Lieutenant Commander Harrison G. O. Colby, the hydrographic inspector for the survey, wrote of Benson: "An excellent officer in every respect, zealous, intelligent, and of good judgement, has a high sense of duty always looking for something to do and loyal to his superiors in rank." In response to a stock question asked of a rating officer about whether he would like to have Benson under his immediate command, Colby stated: "I should consider myself fortunate to get him."[13]

Benson was happy to receive another assignment to the Naval Academy in 1896—this time as a discipline and drill officer as well as an instructor in seamanship—because it permitted a long stay with his growing family. The firstborn, Mary, nicknamed May, was now fifteen, and Howard was eight. Benson's third child, Francis Wyse, had been born on 21 April 1895. The family was close and shared many interests. William and Mary were fond of horses, and the entire family enjoyed sailing. Benson was skilled at handling small craft. Another favorite recreation was taking nature walks at Deer Park during weekends spent with Mrs. Benson's brother, a country doctor. Lieutenant Benson proved adept at identifying birds and trees. The family played penny ante poker together and shared a fondness for good music.

The elegant, soft-spoken Mrs. Benson, small in stature, graceful and cheerful, entertained frequently but shared with her husband a strong interest in the children. Their son Howard remembered his parents' affection and their standards: high principles, good manners, and proper behavior, all taught by example. The children thought of their mother as the "most perfect . . . in the world," and they idolized their father.[14]

During the summer of 1897 Benson sailed with the midshipmen to the Madeiras aboard the practice ship *Monongahela* amid talk of possible hostilities with Spain over Cuba. On the return voyage a strange vessel was sighted, and the ship's captain, assuming that war might have been declared, ordered all hands to general quarters until he ascertained the identity of the unknown ship. When unfavorable winds slowed the return to Annapolis, news of the delay was sent ashore by carrier pigeon. Radio communication and many other remarkable innovations still lay ahead.[15]

The brief war with Spain in 1898 frustrated Benson terribly. When the *Maine* went to the bottom of the Havana harbor, Benson was engaged in revising Admiral Stephen B. Luce's respected textbook *Seamanship*, an undertaking that involved a considerable professional compliment. As soon as hostilities began, Benson asked for sea duty, but the Bureau of Navigation merely placed his request on file. Luce proved sympathetic, and encouraged his associate to make a second request. Once again Benson failed to obtain orders, but he was promised assignment to the *Chicago*. Of this development he wrote hopefully to Luce: "I shall be reconciled though greatly regretting the experience being gained now by those in the fleet." Delays in readying the *Chicago* for active service slowed Benson's work on Luce's volume. He apologized in agitated language: "I am sorry to give you annoyance of waiting and uncertainty, but if you know the galling humiliation I feel each day as I read of what Service is doing, you would certainly pardon me. I would be delighted to have the opportunity to take a torpedo into Santiago." He was not so contrite as to forgo questioning Luce's opposition to hydraulic steering gear: "It has some very strong advocates and is in use on nearly all if not all of our vessels built on the Pacific." He submitted suggested changes—the admiral could "put them in or not as [he thought] best."[16]

Benson's only contribution to the war effort in 1898 was to receive Spanish prisoners of war at Annapolis. Admiral Pascual Cervera, his son Angel, and other naval prisoners taken during the naval battle at Santiago de Cuba were transported to the United States on the cruiser

St. Louis. Benson boarded the receiving ship *Vermont* on 16 July and took charge of fifty-nine Spaniards. A brief contretemps occurred when one of the prisoners, Captain Enrique Caprilles, refused to sign a parole stipulating that he would observe the rules of the vessel and refrain from damaging it. Captain Caspar Goodrich of the *St. Louis* had segregated Caprilles, but Benson proved willing to accept an oral parole. Eventually Benson's decision was upheld. The matter was referred to the superintendent of the Naval Academy, Captain Philip H. Cooper. He consulted the secretary of the navy, John D. Long, who authorized acceptance of the oral parole.[17]

Soon thereafter, Benson completed work on Admiral Luce's book. On 1 August he mailed the remaining revisions to Luce, confessing his terrible disappointment at having missed the war: "The close of this war without being at the front leaves my heart and spirit broken. I wonder of what value is professional reputation!" He consoled himself with the thought of Luce's example: "But when I think of the active interest you take in the good of the profession after being no longer actively engaged, I am fortified against the temptation of becoming indifferent." Luce consoled Benson with compliments. In the preface to the new edition, Luce wrote: "The work of revising the late edition and preparing the present for the press was undertaken by Lieutenant W. S. Benson ... [whose] labors have been attended with marked success notwithstanding those distractions due to the breaking out of the war with Spain."[18]

Benson's first twenty-eight years of service ended with a flourish. He finally reported for duty to the *Chicago*, which sailed first to the Caribbean Sea and then to European waters for duty as the largest vessel in the White Squadron. Soon, however, Benson became the flag lieutenant of Rear Admiral Norman H. Farquhar, commander in chief of U.S. naval forces on the North Atlantic Station. At this time Admiral Farquhar commanded three vessels that were engaged in testing the new invention of the Italian Guglielmo Marconi. Benson was aboard the cruiser *New York* on 2 November 1899 when Marconi transmitted the first official radio message sent from a ship of the U.S. Navy.

Lieutenant Benson, now forty-five years of age, entered the new century with solid but hardly striking credentials. Although he had compiled a sound service record unmarred by a serious blemish, he had accomplished nothing that placed him ahead of many other serving officers—nothing that appeared to mark him for special responsibilities in the future. Nevertheless, he might have looked forward to participating in the modernization and expansion of the U.S. Navy that resulted, in large part, from the nation's assumption of extensive new responsibilities. The war with Spain, which had brought Benson so much disappointment, served him well in the long run, changing the nation's course and opening unprecedented career opportunities for seasoned officers who had toiled faithfully but quietly during the stillness of the late nineteenth century.

CHAPTER II

FIFTEEN YEARS OF SENIOR SERVICE
1900–1915

On 1 July 1900 Lieutenant Benson at last achieved promotion to the rank of lieutenant commander, at the beginning of a busy era for ambitious naval officers. While he continued to acquire valuable experience, the U.S. Navy underwent significant changes that brought a number of reforming officers to prominence, among them Bradley A. Fiske and William Sowden Sims. Although Benson did not seek notoriety and avoided being identified with the more strident proponents of naval reform, he demonstrated considerable interest in various aspects of the movement. Perhaps one reason for Benson's relative obscurity was the nature of the assignments he received during the first years of the new century. He was often at sea, but when he was ashore, he usually secured duty at the Naval Academy or elsewhere in the vicinity. For example, after a brief stay on the battleship *Kearsarge* as a staff officer, Benson in June 1901 became senior assistant to the commandant of midshipmen at the Naval Academy, Commander Charles E. Colahan. In this position he devoted himself, among other things, to the task of eliminating the hazing that took place among the midshipmen. This interlude at Annapolis also allowed him another relatively long period of residence with his growing family.

On 1 October 1903 Lieutenant Commander Benson was ordered to the battleship *Iowa*, one of the principal vessels in the force that had destroyed Cervera's squadron at Santiago de Cuba in 1898. His performance as executive officer of the *Iowa*, which was in the North Atlantic Squadron, brought him praise from his commanding officer, Captain Benjamin F. Tilley, as an "excellent executive officer of a battleship which position exacts the highest qualities." The result was promotion to the rank of commander. His regular commission was dated 26 February 1906.[1]

In 1905, much to the satisfaction of Benson, his son Howard entered the Naval Academy; the proud father seized this opportunity to instruct his son in the nature of the naval profession. His comments reveal his philosophy: "You have chosen a noble profession, a careful perusal of history will convince any thinking man that the noblest and bravest deeds fraught with most important results have been performed by Naval Men." Recognizing the difficulties that attended a naval career, Benson continued:

> A Naval Officer is exposed to many temptations. Another reason I have not been more earnest in advocating your cause is because so many apparently good Catholic boys have gone there [Annapolis] and made a shipwreck of their faith and I feared for you. I would have shielded you, in the tender love I have for you, from all these temptations, but as the years come you must be a man and take a man's place in the world.

He felt that his own life had "always been rather stern and hard" and that he had taken "too serious a view of it." He enjoined Howard to avoid this course. Just before his son began his training, Benson cautioned him: "Your fate, your whole future is in the balance and will be decided entirely on your actions, your efforts[,] with as little left to chance as the laws of nature, as relentless as fate." If Howard left nothing to chance, he would achieve success. "Never put off[,] hoping to make up in the future." Many years later Commodore Benson noted: "My father wrote me wonderful letters for guidance and advice[,] particularly when I was a midshipman."[2]

Benson's next tour of duty was with the Light-House Board, at that time a part of the Department of Commerce and Labor. After making brief inspection tours, he took charge of the Sixth Light-House District at Charleston, South Carolina, on 30 September 1905. His jurisdiction extended from Cape Fear, North Carolina, southward to Jupiter Inlet, Florida. For two years he supervised such matters as anchoring buoys, lightships, and other navigational aids. At the same time he served as the naval member of the Board of Defensive Sea Areas. This organization prepared reports and recommendations concerning coastal defenses in time of war.

During the summer of 1906 Benson attended a two-month session at the Naval War College in Newport, Rhode Island. Long courses were not offered until 1911. During the interim between summer sessions prior to 1911, the War College staff prepared for the oncoming session and drafted war plans and staff studies at the instigation of the Navy Department. Benson was later erroneously criticized for his lack of War College experience. Although he never had an opportunity to take the long course, he did attend the college.[3]

Benson's interest in naval improvements intensified during this period. In a letter to William S. Sims, an advocate of the one-caliber, all-big-gun battleship, Benson endorsed the concept heartily. "I have long advocated the reduction of the number of calibers. My cruise in *Iowa* convinced me of the real injury to a vessel's efficiency so many calibers caused. . . . It seems strange that sensible men hesitate about such vital and important matters." Benson also supported another pet project of the reformers, the creation of a naval general staff. He believed that such a staff was "vital to any system of improvement either in the personnel of the Navy or its organization. Until this [a naval general staff] is brought about[,] any [personnel] system suggested or established will be temporary and unsatisfactory." If a general staff could be established, "most, if not all, the vexing and disturbing questions now arising will disappear and cease to come up."[4]

Benson practiced his adopted religion devoutly. In 1907 he had an opportunity to act as President Theodore Roosevelt's personal representative to a number of Roman Catholic dignitaries, serving as their host and guide. The occasion was the Tercentenary Exposition at Jamestown, Virginia, where the first English colony in America had been established in 1607. Benson provided quarters and transportation on the lighthouse tender *Holly*, which was under his command. In attendance were the apostolic delegate to the United States, Diomede Cardinal Falconio, the American James Cardinal Gibbons, the presidents of Georgetown University and Catholic University, and many American diocesan bishops. Activity of this nature made Benson a leading Roman Catholic layman.

In July 1907 Benson once again returned to the Naval Academy, this time as commandant of midshipmen. Something of a modernist in educational matters, he supported an honor system but opposed the practice of encouraging the midshipmen to report observed violations. He sought to combine fairness and kindness with firm discipline, an approach that gained him the reputation of having a "hand of steel in a glove of silk." The yearbook for 1908, the *Lucky Bag*, was dedicated to "Commander William Shepherd Benson, United States Navy, whose forbearance, sympathy, and justice we count our greatest aid on the road to true and honest manhood."[5]

During the summer of 1908 Benson took command of the Naval Practice Squadron, which included the cruiser *Olympia*, Dewey's flagship at the battle of Manila Bay; the cruiser *Chicago*; the monitors *Arkansas* and *Nevada*; and the ancient *Hartford*. The most memorable incident of this tour was a dispute with the town fathers of New London, Connecticut, who attempted to close a dining and dancing pavilion at Ocean Beach to sailors from Benson's ships. The manager of the pavilion, William H. Wordell, maintained that few parents of New London would "care to permit their daughters to mingle in public halls with

Commander W. S. Benson as Commandant of Midshipmen at the Naval
Academy, 1907. Benson is on the far left.

sailors or soldiers." He wanted to ensure that his pavilion was managed
so that "all respectable people may feel at liberty to attend dances
there." Benson took umbrage, informing Wordell that he would request
a change of station to Newport, thus "wiping New London off the map
of the fleet's itinerary." New London then closed down the pavilion.
This episode did Benson no harm. His commanding officer, Captain
Charles Badger, commended his performance as commander of the
Practice Squadron, writing that he considered Benson among the "most
capable officers in the Navy."[6]

Anticipating promotion to the rank of captain, Benson sought the
command of the new all-big-gun battleship *South Carolina*, but he had
to be content with the third-rate cruiser *Albany*, which was serving as
the flagship of torpedo boats on the Pacific Coast. While in command
of this vessel and its complement of 325 men, Benson gave considerable
thought to gunnery. He had the satisfaction of receiving a gunnery

trophy for vessels of the *Albany*'s class. He corresponded with Commander William S. Sims, who had gained wide recognition as a leader in the field of gunnery while serving as inspector of target practice. Lavishly praising Sims, Benson held: "You have not only made our fighting element what it is, but you have shown to all officers what any one prompted by right motives and high ideals, with a thorough knowledge of the subject and the best interest of the service at heart, can accomplish against all odds." However, Benson also saw fit to comment negatively on Sims's assignment to the command of the battleship *Minnesota* before attaining the rank of captain. He would have preferred to see him "promoted to the next higher grade and then given a battleship than to have established the dangerous precedent of giving battleship to commanders." He feared an adverse effect on discipline.[7]

Sims replied some three months later with a sturdy defense of his views on the naval officer corps. He saw the group as divided between senior officers, who tended to resist criticism of their efficiency and to defend defects for which they were responsible, and junior officers, who resented the inefficiency of their seniors and sought remedies:

> If you can imagine a service in which all of the upper officers would carefully study and easily comprehend all criticism, and cheerfully and openly acknowledge all defects for which they were either actively or passively responsible, then there could be no such condition as that which we deplore. If these officers had all been Remeys, who backed up the reports of our defects to the limit of permissible strenuosity in the use of official language; or Stocktons, who advised that we "stand in the light and not be afraid of the truth no matter how unsatisfactory"; or Wainwrights[,] who acknowledged "I now understand for the first time the depth of the ignorance into which we had fallen concerning our weapons and their proper use"; . . . or Bensons[,] who generously encouraged the well intended (though doubtless often mistaken) efforts of their juniors, they (the seniors of the service) would at once have commanded the respect and loyal support of their juniors. But they did not do so, and, in the very nature of the case, it could not have been expected, simply because in all walks of life the Remeys, Stocktons, Wainwrights, and Bensons are always a small minority.[8]

Benson responded in praise of Sims's views. He thought the letter a "most excellent exposition of the real underlying causes" of trouble in the Navy. "I shall use it on all possible occasions when I find that the right kind of an officer—one who will appreciate it—to show the true state of affairs." He went on to press an issue that concerned him, the undue time spent in cruising: "I think we do entirely too much cruising; our ships should be constantly under trial." He wanted to put ships into condition for battle as rapidly as possible and send them out by divisions, squadrons, or fleet under simulated combat conditions. "If defects are developed, immediately upon return remedy the defects. . . . Of course, I would not make it all work, but that is the general idea."[9]

Benson also interested himself in the pet project of another naval reformer, the range finder advocated by Bradley A. Fiske. In April 1909 Benson wrote to Secretary of the Navy George von Lengerke Meyer in criticism of the extant spotting system and in favor of the range finder. He proposed that "each [gun] turret be fitted with a range finder installed on the inside, whose base line is as nearly equal to the diameter of the turret as conditions will permit and as much attention be given to its installation and proper arrangement as to the guns themselves." Opposed to placing spotters high in the masts, where they were likely to receive enemy fire, he explained to his son Howard the need for a fire control system that would "last just as long as your guns and ships will." A system such as Fiske advocated, Benson wrote, "has got to come and is coming. In a few years, the fewer the better, we will be ashamed to acknowledge how stupid we have been."[10]

Benson's tour in the *Albany* was notable for a taste of gunboat diplomacy. While cruising off Nicaragua in 1909, Benson learned of an expedition that President José Santos Zelaya of Nicaragua was planning to send against El Salvador. Benson quickly notified Zelaya that "any expedition across the Gulf of Fonseca would be stopped and force used if necessary." Faced with this announcement, Zelaya halted the offending enterprise. The *New York Herald* for 27 April 1909 praised Benson for "prompt and determined action" that had "nipped [Zelaya's action] in the bud." Benson strongly approved the presence of the U.S. Navy in Central American waters as a deterrent to aggression by Zelaya. He encouraged his officers to mingle with the local people as much as possible in order to obtain useful information. This practice eventually created a problem for Commander Benson. A consul at Managua, José de Olivares, made no objection to the attendance of some of Benson's officers at a private ball at Jinotepe when the group visited him on their way to the affair, but later he asked Benson to recall them. Benson refused. Meanwhile, at the social affair, circumstances had required the officers to participate in a toast to President Zelaya. The consul protested to the Department of State, which forwarded the matter to the Navy Department. Benson defended his actions as being in accordance with naval regulations and a useful means of obtaining intelligence about the local situation.[11]

Benson's next assignment also had a political flavor. This was a cruise to Japan with the Pacific Fleet to repair damage to Japanese-American relations that stemmed from President Theodore Roosevelt's mediation of the Russo-Japanese War and measures taken to limit Japanese emigration to the United States. While awaiting his next assignment, Benson learned of a retirement that opened the way to a captaincy. After appearing before a naval examining board on the *Tennessee,*

In Japan, January 1910, with Japanese guests. *Seated, left to right:* Rear Admiral Wada, Captain Fiske, Mrs. Niiro, unidentified, Baron Uriu, Rear Admiral Sebree, Mrs. Koizumi, Captain Benson, Rear Admiral Ijichi, and Flag-Lieutenant (to Rear Admiral Ijichi) Shimomura.

Benson was promoted to captain, with 16 December 1909 as his date of rank. His duty with the fleet was to serve as chief of staff to the fleet's commander, Rear Admiral Uriel Sebree. Benson had an opportunity to visit the Hawaiian Islands, the Philippine Islands, and the Chinese port of Woosung before the fleet called at Yokohama in January 1910. Once again Benson received praise from a superior. Sebree's evaluation stated categorically: "Captain Benson is, in my opinion, an ideal chief of staff. He knows our profession thoroughly and is competent for the command of any ship, squadron or fleet."[12]

Benson now sought the command of one of the navy's new battleships. Initially he hoped for the *North Dakota* or the *Delaware.* In the interim, Benson delivered a course of lectures at the Naval War College on strategy in the Pacific Ocean. Eventually he was sent to the *Utah,* then under construction at a shipyard in Camden, New Jersey. He first served as her general inspector, presiding over the trials of the new vessel, which began on 20 June 1911. This ship displaced 21,825 tons with a draft of over 28 feet. More than 521 feet in length, it could operate on either coal or oil at a contract speed of 20.75 knots. Its main armament consisted of ten 12-inch guns in five modern turrets. On 31 August 1911 Captain Benson had the satisfaction of reading orders that placed the *Utah* in commission to a crew of 950 seamen and 50 officers.[13]

As was the custom, the people of the state of Utah presented a silver service to the ship, but in this instance, the act involved a certain

The USS *Utah*. Captain William S. Benson was in command of the *Utah* from August 1911 to June 1913.

controversy. The various plates in the service that had been chosen depicted scenes of structures and people of Utah. Although it was hardly distinguishable, being only two inches in height, a picture of a statue of Brigham Young appeared on the fish dish, and the Daughters of the American Revolution protested this honor to a practitioner of polygamy. So infuriated were the citizens of Utah that they raised an extraordinary sum of money to purchase the silver service, and presented the largest set ever given to a ship at that time. A well-known actress of the time, Hazel Dawn, made the presentation on 6 November 1911. The service included about thirty cups, representing the counties of the home state. Some of the junior officers engaged in an unsuccessful attempt to "tour the state"—to drink from each of the cups in succession without stopping.

The *Utah* began its service with a flourish, setting a speed record for ships of its class of 22 knots on a test run, and then participating in a huge naval review held in New York harbor in November 1911, before joining the Atlantic Fleet. Benson proved most successful as the commander, combining strict discipline with close attention to the welfare of the crew. A member of the crew, Robert M. Griffin, later a rear admiral, remembered that the crew included a "hard core of experienced petty officers with the rest of the young men fresh from the training stations and eager to succeed." Benson assigned them to positions of responsibility for which they had not been trained, a means of hastening their development. Later on, when Griffin had gained "more experience and a better realization of the responsibilities the C. O. bore, I marvelled at [Benson's] patience and courage." Benson's efforts to train his crew were rewarded; the *Utah* placed second in battle efficiency during the period from 1 July 1912 to 30 June 1913. A letter from the assistant

Captain and Mrs. Benson on board the USS *Utah*, 6 November 1911, the day the silver service was presented.

secretary of the navy, Franklin D. Roosevelt, contained notice of another honor: "The Department takes pleasure in informing you that the U. S. S. *Utah* of which you were commanding officer in competition with twenty-five vessels of her class, attained the highest multiple in engineering for the year, and is awarded the engineering trophy in recognition of her excellent service." Benson was singled out for special praise: "The Department commends you for the efficiency of the U. S. S. *Utah* as evidenced by the results attained."[14]

While in command of the *Utah*, Benson seized an opportunity to demonstrate his ability and his courage by undertaking a difficult entry into the harbor at Charleston, South Carolina. The old channel was not deep enough to permit the passage of the *Utah* and three other first-class battleships in the division (*Florida, North Dakota,* and *Delaware*), all of which drew about 29½ feet of water, but a new channel might permit entry. Benson persuaded his commanding officer to allow him to lead his division into the Charleston harbor through the new channel. He performed this duty efficiently, never getting into less than 33 feet of water.

Performance such as this once again earned Benson praise from his superiors. Rear Admiral Bradley A. Fiske rated him as "moderate" in initiative, but as possessing "very good intelligence, excellent judgment, and thoroughness." After Benson was detached from the *Utah* on 13 June 1913, the commander of the Atlantic Fleet, Admiral Charles Badger, wrote: "It is needless I trust for me to say that your departure from the Fleet is a matter of very great regret so far as efficiency of the fleet itself is concerned. Your ship has been all that a ship could be and you certainly may look back with pride upon the condition in which you maintained her and the condition in which you left her."[15]

Benson never went to sea again, but he had served on ships ranging from one of the oldest ships in the navy, the *Constitution*, to one of the most modern battleships. Although he never experienced combat, he was, by 1913, one of the most qualified ship commanders in the navy. One more assignment lay ahead before he took up the duties that transformed him from a competent but relatively obscure captain into one of the foremost naval officers in the world.

Once again Captain Benson sought duty at the Naval Academy, this time as its superintendent, and he received support from Admirals Fiske and Badger, but instead he was given an important administrative assignment, the command of the Philadelphia Navy Yard. Associated with this role was the supervision of three naval districts: the third, with headquarters in New York, for the coast from New London, Connecticut, to Barnegat, New Jersey; the fourth, with headquarters in Philadelphia, from Barnegat to Assateague, Virginia; and the fifth, with headquarters in Norfolk, from Assateague to New River Inlet, North Carolina. Later Benson surrendered command of the third and

In Philadelphia, summer of 1914. *Left to right:*
French Ambassador Jean Jules Jusserand, Captain W. S. Benson,
and Mayor Rudolph Blankenburg of Philadelphia.

fifth naval districts. This change reflected the growth in his workload
after World War I began in 1914. By 1915 Benson commanded about
five thousand officers and men, whereas when he undertook his duties,
he commanded only about one thousand.[16]

Beginning on 15 August 1913, Benson plunged energetically into
the varied responsibilities associated with the Philadelphia Navy Yard.
His early concerns ranged from taking a position on the construction
of a dry dock in the Philadelphia area to seeking removal of unsanitary
pigpens in the vicinity of his command. Typical of his tactful approach
to delicate matters was his handling of a request made by Roman
Catholics at the navy yard to hold a Catholic Memorial Day service.
It seemed possible that other religious denominations might raise objections, so Benson arranged for the service to be held under the auspices
of the Army and Navy Union. All preparations were made without cost
to the government, and attendance was completely voluntary. The occasion passed without incident, earning Benson the thanks of Secretary
of the Navy Josephus Daniels.[17]

Benson's relations with Daniels matured into a close association
during the captain's service in Philadelphia, something that could not

Captain W. S. Benson as Commandant of the Philadelphia Navy Yard, November 1914.

be said about the secretary's dealings with some of the leading naval reformers—for example, Rear Admiral Bradley A. Fiske, one of the more outspoken proponents of change in the navy, who had become aid for operations and, as such, the principal uniformed adviser of the secretary of the navy. Initially hopeful of working effectively with Daniels, Fiske became increasingly alienated from his civilian superior. The new secretary was associated with the William Jennings Bryan wing of the Democratic party. A newspaper editor and publisher from North Carolina, Daniels was a vigorous proponent of temperance. Once in office, he failed to support many projects of the naval reformers, including extensive ship construction and the creation of a general staff. He also eliminated the traditional officers' wine mess aboard ship and championed educational opportunities for enlisted personnel. Fiske did not improve his standing with Daniels when he clashed with him over the elimination of the wine mess and the policy of the federal government toward Japan. A disagreement over Daniels's refusal to promote Captain Templin M. Potts further alienated Fiske. Of greater import, probably, was the unwillingness of the secretary to enhance the authority of his aid for operations; Fiske wanted to enjoy powers commensurate with those of the First Sea Lord in the Royal Navy of Great Britain or the chiefs of staffs in other leading navies.[18]

As Fiske and other activists lost favor, Benson successfully culti-
vated Daniels. He was assiduous in responding to the desires of the
Navy Department. For example, when the secretary asked Benson to
speed work on a destroyer, he responded that he would complete the
task in six days. At the same time, he complimented Daniels on his
efforts to develop educational opportunities for sailors. A few days later
Benson lent support to the secretary's plan for dealing with cases of
absence without leave among enlisted personnel. He also fell in with
the secretary's desire to assemble a force of Marines at the Philadelphia
Navy Yard, despite considerable opposition to that service within the
navy. Benson was quick to support the Wilson administration's effort
to prevent arms supplies from reaching the regime of General Victoriano
Huerta in Mexico, an effort that helped U.S. naval operations at Vera
Cruz. When some new ship construction was begun at the Philadelphia
Navy Yard, Benson took advantage of the opportunity to invite Daniels
to the yard.[19]

Captain Benson's loyalty to the secretary of the navy culminated
in a most unexpected denouement. A serious confrontation between
Fiske and Daniels over the creation of a naval general staff opened
opportunities for which Benson was well prepared. No one could have
foreseen that these opportunities would fall to Benson, even though his
forty-three years of competent professional service spanned the transition from the old sailing navy to the modern fleet that was destined
to participate in the First World War.

CHAPTER III

THE CHIEF OF NAVAL OPERATIONS

At the onset of the First World War in August 1914, President Woodrow Wilson initially proclaimed U.S. neutrality and soon thereafter attempted to mediate the conflict. For more than two and a half years he devoted himself to searching for peace in Europe. This policy initially militated against improvements being made in the United States Navy, especially those espoused by naval reformers such as Rear Admiral Fiske. Wilson feared that the belligerents would construe martial improvements as unneutral behavior. As early as 1 August 1914 the General Board of the Navy discussed the proper disposition of American battleships, recommending that the secretary of the navy recall all such units to home waters for repairs, excepting only the ones stationed in the Caribbean Sea. To this proposal Daniels made no response, reflecting the inertia of the administration. In September the General Board reiterated its recommendations, and again Daniels failed to act. The public showed little interest in naval activism, a circumstance that frustrated the navalists.[1]

This situation began to change after congressional exponents of what became known as "preparedness" leveled criticism at the armed services. A Republican congressman from Massachusetts, Augustus P. Gardner, who was the chairman of the House Committee on Military Affairs and the son-in-law of the influential senator Henry Cabot Lodge, broke the silence on 16 October, calling for an investigation to determine whether the United States was ready for war. Because a congressional election campaign was then in progress, this action, popular among Republican legislators from northeastern states, was interpreted as a partisan enterprise. In a headline on 20 October, the *New York*

Times reported that President Wilson was "Calm to Our War Needs." On the same day Secretary Daniels expressed the opinion that one aspect of preparedness, the creation of a general staff for the navy, was inconsistent with the ideals of the nation. Nevertheless, the impatient leader of the naval reformers, Admiral Fiske, thought that a "fight" would "start on the subject very soon."[2]

Fiske immediately began a campaign to engender congressional support for a naval general staff. First he consulted Senator George C. Perkins (R-Calif.), who chaired the Senate Naval Affairs Committee. Perkins agreed to discuss the matter with Gardner but expressed his doubt that anything could be accomplished without the support of the administration. Fiske and Gardner then sought help from Assistant Secretary of the Navy Roosevelt, whose loyalty to the president on these issues was in some question because the administration had failed to support Roosevelt's attempt to gain nomination as the New York Democratic party's candidate for U.S. senator. Perhaps more to the point, FDR was in favor of expanding the navy. Roosevelt did two things: he gave Fiske a report that showed the disparity between the present strength of the navy and the recommendations of the General Board, and he helped Fiske draft a statement claiming that a shortfall of eighteen thousand men kept the navy below authorized strength and that thirteen second-line battleships could not be kept in commission. FDR's behavior skirted disloyalty, especially since other naval enthusiasts opposed a confrontation with the president. For example, Admiral Mahan called for the creation of a council of national defense that would counter the more extreme activists on either side of the issue.[3]

Fiske refused to turn away from his campaign. On 9 November he wrote at length to Daniels, listing no fewer than sixteen instances of unpreparedness. He claimed, among other things, that, while American ships were "well organized and pretty well drilled," the fleets were not. Moreover, he wrote, the Navy Department was "neither organized nor drilled in a military way." To improve the situation, he advocated a "general staff," but to this plea the secretary of the navy paid no attention. (Later Daniels claimed not to remember receiving Fiske's missive.) On 1 December Daniels insisted that the navy was "always ready—it lives in a state of preparedness." For the next fiscal year he proposed a small building program and ignored naval reorganization.[4]

Fiske did not give up. First he prevailed on Congressman Richmond Pearson Hobson (D-Ala.), a naval hero of the war with Spain, to testify before the House Committee on Naval Affairs in favor of naval reorganization. Hobson's appearance before the committee stimulated some newspaper reports but little else. Fiske then brought together a group of naval reformers who called on Hobson to urge the establishment of an office of naval operations, which would include fifteen "assistants" who would accept responsibility for the readiness of the navy and its general direction. In so doing, the reformers—among them Captains Harry S. Knapp, John Hood, and James H. Oliver, along with Lieutenant Commanders William P. Cronan, Zachariah H. Madison, and Dudley W. Knox—issued a direct challenge to the secretary of the navy.

The civilian leaders of the Navy Department traditionally opposed a general staff because it was deemed likely to place control of the navy in the hands of uniformed line officers. Daniels's predecessor, George von Lengerke Meyer, had warned him against any such measure. He decried an "organization like that in the Army or some foreign Navy" because the "present organization makes the Secretary of the Navy controller of everything." When Hobson presented the reform proposal to Daniels, the secretary indicated that, should it pass, he would "go home."[5]

When it became evident that the Fiske-Hobson scheme might lead to the creation of a powerful naval staff, Secretary Daniels proved equal to the challenge. On 19 February he arranged for an amendment to be made to a naval construction bill that authorized the appointment of a chief of naval operations who would control the operations of the fleet and prepare war plans but who could not issue orders except through the secretary of the navy. This amendment proved acceptable to the Senate, and when the bill went to a conference committee, the House accepted the Senate's action. In its final form, the provision for a chief of naval operations in the Naval Appropriations Act of 3 March 1915 specified:

> There shall be a Chief of Naval Operations, who shall be an officer on the active list of the Navy appointed by the President, by and with the advice and consent of the Senate, from among the officers of the line of the Navy not below the grade of captain for a period of four years, who shall, under the direction of the Secretary of the Navy, be charged with the operations of the fleet, and with the preparation and readiness of plans for its use in war: *Provided*, that if an officer of the grade of captain be appointed Chief of Naval Operations, he shall have the rank, title, and emoluments of a rear admiral while holding that position.
>
> During the temporary absence of the Secretary and the Assistant Secretary of the Navy, the Chief of Naval Operations shall be next in succession to act as Secretary of the Navy.

Thus, the reformers gained little; Daniels had largely outmaneuvered them. Congress authorized an office that might head a naval general staff, but it did not provide the staff itself, and it maintained the principle of civilian supremacy.[6]

Rear Admiral Fiske appeared to be the logical choice for the new position, but he had clashed frequently with the secretary of the navy, and Daniels proved recalcitrant. He sought an officer who would act within the framework of the existing structure of government and who would show loyalty to the civilian head of the navy. Adamantly opposed to anyone who might "Prussianize the American Navy," Daniels feared those who possessed a "consuming passion to confer all power on the head of Operations," preferring an "officer of practical judgment who believed in the American system." These considerations ruled out leading members of the reform faction—officers such as Rear Admiral Thomas B. Howard, Captain Harry S. Knapp, and Captain William S. Sims. Daniels seriously considered Rear Admiral Cameron M. Winslow, the head of the Naval War College, but Winslow's candidacy collapsed when he expressed unwelcome views of the office. Daniels wrote that "Winslow, the soul of frankness, told me he believed the Navy should be organized according to the German idea of bureaus reporting to and acting under the direction of the Chief of Operations. That eliminated him from consideration." Another potential appointee, Admiral Frank F. Fletcher, the commander in chief of the Atlantic Fleet, unsuccessfully urged Daniels to name Fiske. When asked about Captain Benson's fitness, Fletcher argued that Benson did not have the "necessary knowledge or experience or ability, and was exactly in the position *now* he is fitted for."[7]

Meanwhile, Benson prepared to launch the first vessel built at the Philadelphia Navy Yard. Earlier in his career he had favored a general staff, but he kept silent during the debates of 1915, avoiding expressing an opinion to Daniels. In April he invited the secretary to attend the launching, which was scheduled for June. At this point he encountered difficulties with labor leaders. Assembling the civilian workers on the parade ground on 24 April, he forthrightly said that he intended to control matters at the navy yard as long as he was in command and that the dissatisfied were at liberty to seek employment elsewhere. That same afternoon he received an order to report to the secretary of the navy immediately. To his wife he said, "I did not believe it possible that the 'Labor People' could get such fast action. I guess this is it. I will probably be sent to Guam."

Benson arrived at Daniels's home that evening. The secretary put aside a book, and the two exchanged pleasantries. The secretary then told Benson, who had been expecting a reprimand: "I have been planning a reorganization of the Navy Department with a Chief of Naval Operations to head it up. I have selected you to be the first Chief of Naval Operations." The astonished Benson had to "hang on to his chair to keep from falling off." He had not sought the assignment, and had hoped instead for an important command at sea. The "most surprised person in Washington" then asked for a few days to consider the move. Daniels had passed over twenty-six rear admirals and five senior captains in making his choice.[8]

At length Benson accepted the assignment, recognizing that in so doing he must abandon his ambition to command the fleet—unless, as he jokingly remarked to his son, he appointed himself to the position.

After Daniels cleared the matter with President Wilson, he informed Benson that he had talked at length "with the President about the Chief of Operations and conveyed to him your views and your spirit. He was so greatly pleased and warmly approved my suggestion and the appointment will be announced from here in a few days." Then came a personal comment: "Your coming here in this important position makes me happy. We will have real team work in earnest work for steady improvement of the service." The next morning, 28 April, Daniels told Fiske, not the best of team players, that he had chosen Benson as CNO, and that afternoon he made the news public. Putting the best face on Benson's experience, which, although extensive, did not match that of some other officers, he highlighted the appointee's command of "one of the greatest and most modern battleships" and of a division of the Pacific Fleet, as well as his work at the Philadelphia Navy Yard "rapidly developing and fitting out to do shipbuilding on a large scale." Among those who sent letters of congratulation were Admiral Fletcher, commanding the Atlantic Fleet, Colonel John A. Lejeune, Assistant Commandant of the Marine Corps, and Captain William F. Fullam, Superintendent of the Naval Academy, but that neither Fiske nor Sims did so is an indication of the reform faction's views.[9]

Fiske was quite unhappy. To his diary he confided sourly: "N.Y. *Sun* has editorial on Benson's appointment, which speaks well of him, but makes comparison between him and me far from favorable to Benson." Much later he commented in his biography: "Benson was a handsome dignified gentleman of thoroughly correct habits, very religious and conscientious, and an excellent seaman; but I had never heard that he had ever shown the slightest interest in strategy or been on the General Board *or even taken the summer course at the War College.*" Fiske was correct in that Benson had not served on the General Board, but he had attended the summer course at Newport in 1906 and had presented a series of lectures on strategy in the Pacific at that institution in 1910.[10]

Benson's classmate Captain Fullam indirectly expressed the frustration with Secretary Daniels that pervaded the officer corps—which greatly influenced Fiske and other reformers. Fullam was glad to see a member of the Class of 1877 assume the "*most important* [position] *in the Navy*," but he admonished Benson: "I am sure you will stand up to it, and that you will stand immovable for a *military control of the Navy.* Of course, you know there has been for some time past a feeling of great discouragement throughout the service—a feeling that the line and the military element in the Navy has been more or less discredited or subordinated." Fullam surely had in mind the activities of Daniels, who had opposed most reform proposals and had ordered a number of unpopular measures, including the abolishment of the traditional officers' wine mess and the provision of educational opportunities for enlisted personnel.[11]

W. S. Benson in Washington, 1915.

Another of Benson's correspondents, Rear Admiral Uriel Sebree, offered advice that was much closer to Benson's line of thought. Recognizing that the CNO would have to cope with the factional struggle between the reformers and the moderates, Sebree contended that "we cannot afford to have you get peeved, and say you will get out etc. You *must* keep working. There should not be any politics in the Navy, and right now both Parties ought to be for a very strong Navy."[12]

Daniels had certainly frustrated the more extreme proponents of an influential naval staff, but by selecting a sailor of solid professional credentials for the position of CNO, he effectively silenced the critics. Benson fully accepted the principle of civilian control, and he had every intention of rendering loyal service to the man who had chosen him for important national duties. However, his sense of responsibility to a civilian superior did not mean that he would fail to strengthen the office to which he had been called, an office that at the beginning was a far cry from the ideal of those who desired a strong uniformed leader to offset the secretary of the navy and the powerful bureau heads who dominated the Navy Department.

On 11 May 1915 Secretary Daniels installed Benson as chief of naval operations in the presence of the bureau chiefs and Mrs. Benson. Surely Benson looked the part. Tall, erect, and of powerful build, he was both dignified and commanding, but his cheerful eyes belied his stern mien. The CNO was retiring by nature, but his wife, Mary Augusta, who was thoroughly familiar with military life, compensated for her husband's tendency to shun publicity. They made a handsome and amiable couple. By virtue of office an interim rear admiral, Benson was now eligible for an annual salary of six thousand dollars and free quarters. He was offered the residence on Massachusetts Avenue provided the officer who commanded the Naval Observatory, but he declined because he did not wish to displace its occupant. Instead, he rented an eight-room apartment on Columbia Road for ninety-six dollars a month.

Even before he took his oath of office, Benson began to accumulate a group of assistants to his liking. On 4 May he ordered Captain Volney O. Chase, a graduate of the Naval War College, Lieutenant Byron McCandless, an ordnance specialist, and Lieutenant Wilson Brown, then serving on the *Connecticut*, to report for duty on 11 May. A number of existing organizations within the Division of Operations automatically became part of the CNO's domain. These included the Office of Naval Intelligence, the Naval War College, the Office of Target Practice and Engineering Competitions, the Naval Radio Service, the Office of Naval Aeronautics, and the Board of Inspection and Survey.[13]

Benson moved into Fiske's cramped and ill-equipped office in the State, War, and Navy Building adjacent to the White House. The office was a fair indication of Benson's equivocal status at the beginning of

Rear Admiral W. S. Benson as CNO, 1915.

his service; it consisted of two small rooms in addition to a main room that was just large enough to accommodate a flat-topped desk and a few chairs. Benson was provided no clerical support. The only available records were the war plans prepared by the General Board. Shortly after Benson assumed office, he was required to order some vessels from Hampton Roads to New York, and several hours were required just to ascertain what ships were available for this transfer.[14]

The task of converting the Office of the Chief of Naval Operations into an effective institution required the support of Secretary Daniels and President Wilson, and obtaining their support was a daunting challenge, given the administration's antimilitary stance and its antipathy toward the reformers. Benson shared the reformers' zeal for naval reorganization and preparedness, especially because of the Great War in Europe, but he did not approve of their methods. He was notably sensitive to the imperatives of the naval chain of command, which subordinated the military establishment to the civilian authority ultimately vested in the president. Unlike Fiske, Benson was prepared to work within the constraints of the established system, manifesting patience and accepting unavoidable delay in the interest of achieving eventual change. Teamwork appeared to him more efficacious than defiant opposition. For these reasons, he refused to act in any way that might undermine Secretary Daniels. When naval officers were "excessively or obnoxiously critical" of the secretary in his presence, he left them, deeming such expressions a violation of professional ethics.[15]

Shortly after Benson took office, Fiske reaffirmed his views before the annual alumni dinner of the Naval Academy. The navy was unprepared for war, he asserted, and was culpable because of its failure to establish a "General Staff or some similar agency." The legislation establishing a CNO he deemed a step in the right direction, but he was critical of naval officers who failed to take sharp and public issue with the secretary of the navy, a veiled reference to Admiral Benson and others of like mind. "If we fear to do this, lest we incur displeasure and spoil our individual careers, we are unworthy of the uniform we wear, and we fail our country in her hour of need, just as effectively as if we deserted her flag in war." Thus began a slur on Benson that persists to the present day. It avers that he was more concerned with place and position than with his responsibilities to the naval service, and that he was prepared to make whatever concessions to civil authority were required to remain in office. After the dinner, Captain Sims wrote to Fiske admiringly: "At exactly the right time, you said exactly the right thing, and it will do a heap of good to our poor Navy." He stressed the importance of public frankness, perhaps thinking back to the reprimand he had received from President Taft in 1910 for an injudicious pro-British speech he had delivered at the Guildhall in London. "I think it particularly valuable that you brought out so strongly the duty of a naval officer to tell the truth about our deficiencies and to hell with personal consequences. Our trouble has always been that the politicians have been able to find naval officers to say what they wanted to say."[16]

Admiral Benson replied to these assertions during a public appearance in Philadelphia. He warned against assigning the responsibility for unpreparedness to any one person. Asserting that preparedness was the surest guarantee of peace, he averred that the navy had not made the most effective use of existing resources. He intended "to get every unit in the best shape possible"; then, he said, "We will be in a position to go to Congress and ask for more."[17]

The reformers naturally took issue with this approach, and the partisans of Benson just as naturally lent support. Fiske's coterie ever after considered Benson a mere "yes man." Its outlook has largely prevailed among historians, probably because the views of Fiske, Sims, and others were effectively recorded in memoirs and biographies, whereas Benson never wrote extensively in his own defense. William Veazie Pratt, one of Benson's closest associates in the Navy Department, supported his chief. According to this officer, who later became chief of naval operations, Benson's "sterling character . . . fitted him to hold the position of our war Chief of Naval Operations, perhaps as no other man was fitted." Harold C. Train, a subordinate who became a rear admiral, argued that Benson was never a "yes man." This view of Benson originated among Fiske's supporters, according to Train, because their leader, "sort of famous at that time, had not been apppointed to be the first chief under the law. As Chief, Benson headed us all. I thought he was a very, very effective man." Royal E. Ingersoll, a young officer at the time of Benson's appointment who later became an admiral, remembered that Benson "was no timber for a yes man. He was a strong character and that was that."[18]

Some of Benson's critics have maintained that the chief of naval operations and the uniformed heads of the other armed services should resign to publicize their most important differences with civilian leaders, but others, including Benson, have taken a different view. Rear Admiral Hilary Jones expressed this position clearly in a letter to Admiral Fiske after Benson had left office. "It has been said that in matters of more or less serious policy the Chief of Naval Operations might well throw his position in the balance, and resign if his views are not supported." Nevertheless, there was another side: "Very often a man must balance against the question at issue . . . the possibility of his achieving results in other directions; in other words, to save what he can out of what promises to be a wreck." Probably thinking of Benson, he concluded: "I am convinced that Chiefs of Operations in the past have had this in mind when we on the outside have wondered how they could allow certain policies to be put over."[19]

At least on some occasions, criticism of incumbents who submit to higher authority stems from professional jealousy. Admiral Pratt thought that the antagonism toward Benson "was all small stuff; too much of personal equation." He once wrote to Admiral Benson's son in explanation of this view: "At the time of his appointment [as] CNO many officers in our Naval service were jealous of him and thought that they would make better CNO's than your father; and because he was chosen over them . . . they could never quite forgive him." After many years of reflection, Pratt stated: "If I had to do it all over again I know I would prefer to serve under your father than under any of those others who were so jealous of him and who on that account never gave him the full credit which was his due."[20]

One of the most unfortunate difficulties that confronted Admiral Benson in his early days as CNO was the animosity of the elderly naval hero Admiral George Dewey, then serving as the president of the General Board. This duty was neither time-consuming nor taxing, but it was deemed the most prestigious position in the United States Navy until it was eclipsed by the position of chief of naval operations. At seventy-eight, Admiral Dewey did not aspire to the new office, but he continued to covet public notice. Probably in consideration of the ancient hero, Daniels went out of his way to explain that the establishment of a chief of naval operations did not mean that he wished to abolish the General Board or to curtail its functions; he had no intention of minimizing the value of Admiral Dewey's service to the navy. This statement did not placate Dewey, who recorded his views in no uncertain terms: "It has been my opinion for many years that we have in the General Board of the Navy a better General Staff than the Army; and the work as conducted by the Board in its advisory character, based upon mature thought and experience by the best talent in our Navy, I believed to be of inestimable value as an asset in times of peace or war."[21]

The depth of Dewey's irritation was revealed when he unexpectedly encountered Benson in Secretary Daniels's office. As Benson attempted to shake hands with the admiral, Daniels saw a "baleful light come into Dewey's eyes," and he heard him say bitterly: "How dare you speak to me, you damned hypocrite and snake who has been seeking to undermine me, you blankety-blank God damned blankety-blank." Daniels was dumbfounded; he knew Dewey as a man of "courtesy, kindness, and equable temper." Moving toward Benson, Daniels said, "For God's sake, say nothing, leave it all to me," but Benson chose to respond. Indignantly but with great control, he expressed amazement and said that some enemy must have spoken falsely of him; he assured Dewey that he had always regarded him as an "inspiring naval leader" and that he was glad "to follow where he had led." Dewey remained adamant, enjoining Benson "not to add falsehood to treachery." At Daniels's request Benson left, but not before firing a parting shot: when Dewey learned the truth, Benson remarked, he would regret having spoken so to a "warm admirer." Dewey then departed in a huff, walking down a staircase to his car rather than waiting for an elevator. Daniels called in Benson and congratulated him for his restraint in the face of such grave provocation. Benson was bewildered, because he had done nothing to earn such condemnation; he suspected someone of having told Dewey that he sought to become president of the General Board on the ground that the incumbent was too old to continue.[22]

Daniels finally managed to restore order. He called on Dewey that evening and discovered that the admiral had "recovered his equanimity." The secretary assured Dewey that he would not consider replacing him on the General Board as long as he lived, and he argued that someone had misrepresented Benson, a man who was "incapable either of hypocrisy or lack of loyalty" to him. Dewey responded only that he knew that no conspiracy could succeed as long as Daniels remained in office. Later on, however, the secretary's mediation bore fruit in an unexpected fashion. When Daniels sought to retire Rear Admiral Charles Badger, an officer from the General Board who favored naval expansion, Benson enlisted Dewey's assistance in preventing the removal. This tactic achieved its purpose, as Daniels decided not to force Badger to retire.[23]

During Benson's first year as CNO, he became involved in a controversy with Admiral Fullam that adversely affected their association thereafter. When Fullam was superintendent at the Naval Academy, Benson's son Francis was punished for violating a prohibition against hazing. Francis, who denied the allegations, was put back a year. Benson believed his son but did not intercede. Later, when Fullam assumed command of the U.S. Pacific Reserve Fleet, he attributed the withdrawal of certain ships from his command to Benson's appetite for revenge. Astonished at this charge, Benson asked to be excused from making any reply. Fullam proved unrepentant: "I should not have written . . . had it not come to me from more than one source that you were *no friend of mine*, and in one case that 'he will do all he can to keep you down.'" Benson thus learned that even the oldest associations might not survive the stresses of senior responsibilities in the navy.[24]

Some of Benson's difficulties stemmed from the accepted habits of bureau heads in the Navy Department. The several bureaus were largely independent of each other, and bureau chiefs tended to magnify the work of their organizations and to establish special relations with the secretary of the navy. Jealous of their power, they instantly contested any efforts, real or presumed, to curb their activities. To foster improved cooperation among the bureaus, Benson organized an advisory council, which was established on 24 June 1915. Meeting weekly to discuss naval policy, including the question of preparedness, the council received the approbation of Daniels, who thought that it recognized the bureau chiefs as "masters of the professional work under their direction." Benson contended that the "idea of the Council is meeting with even better results than were anticipated."[25]

Nevertheless, Benson did not ignore opportunities to expand the scope of his own office. For example, when Daniels showed reluctance to name a successor to a departed aide for materiel, the CNO suggested that the duties of this officer be assigned to an "assistant for materiel" located in his office. This arrangement would unify authority for operations and the supply of the fleet. On 1 August 1915 Captain Josiah S. McKean, an expert in logistics who had been a staff member at the Naval War College, became the first assistant for materiel. Sims informed a friend that he rejoiced at this development, "as do all hands, who consider him the best man in the service for the job."[26]

Despite a growing workload, Benson moved slowly in adding personnel to his staff because experienced naval officers were in short supply throughout the navy. He did not want to disrupt fleet operations unduly by ordering wholesale transfers to the Navy Department. To compensate for shorthandedness, the CNO and his assistants often worked after normal duty hours. Benson also took work home, where two telephones connected him to the State, War, and Navy Building. Despite the burdens of his office, he encouraged naval officers to correspond directly with him, a policy that generated a tremendous volume of mail. When Sims complained about the training of militia on destroyers (Sims was then in command of the destroyer flotilla), Benson responded with a long memorandum on the subject. He wrote separately to express pleasure at the receipt of Sims's letter and to solicit his views on any subject, a consequence of Benson's desire "to consider always the other fellow" and to try to put himself in the place of others. Sims welcomed this give and take: "It is a great satisfaction to have even an ill-natured growl treated with such frankness and fairness. I believe you can hardly realize how much it means to the service to have as Chief of Naval Operations a man of your uncompromising squareness."[27]

By early 1916 Benson was able to divide his work as CNO into five categories. He was much involved in the collection of intelligence, the function of the Office of Naval Intelligence. Officer education was another preoccupation, delegated to the Naval War College at Newport. Planning also required considerable attention, especially because Benson was an ex officio member of the General Board. Like most senior officers, Benson monitored inspections, the function of the Inspection Board. Finally, he exercised operational responsibility, carrying out "approved policies and plans."[28]

At this time Benson worked through eight organizational entities in the Office of the Chief of Naval Operations. The Division of Operations provided overall guidance for the fleet. "Plans" prepared reports on readiness. A group dealing with naval districts supported the shore establishment of the navy. Regulations and Records maintained the governing documents of the Navy Department and maintained communications with other parts of the government. Another unit dealt with movements of ships, and still another with communications of all types: radio, cable, telegraph, and telephone. A publicity section provided general information and undertook to censor departmental communications. Finally, the Materiel Division oversaw logistical matters.[29]

Despite the workload, Benson managed some recreation. Following the custom of the day, the Bensons called on the families of naval officers who lived in Washington and received return visits. Benson was expected to return the calls of senior officers, but he also followed this practice with junior officers, who were both surprised and pleased at this consideration. On occasion he indulged his love of the outdoors, exploring Rock Creek Park. He also enjoyed drives in his automobile to seek out unfamiliar areas and roads. His wife and elder son frequently accompanied him. "I don't think," recalled Howard Benson, "that my mother enjoyed these trips as much as my papa and I did, but she loved being with us." When time allowed, Benson visited his daughter and son-in-law in Annapolis.[30]

Some reward for his labors came on 24 January 1916, when Benson learned that he had been promoted to the regular rank of rear admiral as of 25 November 1915. Secretary Daniels had testified in fitness reports to his resourcefulness and administrative ability: Benson met the "highest tests demanded of a naval officer afloat and ashore"; "under his leadership the Operations has set a new pace in naval preparedness and strategy."[31]

After one year in office, Benson could claim measurable accomplishment. His enlarged staff now occupied nine properly renovated and equipped rooms. His organizational initiatives, notably the advisory council, had enhanced the efficiency of the Navy Department and improved relations between the CNO, the secretary, and the bureau chiefs. Benson's unobtrusive, steady, and flexible approach to his work contributed a great deal to these improvements, although he thereby sacrificed public notice.

Even as Benson sought to create a more efficient administration of the Navy Department, he was plunged into a myriad of day-to-day activities that enhanced the readiness of the United States Navy—which had become all the more important given the foreboding course of the devastating European war. The war had evolved into an excruciating stalemate that made American intervention likely in one form or another. This circumstance greatly affected the continuing attempts to enlarge the naval establishment.

CHAPTER IV

READINESS AND EXPANSION 1915–1916

During the first phase of his service as chief of naval operations, Admiral Benson emphasized the necessity of fleet readiness and naval expansion. Both topics gained priority within the Wilson administration as the war in Europe moved into a second year and then beyond with no sign of a decision. Some politically tinged issues came to Benson's attention, principally the operations of the navy in the Caribbean Sea associated with several interventions in that area, but the most important of all such questions was the naval building program. Benson played a congenial role in the sequence of events that led the Wilson administration eventually to sponsor the greatest program of naval expansion in the nation's history. The CNO strongly endorsed the view that the best means of assuring peace was to be prepared for war, and he was able to put this view into practice during the anxious period of neutrality that preceded the armed intervention of April 1917.[1]

One of Benson's first acts as CNO was to gain approval of a plan to ensure that the navy could mobilize at short notice. Admiral Fiske had recommended such a plan, but Daniels had refused to act on it. Benson proposed that each bureau take action within its jurisdiction to ensure that the entire naval force could be "manned, fitted out and mobilized within two weeks." The bureaus were to render reports on their progress at the end of each quarter. In this instance the secretary of the navy quickly gave approval, a reflection of his confidence in Benson. One authority suggests that the CNO's "forthrightness, patience, and courtesy undoubtedly influenced Daniels to accept changes that the nagging Fiske had failed to win."[2]

Benson took full advantage of the secretary's order. When he received the first group of reports from the bureau heads, he sent them to Daniels, who passed them on to the General Board. One month later the board submitted comments and recommendations to the secretary over Benson's signature. This procedure elicited complete information about the status of all vessels and directed attention to the measures required to prepare for wartime duty at sea. Associated with this program was Benson's decision to discontinue the annual overhaul of all ships in commission. This task, a costly process that lowered morale, consumed three months of the year. Vessels were henceforth to go to a navy yard for needed work "only when absolutely necessary to maintain their military efficiency. They would not be ordered to yards until all plans and material were ready to begin actual work."[3]

Another aspect of readiness was inspection of American merchant vessels to determine their fitness for use as auxiliaries in time of war. Benson increased the personnel of the Board of Inspection to accomplish this purpose. When the inspectors presented recommendations for alterations or improvements, Benson referred the subject to the appropriate bureau. In due course, blueprints of required changes were prepared, and a navy yard was charged with the task of completing necessary repairs. At the beginning, the army and the navy, each with an interest in the merchant fleet, conducted separate inspections. Benson played a leading role in arranging through the Joint Army-Navy Board for a combined Army and Navy Inspection Board, a measure that minimized confusion and competition.[4]

In one instance Benson encountered unexpected resistance from Daniels; the secretary objected to a plan to reorganize the battle fleet. On 24 May 1915 Benson recommended to the General Board a scheme for the "Organization of the Active Battleship Fleet" which sought to "advance the development of fleet tactics and to give increased opportunity for the exercise of flag commands." On 2 June the General Board discarded a plan of its own and adopted Benson's scheme, which established three squadrons of three divisions. Each division included three ships. Daniels took exception to the recommended terminology. He deemed the word *force*, as used in Cruiser Force, Destroyer Force, and Battleship Force, to be overly antagonistic. Benson persisted, and his views prevailed after considerable delay. Much later he looked back at this achievement with satisfaction. "Several months of diligent work were devoted to this particular effort but the result was most satisfactory. . . . Notwithstanding the many changes of scene of operation, the size of the forces engaged in the various operations, etc., there was never at any time the slightest confusion or signs of disorganization."[5]

Benson was concerned about the deterioration of gunnery in the fleet, and soon after becoming CNO he sought to make improvements. First he attempted to reappoint "his old friend" Sims as director of target practice. Earlier Sims had greatly improved naval gunnery. Sims proved uncooperative. In rejecting the position, he expressed appreciation for flattering opinions of his previous work but denied credit for having developed the modern system of gunnery training: "I did not initiate any part of it," he wrote. "It was taken bodily from Sir Percy Scott [a British gunnery expert]. . . . I was never anything of an expert in this question of the development of the details of gunnery training." Undeterred by this setback, Benson took advantage of a controversy that arose during a conference held at the Naval War College in October 1915 to press for continued emphasis on gunnery. Sims had disagreed with the Commander in Chief of the Atlantic Fleet, Admiral Frank F. Fletcher, about the effectiveness of destroyer tactics during fleet exercises. He and Fiske hoped for the removal of Admiral Fletcher, a measure that Benson opposed, but Sims was pleased that his candidate for director of the Office of Target Practice and Engineering, Captain Charles P. Plunkett, received the billet.[6]

Admiral Benson's concern for readiness extended to the shore establishment. Well-acquainted with the activities of the naval districts, he considered the districts' organization "nominal" and decided to make improvements. Captain Volney O. Chase was made chairman of a board set up to review the "Regulations for the government of Naval Districts." This board recommended the creation of an office of naval districts to ensure improved organization. Secretary Daniels at length established, under Captain George R. Marvell, the Division of Naval Districts, which thereafter administered the shore establishments.[7]

The CNO showed unusual interest in another critical aspect of readiness, technological development. The extraordinary changes that had come about during the early phases of the war in Europe forced the Navy Department to act. In July 1915 a Naval Consulting Board came into existence, with Thomas A. Edison as the chairman. Its members were experts who could mobilize the scientific and technical expertise of the nation in behalf of naval improvements. Benson drafted the rules and regulations for the Consulting Board. Edison's group was part of the effort of the navy to keep abreast of three important innovations: the radio, the submarine, and the airplane.[8]

Early efforts to upgrade radio communications had come to naught; in 1916, Admiral Benson took steps to enhance the readiness of the Naval Radio Service. On 28 July 1916 the inefficient Naval Radio Service was abolished, and the Naval Communications Service was established in the Office of the Chief of Naval Operations. It operated around the clock, providing telephonic and telegraphic communication to shore establishments, and radiotelephonic communication to ships at sea.[9]

The extraordinary accomplishments of Germany's U-boats created great concern in the United States; Benson took decisive action to up-

"*Wireless Telegraphy.*" ©T.A.E.

To my friend Rear. Admiral William S. Benson U. S. N.

MRHutchinson 10/19/15

Thomas A. Edison with his assistant, Miller Reese Hutchinson, 19 October 1915.

grade the American submarine service. Soon after becoming CNO, Benson arranged for Captain Albert W. Grant, the commander of the *Texas,* to lead the Atlantic Submarine Flotilla, and gave him authority to exercise general supervision over submarines elsewhere in the navy. Grant's charge was to develop to the utmost the "submarine as one of the most valuable instruments of our national defense." He was expected "to put every unit of the submarine flotilla in first class condition to perform all the functions for which it is designed." Benson made certain that Grant received sufficient authority to act decisively. This initiative resulted in the establishment of a submarine base and a submarine school at New London, Connecticut, and the authorization of the first 800-ton submarines. In a departure from the practice of obtaining plans from private shipbuilders, the Navy Department produced the design for these boats.[10]

Because the navy had been as laggard in developing its air arm as it had been in improving the submarine service, Benson also interested himself in this area. The Office of Naval Aeronautics consisted of just three people, with Captain Mark L. Bristol in charge. The sole naval air station, located at Pensacola, Florida, had only fourteen aircraft, none of them ready for regular service. There were only eleven naval pilots. The armored cruiser *North Carolina* was the only designated aeronautical vessel in the fleet. To energize the air arm, Benson first placed jurisdiction over the program in the Materiel Division within his office. Some have criticized this arrangement, but it resulted in Bristol's designation as commander of the Air Service. He was given command of the *North Carolina* and authority to supervise all aircraft and aircraft stations and to preside over further development of naval aeronautics.[11]

Despite these beginnings, naval aviation did not fare well. Bristol encountered difficulties with a subordinate officer, and his responsibilities were restricted to "development of tactics and use of aircraft afloat." Meanwhile, there was turnover in the position of assistant for aviation in the Materiel Division. At this stage, an association with naval aviation did not appear to officers to be career enhancing; furthermore, promotion was slow, and no incentives were offered to compensate for dangerous duty. Controversies raged over many issues, among them whether to develop lighter-than-air dirigibles or heavier-than-air craft, and whether to encourage private or public production. The *Liberty* motor for airplanes was as yet undeveloped, the first catapult had just been installed on the *North Carolina*, and air doctrine was in its earliest stages of development.[12]

Under these dubious circumstances, Congress debated the naval appropriation bill for 1916. Bristol sought $13.5 million for naval aviation, hoping to expend $6 million on the construction of two aircraft carriers. Benson opposed a major commitment until more was known about the requirements for aircraft carriers, suggesting an appropriation of $2 million. Ultimately Congress authorized $3.5 million. Commenting later on his position, Benson admitted that "it would unquestionably have been well to have devoted more money" for naval aviation, but he defended his decision: "In view of the situation as it was then and that is what we had to go upon in my judgment, . . . I felt that that was the best thing to do in the light of what we then had." Benson was accused of "butchering" Bristol's request, but the appropriated sum, while not providing funds for carriers, represented a considerable increase over prior grants. The steps taken in 1916 provided a foundation for the expansion that was to come very soon.[13]

Benson's early service as CNO coincided with significant armed interventions in the Caribbean region, notably in Haiti and the Dominican Republic, and in the annexation of the Virgin Islands. President Wilson sent naval forces into Haiti and the Dominican Republic to ensure stability. After the Marines restored order in Haiti, Benson expressed his approval of creating a Haitian constabulary to provide permanent security. A treaty negotiated in September 1915 reflected Benson's advice. In 1916 Benson gave considerable attention to the situation in the Dominican Republic, where a military government was established in November. Of greatest long-range significance, however, was Benson's involvement in the process that led to the purchase of the Danish West Indies. Fearful that Germany might obtain this territory and thus gain a base in the Caribbean Sea, Benson obtained the support of the General Board for its purchase. The Department of State negotiated a treaty in August 1916 that arranged the purchase of the Danish West Indies for $25 million. After the Senate gave its consent to this treaty in January 1917, President Wilson placed the acquisitions temporarily in the care of the U.S. Navy; they were renamed "The Virgin Islands of the United States."[14]

Benson made energetic contributions to the readiness of the fleet and to naval-political activity in the Caribbean Sea, but by far his most important concern during 1915 and 1916 was naval expansion. The war in Europe seemed to mean that the United States should expand its fleet. This subject became ever more pressing as both Great Britain and Germany posed challenges to the freedom of the seas. How many new ships should be authorized? What types were required? These and many other questions increasingly preoccupied Wilson and his principal naval adviser, Secretary Daniels, who shared the president's desire to avoid war. This desire, along with public apathy, inhibited preparedness.

The behavior of Germany, particularly after the sinking of the British ocean liner *Lusitania*, ultimately forced the president to conclude that the United States must expand its naval power. His closest adviser had similar thoughts. Edward M. House wrote as early as July 1915: "I wonder . . . whether we did not make a mistake in not preparing actively when this war first broke loose. If we had, by now we would have been in a position almost to enforce peace." President Wilson proved much more prepared to consider naval growth in 1915 than he had in earlier years. He asked Daniels to seek "professional advice" in drafting a program that would ensure "consistent and progressive development" of the navy. This step has justly been called an important turning point in the growth of the preparedness movement, which gained momentum as the war in Europe dragged on.[15]

Daniels asked the General Board to draft a program of naval construction for presentation to Congress, and on 30 July the group reported its findings. Asserting that the navy "should ultimately be equal to the most powerful maintained by any other nation in the world," the board insisted that the building program "should be gradually increased . . . by such a rate of development, year by year, as may be permitted by the facilities of the country, but the limit . . . should be attained not later than 1925." Estimating that the total cost would be over $285.6 million, the board's proposal called for construction of seventy-eight ships of war, including four dreadnoughts, four battle cruisers, six scout vessels, thirty coastal submarines, seven fleet submarines, twenty-eight destroyers, and six gunboats. Construction of various other units, such as tenders and a hospital ship, was also recommended. Construction would begin during the next fiscal year with an appropriation of $6.6 million. Appropriate increases in personnel and shore facilities were included in the program.[16]

On 19 August Benson provided detailed descriptions of the recommended ships and his justification for their inclusion in the building program. Four battleships were needed "to meet corresponding vessels of probable enemy." The nation had no battle cruisers, but all other large navies had added them: Britain had ten, Germany eight, and Japan four. The scout ships "would carry aircraft that go out from them and thus extend the area covered." Benson described the submarines as integral parts of the fleet rather than as independent units.[17]

Daniels suggested to the president that he discuss the naval proposal with Benson, but the cautious Wilson failed to do so. Benson maintained pressure on the secretary, on 22 September forwarding a justification for building four battleships armed with large-caliber guns. On 25 September he reiterated his earlier arguments for the overall program, stressing the importance of "putting the Navy in the best possible condition of preparedness to meet with possible enemies of the United States." Included in this communication was a proposal to appropriate at least $2 million "for the purchase of aircraft and motors, the development of fittings for their use on board ships, and the establishment of stations along the coast." Special mention was made of the need to add at least ten thousand personnel.[18]

Consideration of the building program entered a new phase when Secretary Daniels spoke through Benson to the General Board, asking that group to recommend a program of construction that would require an expenditure of about $100 million a year for five years. No secretary of the navy had ever before supported a continuing program of naval construction, although the General Board had called for such a program since 1903. By 12 October, after frequent meetings that usually included Benson, the board suggested a five-year program that provided for 157 new vessels. Three days later Daniels sent the naval estimates for the next annual budget to the secretary of the treasury, indicating a desire to begin construction of 55 vessels in the first year of a five-year program at a cost of about $502.5 million.[19]

The administration then prepared to push the program through Congress. On 4 November President Wilson endorsed the proposals of the General Board during a speech before the Manhattan Club in New York City. On 1 December Daniels included a recommendation for a five-year building program in his annual report to Congress, and the president followed suit in his annual message of 7 December.[20]

This unprecedented building program encountered difficulties in Congress. Republicans in the minority favored an even larger program, and they also wanted to augment the Office of Naval Operations. The Democratic majority was divided, some members supporting the president and others objecting to the large size of the program. To publicize the program, President Wilson spoke at St. Louis on 3 February 1916. The authorized text called for the "most adequate navy in the world," but Wilson actually said that he favored "incomparably the greatest navy in the world." When asked at a cabinet meeting whether he had spoken as reported, he replied: "Yes, and it is one thing I said in my swing around the circle that I absolutely believe." Wilson's ringing endorsement reflected not only a need to respond to the rising agitation for preparedness, but also a recognition that his diplomatic efforts to arrange a European peace settlement were likely to fail without the backing of respectable armed forces.[21]

Admiral Benson testified in behalf of the naval bill before the House Committee on Naval Affairs on 16–17 March, bearing in mind that the "small-navy" faction within the Democratic party held the balance of power in Congress. He lent support to the building program, arguing that a navy at least equal to that of Great Britain could meet the largest conceivable opponent, the British Grand Fleet, or a combination of the next two navies, those of Germany and Japan. To placate the small-navy advocates, he criticized the Republican plan to expand his own office, stating that the existing arrangement would soon accomplish "all that by human foresight it is possible to do by any system that could be designed."[22]

The contentious Admiral Fiske testified on 24 March in support of the provision to expand Benson's staff, an act that stimulated a campaign in the press for a naval general staff and elicited a rejoinder from Benson. Fiske advocated a plan to place fifteen assistants in the Office of the Chief of Naval Operations, thus reviving the key element in the proposal that he had favored in 1915. Benson took an opportunity in June to reiterate the views he had expressed to the House Committee on Naval Affairs. Speaking at the Naval Academy about his accomplishments, he maintained that the results were what "could be reasonably expected from a so-called 'General Staff,'" and that the work in operations was proceeding "in a purely American and businesslike manner." The existing organization ought to remain in place. Fullam wrote disparagingly to Sims, reflecting the reaction of the naval insurgents: "Did you read Benson's speech? . . . It would appear that the only way to get anything these days is to truckle and trim, and I am not prepared to do that by any means."[23]

When the House acted on the naval appropriation, it adopted a compromise that fell far short of the administration's desires. The small-navy Democrats agreed to support a one-year program that included funds for five battle cruisers, four scout cruisers, ten destroyers, twenty submarines, and three auxiliaries. In return, they exacted support for the Hensley amendment, which authorized the president to convene a disarmament conference by the end of the war. The one-year program of 2 June 1916 far exceeded the first-year recommendations of the General Board, but Benson and the members of the board were disappointed because it abandoned the continuous five-year program and ignored dreadnoughts, the backbone of the modern battle fleet.[24]

At just this moment, however, several fortuitous developments allowed the Wilson administration to revive the long-term approach. News of the battle of Jutland arrived just after the House passed its version of the naval bill. That engagement graphically demonstrated the importance of sea power. The chairman of the Senate Committee on Naval Affairs, Benjamin R. Tillman (D-S.C.), was now convinced of the need to build battleships as well as battle cruisers. Meanwhile, the news that Russia and Japan had renewed their political ties caused concern. This event raised the specter of a Russo-Japanese-German combination against the United States at some later date. Colonel House saw in it justification for an expanded navy. To Wilson he wrote: "If we do not [enlarge the navy], some such trouble may come. . . . If after all the warning we have had, trouble should follow this war, the people would feel that their interests have not been properly protected." Still another consideration arose: continuing difficulties with Mexico drew attention to the limited capacity of the fleet. After American forces clashed with Mexican troops on 22 June, Benson informed Secretary Daniels that war with Mexico would force the recall of all vessels in Chinese waters and weaken the naval force in Haitian and Dominican waters.[25]

President Wilson assumed the initiative on 27 June, coming out for the original program of naval construction and even reducing the time to three years, an action that finally led to acceptable legislation. The Senate passed a bill with these provisions on 21 July. Wilson then exerted pressure on the House, and that body acted on 15 August. The Naval Appropriations Act, signed by President Wilson into law on 29 August 1916, accepted the General Board's proposals for construction but specified that 157 ships were to be laid down before 1 July 1919 rather than by 1921. Congress appropriated $312,678,000 for the first year of construction and permitted an increase in enlisted strength from 51,000 to 74,000. Congressman Claude Kitchin (D-N.C.) exclaimed that the program required an *"increase of appropriations over 7 times more than the total increase by Great Britain in the 10 years prior to the European War . . . 60 times more than the total increase by Ger-*

many in the 5 years preceding the war, and 100 times more than the total increase by Germany in the 3 years preceding the war." Nothing like this legislation had ever before been realized; the nation was now definitively committed to build a navy second to none.[26]

The law of 29 August 1916 also provided for an enlargement of Benson's staff. After the change in mood during June, Benson had urged the secretary of the navy to authorize four changes: specify the rank of full admiral for the CNO; give the CNO power to issue orders to the fleet for the secretary of the navy; designate a certain number of officers as the CNO's assistants; and authorize retirement of the CNO at his permanent lineal rank. Daniels did not oppose these aggrandizing recommendations, a measure of the trust and confidence he had in Benson. The CNO's loyalty to the administration, a commitment that estranged him from many of his fellow officers, led to achievements that the reformers had sought in vain for many years. Legislative arrangements for the Office of the Chief of Naval Operations reflected Benson's proposal:

> Hereafter the Chief of Naval Operations, while so serving as such Chief of Naval Operations, shall have the rank and title of admiral, to take rank next after The Admiral of the Navy [Dewey], and shall, while so serving as Chief of Naval Operations, receive the pay of $10,000 per annum and no allowances. All orders issued by the Chief of Naval Operations in performing the duties assigned him shall be performed under the authority of the Secretary of the Navy, and his orders shall be considered as emanating from the Secretary, and shall have full force and effect as such. To assist the Chief of Naval Operations in performing the duties of his office there shall be assigned for this exclusive duty not less than fifteen officers of and above the rank of lieutenant commander of the Navy or major of the Marine Corps.

Benson now outranked all fleet commanders. On 7 September 1916 President Wilson signed a commission that made Benson a full admiral with date of rank from 29 August 1916.[27]

Admiral Benson contributed significantly to the process that produced the great naval legislation of 1916. The confidence they had in Benson was not the least of the circumstances that helped convert President Wilson and Secretary Daniels to the cause of naval expansion. When Benson informed Daniels that the appropriations bill had been signed, the secretary responded from Maine: "Glad to receive your telegram that the best Navy Bill ever enacted is now a law and that you have taken prompt steps to secure the building of the ships authorized." In less than two years of service, Benson could point to a significant improvement in the readiness of the navy and to a charter for the future that no one had anticipated, least of all his critics among the naval reformers. Benson's tactful relations with his civilian superiors and his willingness to accept the compromises essential to the legislative process, dismissed by his opponents as self-serving, had, in the end, contributed greatly to the nation's well-being.[28]

A supreme challenge lay ahead. The armed intervention by the United States in the European conflict that Woodrow Wilson so desperately wished to avoid took place a mere seven months after the passage of the epochal naval bill. When war came, the navy was much better prepared to fight than the army, in great part because Benson had assigned first priority to readiness and had effectively supported the decision to build a navy second to none.

CHAPTER V

THE END OF NEUTRALITY

President Wilson's desire to mediate the European war led to an unprecedented program of naval and military preparedness, but it also inhibited the progress of war plans and other measures that could have ensured full readiness in the event of war. Britain and Germany pursued maritime policies that violated American interpretations of international law and led to dangerous controversies between the United States and both coalitions. Wilson wanted to develop stronger armed forces in order to give credibility to his diplomacy, but he did not want to jeopardize his standing as an honest broker by taking martial steps that either European coalition might deem unneutral. This policy had the serious disadvantage of leaving the initiative to the Europeans, who had to accept Wilson as a mediator before peace negotiations could begin.

There was, temporarily, another deterrent to energetic activity in the Navy Department and in the other services: the president was deeply involved in a campaign for reelection. Perhaps against Wilson's wishes, the campaign of 1916 turned in part on the appealing slogan "He kept us out of war." Important national initiatives had to await the outcome of the vote in November.

In the constrained circumstances of 1916, Admiral Benson was forced to press for naval preparedness with a naval staff of only seventy-five officers, a talented but overtaxed group. Among them was Captain William Veazie Pratt, who in time became the CNO's right-hand man. Attempting to relieve a shortage of enlisted personnel, Benson sought to attain a strength of eighty-seven thousand sailors. He hoped to encourage general enlistments by developing a regular recruiting service throughout the nation. Rear Admiral Leigh C. Palmer, who was appointed chief of the Bureau of Navigation in August 1916, set up training facilities in colleges and technical schools to supplement conventional training camps. Additional strength became available after 7 September 1916, when Congress created a Naval Reserve administered by the Bureau of Navigation.

Benson worked closely with the General Board in drafting building programs and other elements of naval policy, and thus he was anxious to keep competent officers on it. When Admiral Badger finished a term on the board, Benson decided to retain him, a step that disappointed Admiral Fletcher, lately relieved as commander in chief of the Atlantic Fleet, who wanted the position. To retain Fletcher's good will, Benson explained that he had acted with the support of Secretary Daniels and Admiral Dewey and had taken into consideration "the best interest of the Service at this time." Fletcher responded graciously: "I think that under the circumstances your action was quite logical."

Benson was at pains to discourage undue faultfinding in senior officers. When Admiral Fullam complained about the department's failure to assign additional personnel to his command, Benson reminded him that the Office of the CNO was also staffed minimally and that it was "incumbent upon every officer, especially the older ones, to realize and appreciate this condition and to do everything in their power to inculcate a spirit of united effort rather than a spirit of fault-finding and criticism." He was quick to head off the continuing criticism of Secretary Daniels; for example, he told Rear Admiral Albert Gleaves, the new commander of the Destroyer Force, Atlantic Fleet, that senior officers should try to "neutralize" what he characterized as "too-free criticism of the head of the Navy."[1]

During this period, Benson was particularly concerned with the procurement of future officers. Even before the passage of the Naval Appropriations Act, he arranged a naval cruise for civilians who were interested in obtaining commissions. More than twenty-five hundred volunteers embarked on 13 August 1916 for a training cruise on the six battleships assigned to this duty. Instruction on board ship resembled that given to midshipmen on practice cruises; the civilians took target practice, loaded and fired guns, stoked the boilers, and held naval exercises. In addition, the trainees attended a series of lectures on various subjects of professional interest to naval officers, such as strategy, tactics, gunnery, torpedo craft, defense of naval districts, customs of the service, military character, and the relationship between diplomacy and naval power. When the cruise ended, Benson spoke of it in laudatory terms, stating that the public had gained an improved understanding of naval operations, an outcome that would encourage men to enlist.[2]

Admiral Benson also devoted considerable time to naval construction. The building program authorized in August 1916 required the development of shipyards, including the Philadelphia Navy Yard. In need of attention were technological innovations such as an electric drive for battleships, whose development the CNO supported. To many naval officers, including Benson, the building program provided insurance in the event that the United States encountered serious dangers at sea in the wake of the European conflict—whether or not the United States was drawn in. The General Board met on 13–14 October 1916 to prepare the naval estimates for 1917. It proposed construction of the ships authorized in August and, in addition, twelve minesweepers, two seagoing tugs, and a supply ship.[3]

On 14 November 1916 Congress passed the Shipping Act of 1916 in an effort to encourage expansion of the ailing American merchant fleet; soon thereafter, Admiral Benson expressed himself on one aspect of this enterprise—the protection of coastal commerce. Speaking to the National Waterways Congress on 8 December, Benson drew attention to the need for a protected coastal route. He had in mind a basic strategic consideration: "Our coasts might be assailed by an overwhelming naval force before we could prepare ourselves fully to repel. That being the case, you will easily understand what an advantage it would be if we could move our ships from one part of our coast to another." Benson would return to the subject of protective measures for the coast sooner than anyone anticipated.[4]

In light of increasing tensions resulting from the controversy over neutral rights with Great Britain as well as Germany, Benson did what he could to prepare for mobilization. On 11 December he augmented his earlier arrangements for mobilization, notifying all bureaus, naval districts, and offices in the Navy Department that he intended to issue "mobilization sheets," which would prescribe the actions to be taken in the event of war. If necessary, he directed, the commander in chief of the fleet and commandants of naval districts would issue additional orders.[5]

In November, President Wilson was narrowly reelected, clearing the way for a final, desperate effort to bring the contending coalitions to the peace table. While Secretary Daniels proposed a building program for the next year that exceeded the earlier recommendations of the General Board and called for production of the final ninety ships authorized in August, the president, on 18 December, asked the belligerents to state their war aims, as a basis for possible negotiations. Although he received discouraging responses, he decided to make a public appeal to the belligerents. On 22 January 1917 Wilson delivered one of his most important speeches, calling on the Allied Powers and the Central Powers to accept a "peace without victory." This commitment would permit a boundary settlement based on the democratic principle of self-determination and the creation of a League of Nations to ensure a just and lasting peace.[6]

Unbeknown to Wilson, however, after Lloyd George rejected Kaiser Wilhelm II's peace proposal of 18 December 1916, the German government had decided on a naval initiative that contemplated an early and decisive victory rather than peace negotiations. In 1915–16, President Wilson had threatened war should Germany embrace a policy of unrestricted submarine warfare—attacks without warning against neutral and noncombatant belligerent commerce on the high seas. At that time Germany had decided to desist, but January 1917 saw a change of policy. German naval leaders assumed that Germany's submarines could sufficiently damage the merchant shipping that brought supplies to Britain and France to force the Allies out of the war in six months. This undersea campaign would probably lead to an American intervention, but the German government assumed that the war would end before the unprepared United States could influence the outcome.[7]

Germany's decision placed President Wilson in a wrenching dilemma: he must take decisive action or surrender all influence over the future course of the war and the peace settlement. His first step was to break diplomatic relations with Germany, but as he did so on 3 February, he temporized: "I refuse to believe that it is the intention of the German authorities to do in fact what they have warned us they will feel at liberty to do. . . . Only overt acts on their part can make me believe it even now." He then began to search for a response to Germany that would satisfy American honor but avoid a declaration of war. Secretary Daniels supported this course, and, seemingly, so did Admiral Benson. Daniels reported the CNO's views to the president on 2 February, noting that Benson possessed "the same abhorrence of becoming enlisted on either side of combatants that you expressed. His view is that if we lose our equipoise, the world will be in darkness. He expressed the hope that you would find a way to avert the calamity."[8]

Whatever his hopes, Benson certainly recognized that war was a distinct possibility; he indicated how belligerency might begin in a memorandum of 2 February titled "Regarding Belligerents in Neutral Jurisdiction." The United States, he explained, would not become a belligerent until it declared war against another nation or some other nation declared war against it. If the United States committed warlike acts without declaring war, neutral states would have to decide whether deeds of this nature "were sufficiently grave to warrant such neutral in the projection on its neutrality to declare that we were a belligerent power and must be so considered as far as its own ports and territorial waters were concerned." In this way, Benson opened the door slightly to measures short of war.[9]

Of greater importance was another memorandum of the same date in which Benson reviewed the possible consequences if the United States Navy provided armed escort to convoys of merchant vessels—a form of armed neutrality. Such action was perfectly legitimate, he explained, but a belligerent could legally halt a convoy and its escort on the high seas, presumably to exercise the right to visit the ships and even to search for contraband. What about denial of passage through an area within one of the zones where Germany intended to wage unrestricted submarine warfare? The United States, he insisted, had a right to resist illegal actions prejudicial to its interests, and the German zones were illegal by any measure: international law, maritime practice, and legal precedent. After reviewing the legal issues, the CNO noted that, in all probability, if the United States challenged the German blockade, an armed action would result.[10]

This memorandum was part of a sustained effort to find some means short of belligerency of making a credible response to the German undersea initiative—some form of armed neutrality. One possibility was to arm merchant vessels. The CNO proved responsive to this measure after discussing the subject with Secretary Daniels and President Wilson on 5 February. He noted that an armed merchant vessel was equivalent to an escorting patrol vessel. On 14 February he was most positive in his endorsement, as the concluding words of a memorandum he wrote to Daniels indicate: *"Arm the merchant vessels and train their gun's crews to the highest efficiency."*[11]

President Wilson's hand was forced when Germany sunk two American merchant ships and when it became known that Germany had attempted to enlist Mexico in the cause of the Central Powers in return for restitution of territory Mexico had lost to the United States in the nineteenth century. The president decided to arm merchant vessels, and on 26 February he asked a joint session of Congress to give him such authority. This proposal pleased neither those who opposed war nor those who favored it. Pacifists viewed the expedient of arming merchant ships as simply a stop on the way to belligerency, whereas those who wanted to fight preferred an immediate declaration of war. The outcome was a prolonged filibuster in the Senate. Congress ended its session on 4 March without taking action on the armed-ship resolution. Unwilling to accept congressional inaction that he attributed to "a little group of willful men," Wilson determined that he possessed sufficient executive authority to act without legislation. The Navy Department then prepared regulations to guide the conduct of armed merchant ships. According to Secretary Daniels, Chief of the Bureau of Navigation Palmer thought that Germany would construe the arming of merchant vessels as an act of war, but Daniels informed the president that Benson proposed to give due notice to the German government, believing it "barely possible that Germany might not carry out her threat." The first vessel to leave port with a naval armed guard on board, the *Manchuria*, departed from New York on 16 March.[12]

Meanwhile Benson took all feasible measures to prepare for war. To ensure the security of the Panama Canal, he arranged to augment the Caribbean Squadron with armored cruisers and destroyers drawn from the Pacific Ocean. Of greater importance was the decision to concentrate the battle fleet in the Chesapeake Bay. Captain Pratt suggested that the battleships and armored cruisers not required in the Atlantic be sent to the Pacific, where they would enjoy relative safety and "their potential as a fleet in being might be used to the best political advantage." Both Admiral Henry T. Mayo and Admiral Benson opposed such a move. The CNO held that Pratt's plan might easily be construed as an admission of weakness. The General Board approved the plan Benson preferred, concentrating the fleet in the Chesapeake Bay. Much of this activity reflected an essentially defensive orientation, as did orders from Benson to the commandants of the eight naval districts concerning coastal defense. Nothing more was possible until the political situation was clarified.[13]

On 20 March President Wilson called his cabinet together to consider the nation's future course, recognizing the failure of his efforts to develop a viable policy of armed neutrality. Most of his advisers favored war, including Secretary of State Robert Lansing. The most compelling of the arguments in support of belligerency was Lansing's observation that maintenance of neutrality would deprive the United States of any future influence on the outcome of the war. The president was determined not simply to bring the struggle to an end; he wanted to exercise a predominant influence on the peace settlement. This desire was sufficiently strong to compel him to ask for a declaration of war when it became clear that any other course meant diplomatic bankruptcy. On 21 March he called a special session of Congress for 2 April that was "to receive a communication by the Executive on grave questions of national policy which should be taken immediately under consideration."[14]

During the interim between 20 March and 2 April, the United States finally began extensive preparations for war, including taking immediate naval action. President Wilson's desire to avoid the appearance of belligerency had precluded communications between the United States and the principal naval power, Great Britain, but this constraint disappeared after the decision for war was reached. On 23 March the American ambassador to Great Britain, Walter Hines Page, urged that an American admiral be dispatched to London to take part in naval discussions, and on 24 March Wilson adopted this course. To Daniels he wrote: "The main thing is no doubt to get into immediate communication with the Admiralty on the other side (through confidential channels until the Congress has acted) and work out the scheme of cooperation."[15]

On 28 March 1917 Rear Admiral William S. Sims, then president of the Naval War College, was called to Washington and ordered to proceed secretly to Great Britain. Daniels had considered Captain Henry

B. Wilson for this duty, but others in the Navy Department, especially Admiral Benson and probably also Assistant Secretary Roosevelt, successfully urged the selection of Sims. Sims was well known for pro-British proclivities, having been born in Canada of a British mother and an American father. In his memoir of the war years, *The Victory at Sea*, Sims summarized the instructions he received: the department "wished me to leave immediately for England, to get in touch with the British Admiralty, to study the naval situation and learn how we could best and most quickly cooperate in the naval war." On 31 March Sims embarked on the steamer *New York* bound for Liverpool. He and his aide, Lieutenant Commander John V. Babcock, traveled in great secrecy under assumed names, because the United States had not yet declared war.[16]

However, there was more to the story than Sims revealed in *The Victory at Sea*. In 1920, testifying before a congressional investigating committee, Sims reported that he had received some stern advice from Admiral Benson: "Don't let the British pull the wool over your eyes. It is none of our business pulling their chestnuts out of the fire. We would as soon fight the British as the Germans." Although Sims may have embroidered the statement somewhat, Benson himself said, when queried by the same congressional committee: "Well, I might put it this way. I thought that there were certain things going on that we ought to be prepared for in an emergency. Our ships were being held up and certain things were going on that might make it necessary for us to take a definite stand. I never had any idea that we would have to fight any other country; no." Benson did not deny having warned Sims to guard against British machinations, but he sought to counter the implication that he was as anti-British as he was anti-German.[17]

This story has been recounted many times in support of the allegation that Benson was an Anglophobe and Sims an Anglophile, but these categories may not be helpful in treating the controversies that later developed between the two admirals. A balanced assessment is that Sims reflected the special perspective of a theater commander, and Benson that of an individual in headquarters who was preoccupied with broader political-military concerns. Sims was convinced that close ties with Great Britain best served the national interest, whereas Benson thought that such cooperation might not be desirable in certain contexts.[18]

Admiral Benson's ideas regarding U.S. intervention were faithfully reflected in "The Possibility of War," an extensive memorandum prepared by his staff in February 1917. He entertained views that suggested a naval-political posture that differed from the one Sims came to advocate after arriving in London. Various measures were identified as necessary for ultimate success, most of them relating to mobilization of the fleet and construction of naval vessels. Of greatest interest, how-

Sitting, left to Right - Mr. Hoover, General Bliss, Admiral Benson, Mr. Baruch, Mr. Robinson
Standing, Left to Right - Mr. Lamont, Mr. Stephardson, Mr. Norman Davis, Colnel House, Mr. auchincloss
Mr. Vance McCormick .

Group portrait, 1917. Caption is in Admiral Benson's handwriting.

ever, was a commentary on motives for going to war. Contrary to the view that the United States should fight "for the sole purpose of protecting commerce," Benson believed that the decision should reflect an intention "to secure guarantees for the future." Obviously the United States must align with the Allies to bring about the defeat of Germany, but victory by itself would not protect the future. The only real guarantee was "superiority of fighting power," given the fact that "expediency was the chief motive of warring powers in their international relations." The United States must recognize that the "possible combinations, of powers and circumstances, are too numerous and too pregnant with possibilities adverse to our interest to permit us to consider any plan other than one which will permit us to exercise eventually the full naval and military strength of the United States in the defense of our interests." For this reason, Benson was wary: the United States must act quickly in behalf of the Allies, but it must do so with "full realization that we may eventually have to act alone." In other words, the United States must bear in mind the possibility that the Germans would defeat the Allies and that the United States would have to continue the struggle by itself.

What, then, was the correct naval policy? Three missions suggested themselves: "(1) *To develop the full military and naval strength of the United States as fast as possible,* (2) *To employ our forces in war so as best to build up our fighting power as an independent nation,* (3)

To render the maximum possible support now to the enemies of the Central Powers." The third of these missions held the first priority, given the emergency at hand, but the United States could not "assume any safety not founded on the accomplishment of the first two." This consideration dictated certain practices when aiding the Allies: the United States must maintain full strategic, tactical, and administrative support of its naval forces, and it should employ those forces in waters closest to the United States. It was necessary, Benson contended, to "make war on enemy submarines within the areas assigned and to deflect sufficient commerce to the transatlantic trade to ensure the full support of the entente powers." For this reason the United States should construct antisubmarine vessels, which could be built quickly and which might exercise decisive influence, but, nevertheless, "vessels should be built not only to meet present conditions but conditions that may come after the present phase of the world war." The policy adopted in 1916 of building a balanced battle fleet that would include the required number of battleships and cruisers was necessary to allow the nation "to dispute the freedom of the seas with potential enemies. . . . We may expect the future to give us more potential enemies than potential friends so that our safety must lie in our own resources." The list of possible naval enemies would presumably include Great Britain as well as Japan.[19]

Admiral Benson expressed similar views in March 1917. He argued that the United States must prepare "to render futile and destroy the immediate menace of the German submarine campaign in order to destroy the ultimate menace of her full strength used against us, but at the same time we must prepare ourselves *to meet the ultimate menace* if it comes, for unless we are prepared to meet it the very life of our nation is endangered." Once again the CNO raised the specter of Allied defeat as a reason for maintaining the building program of 1916.[20]

Admiral Benson developed his conception of wartime naval policy well before the United States entered the war in April 1917. Concerning the question of whether the United States should emphasize the immediate threat of the German submarine or the long-range danger that might materialize later on, Benson proposed to adjust naval strategy in the immediate future to ensure that the nation was prepared to respond to both situations. This position reflected his views that Germany could conceivably defeat the Allies and that the balance of power after the war, even in the wake of Allied victory, might prove threatening to the United States.

These considerations, ably developed by Admiral Benson, came under close scrutiny during the early months of the war as the Western coalition sought to counter the unrestricted submarine operations of Germany, which were designed to bring the war to a close before the United States could turn the tide. In due course Admiral Sims's reports from London had a considerable impact on the leadership of the United

States as it determined the character of its wartime assistance to the Entente nations, but the initial leadership decisions stemmed from discussions held with the missions sent by the Allies to Washington shortly after the U.S. declaration of war.

CHAPTER VI

INTO THE WAR

American leaders possessed only the vaguest notion of the military and naval situation in Europe as the United States entered the war in April 1917. Neither the army nor the navy had made extensive efforts to analyze the conflict, a consequence both of Wilson's desire to maintain his credibility as a mediator and of European censorship, which withheld accurate information. The submarine crisis materialized so suddenly that even some members of the British government failed to recognize the extent of the emergency. Admiral Sims sailed for London under the misapprehension that "sea power apparently rested practically unchallenged in the hands of the Allies." The thought that the Entente Powers might lose the war had not crossed his mind: "All the fundamental facts in the case made it appear impossible that the Germans could win the war."[1]

As late as 21 March 1917 British policy makers assumed that "Great Britain should not appear anxious that America should enter the war." The Admiralty did not indicate its requirements until President Wilson decided to send an emissary to London. Captain Guy R. A. Gaunt, the British naval attaché in Washington, then revealed that Great Britain wanted the United States Navy to patrol both the North and the South Atlantic; to send destroyers to Ireland to operate against German submarines; to guard the east and west coasts of Great Britain; and to maintain naval forces in the Far East, compensating for the withdrawal of the Royal Navy from that area. Gaunt communicated this information to his friend Assistant Secretary of the Navy Franklin D. Roosevelt, from whom he learned that the United States wished to avoid official contacts, preferring that Great Britain send a naval officer to Washington as soon as possible for consultations. Roosevelt presumably passed the British message to Daniels, who informed the president. Wilson did not think that the proposed program was especially effective, but he was not prepared to criticize it until something better came to hand.[2]

Meanwhile, France had taken an important initiative in an effort to establish contact with the United States Navy. The French minister of marine, Georges Leygues, directed his naval attaché in London, Rear Admiral Maurice Henry de Lostende, to inform the British Admiralty that France had appointed the commander of the French navy's West Indian Division, Rear Admiral Maurice Ferdinand Albert de Grasset, to represent France in any naval negotiations that might take place. He would proceed to Bermuda and await instructions to go to the United States. The Admiralty then informed de Lostende that it had designated the commander of its North American and West Indian Squadron, Vice Admiral Sir Montague E. Browning, to represent Britain in negotiations that would take place after the United States indicated its intention to enter the war. In the interim, Browning was to confer with de Grasset.[3]

As soon as war was declared, the proposed naval conference was arranged; on 10 April 1917 Admiral Benson, with an aide, Lieutenant Commander Andrew F. Carter, and Admiral Mayo, with a member of his staff, Captain Henry B. Wilson, welcomed the British and French representatives at Hampton Roads, Virginia. This development reflected the presumption, which proved accurate, that the United States would first make its presence felt in the war by deploying its naval power. The United States Army, far less ready for action, would require many months of preparation. The British and French admirals did not dwell on the emergency that had developed in European waters, concentrating instead on a series of specific tasks for the United States derived from the list that Gaunt had passed to Roosevelt in March.[4]

The site of the conference then moved to Washington, where participants took up various British and French proposals. Secretary Daniels presided; Assistant Secretary Roosevelt and members of the General Board were in attendance. Admiral Benson asked: "Where can our Navy render the best service immediately?" Not surprisingly, the first topic of discussion was the proposal to send American destroyers to European waters. Benson showed reluctance to interfere with the American practice of retaining two destroyers for every battleship in the fleet, a procedure that Browning could hardly criticize, because both the British and the French followed it. He also manifested concern about German U-boats in American waters, remembering the appearance of the U-53 off New England during 1916. He wanted to send only one or two destroyers to "show the flag" in Ireland, claiming that this gesture would exercise a considerable moral effect.

Admiral W. S. Benson with Vice Admiral Sir Montague Edward Browning, Washington, D.C., 13 April 1917. Courtesy of Mrs. J. S. Hammill, daughter of Admiral Browning.

Other items were then discussed. The Americans were unenthusiastic about the British suggestion that they establish a South Atlantic Squadron, but everyone agreed that this would be done as soon as possible. Browning thought that armed merchant ships could be used to counter German raiders, but the Americans wondered whether such vessels were not better employed in commerce. During a discussion of the security of the Gulf of Mexico and Central America, Browning consented to American use of Trinidad as a base for the American Patrol Squadron. The Americans agreed to keep their Asiatic Squadron on station.

On 13 April specific terms of an agreement were drafted in Admiral Benson's office. The Americans agreed to patrol in both North Atlantic and South Atlantic waters and to maintain the Asiatic Squadron in Far Eastern waters. Six destroyers were to be sent to European waters. Some small craft were designated for service in France.[5]

As the conference continued, the naval leaders began to form impressions of one another. Browning, who had been unsure of the mood at the beginning, reported later that the Americans were "really anxious to cooperate" and that Admirals Benson and Mayo "became more and more cordial." There was an "anxious desire" for advice and "no trace of any feeling to the contrary." Benson and Browning developed mutual respect for each other at this time, which led to a lifelong friendship, but Benson and de Grasset did not establish comparable rapport, in part because of the language barrier. The French admiral reported that both Benson and Daniels appeared lethargic. Of the CNO he remarked: "His spirit is slow and he does not seem possessed of the moral authority that comports with his rank and functions, . . . a bureaucrat who arrived at the grade of admiral through political changes happening in the [naval] ministry." Browning thought that de Grasset was disturbed because the British gained a great deal by comparison, even if the French received what they had requested: small gunboats to defend their fishing fleet and an armed transport to ferry railroad material to France. This outcome reflected the fact that the United States had to concentrate on naval cooperation with the dominant Allied naval power.[6]

During this conference Benson drew on his established views in evaluating the Anglo-French proposals. Together with the General Board, he supported Admiral Alfred Thayer Mahan's dictum that the United States should not divide its battle fleet. He looked suspiciously at any suggestion to detach integral components such as destroyers for service elsewhere. He also believed that the first responsibility of the navy was coastal defense, as he had argued regularly in his prewar statements on the use of naval power. Finally, he retained the fear that the Entente Powers might have to accept a separate peace, leaving the United States to fight on alone. The General Board associated itself with Benson's views on the most important question, the dispatch of destroyers to European waters, holding that the United States should not strip itself of naval vessels "until the [European] situation was better understood."[7]

The negotiators did not discuss long-range plans or policy. American participants were unprepared to advance such proposals, and the Allies concentrated on immediate concerns. Benson noted much later: "Our forces would have to be combined with their forces in the way that would carry out the plans and policies that they had set out and had been following. Further guidance would have to come from Great Britain."[8]

Admiral Sims arrived in London on 10 April and immediately entered into detailed discussions at the Admiralty. After initial conversations with the First Sea Lord, Admiral Sir John R. Jellicoe, and Rear Admiral Sir Dudley R. S. de Chair (who soon thereafter visited Washington), Sims realized that he and his countrymen were under serious misapprehensions about the situation. "The Germans, it now appeared, were not losing the war—they were winning it." The British Navy was engaging the submarine with "pitifully inadequate forces."[9]

On 14 April, Sims sent to the Navy Department the first in a long series of cables that both revealed the gravity of the naval emergency and proposed countermeasures. The total of Allied and neutral shipping falling prey to the submarine had risen to over five hundred thousand tons in February and again in March, and about two hundred thousand tons had gone to the bottom during the first ten days of April. Pointing to the "dangerously strained" condition of the Royal Navy, Sims emphasized the need for a maximum number of destroyers and other small antisubmarine craft based on Queenstown, Ireland (now known as Cobh), to patrol west of Ireland. Sims wanted to detach destroyers from the fleet, leaving the capital ships without a screen, a measure that violated both Admiral Mahan's teachings and the Navy Department's established practice. He requested repair ships and staff for Queenstown and an advanced base at Bantry Bay. Regarding other types of naval vessels, he wrote: "At present our battleships can serve no useful purpose in this area except that two divisions of dread-noughts might be based in Brest for moral effect against anticipated raids by heavy enemy ships in the Channel out of reach of British main fleet." He argued that the British Grand Fleet, based in North Sea ports, could not be expected to venture out of that general area, because the "German main fleet must be contained, demanding maximum conservation of British main fleet." Other than antisubmarine craft, the "chief other and urgent practical cooperation is merchant shipping." Sims recognized that some U-boats might visit the Caribbean Sea or the American East Coast to lay mines, hoping to force American naval vessels to remain in home waters, but he maintained that minesweeping could easily counter such enemy tactics. He summarized his recommendations dramatically: "Maximum augmentation merchant tonnage and anti-submarine work where most effective constitute the paramount immediate necessity."[10]

Sims augmented his views on 19 April. Although he realized that the enemy might launch diversions on the American coast or elsewhere, he was convinced that the "critical area in which the war's decision will be made is in the eastern Atlantic at the focus of all lines of communications," because Germany did not have enough submarines to employ them efficiently in other places. He then drew attention to public criticism of the Admiralty "for not taking more decisive steps and for failing to produce more substantial and visible results." At that time, one tactical response to submarines was to disperse merchant ships. An alternative was to escort merchant ships in convoys through the danger zone, but the British had not done so because they lacked sufficient vessels. However, Sims was consulting the Admiralty about adopting the convoy method "in case the United States is able to put in operation sufficient tonnage to warrant it." Another possibility was to block the exits from the enemy's principal submarine bases. The British prime minister, David Lloyd George, was interested in this measure, but Sims claimed to have convinced him that such a tactic was impractical. It was impossible to maintain a close blockade and, in any event, this measure would concentrate friendly naval power in an area where the enemy had a distinct advantage.[11]

Meanwhile the United States dispatched its first naval reinforcement to European waters. On 18 April Commander Joseph K. Taussig was ordered to prepare Destroyer Division Eight for "distant service"; his mission was "to assist naval operations of Entente Powers in every way possible. Proceed to Queenstown, Ireland. Report to Senior British Naval Officer present and thereafter cooperate fully with the British Navy." On 24 April the six destroyers left Boston. Sims considered that this effort, which engaged 12 percent of the available fifty-one destroyers, fell short of the requirement. He wanted the United States to send "all the destroyers that could get there."[12]

The departure of the destroyers raised the question of naval command in European waters. Sims had gone to London on temporary duty as a liaison officer, but on 28 April he was given orders to "assume command all destroyers operating from British bases, including tenders and auxiliaries, these to be sent later." Taussig was informed that the destroyer division was now under Sims's command, but that "active command [would] be exercised by the senior officer on the spot, under orders of the Vice Admiral of the Port." This decision for all practical purposes put the destroyer division temporarily into the Royal Navy. Sims recognized the possibility of Anglo-American friction and, to counter possible controversies with Vice Admiral Sir Lewis Bayly, the commander at Queenstown (who was deemed a "peculiarly difficult man to deal with"), he asked Taussig not to mention any problems that might arise: "Criticism can do no good, it may do much harm. Let us set a record among the Allies for cooperation and show what can be done in common cause." All this was the beginning of the process that eventuated in the designation of Sims as the American naval commander in Europe. It also inaugurated his studied efforts to maintain the closest possible coordination with the Royal Navy, a policy that was certain to create friction at home.[13]

These arrangements proved disturbing to Admiral Henry T. Mayo, commander in chief of the Atlantic Fleet, who requested service in European waters. The Navy Department disagreed with Mayo, believing that the situation did not call for an American commander in chief because American naval forces sent to Europe would complement those of the Allies rather than operate independently. Furthermore, the submarine campaign might force the British to settle with Germany, in which case the Atlantic Fleet must be prepared to operate as a distinct entity.

Taussig reached Queenstown on 4 May, and his command received a cordial reception. When Admiral Bayly asked when the American boats would be prepared for service, Taussig set the tone for cooperation, responding immediately: "We are ready now, Sir, that is as soon as we finish refueling." His division was soon at sea. Ambassador Page reported at the time that the British public was "becoming very restive with its half information and it is more and more loudly demanding all the facts. There are already angry threats to change the personnel of the Admiralty; there is even talk of turning out the Government." The prompt American action, however limited, greatly encouraged the British ministry.[14]

The first of a series of missions from the cobelligerent powers— a British group headed by Foreign Secretary Arthur James Balfour— soon appeared in Washington to hold detailed discussions. Twenty-two members represented the agencies of the British government most concerned with the conduct of the war: the Foreign Office, the War Office, the Admiralty, and those organizations concerned with munitions, blockade, and food. The British naval attaché in Washington between 1902 and 1905, Rear Admiral Sir Dudley de Chair, who had participated in the early discussions with Sims in London, represented the Admiralty. When the mission arrived on 23 April, de Chair exchanged calls with Daniels and Benson. Much to the surprise of his British hosts, Benson drove Daniels to the meeting with de Chair. Daniels considered this episode of interest, noting in his diary: "Wasn't that true American democracy—a full admiral driving the car?"[15]

Balfour arrived with specific instructions designed to encourage early American actions. He was directed to press for full development of the American shipbuilding industry and to advocate transfer of American vessels then engaged in coastal trade to the supply of the Allies. Neutrals could provide sufficient shipping on the American coasts. He was also enjoined to request some American troops: they would "show the United States flag [on the Western Front] and give the public of the United States of America a definite stake in the war." Other tasks were to urge adoption of British weapons, a means of ensuring the greatest efficiency in arming the American army; to obtain much-needed wheat; and to suggest a reduction in civilian use of steel.[16]

Of greatest immediate import was the discussion of naval questions. Balfour later remembered: "Things were dark when I took that trip to America. . . . The submarines were constantly on my mind. I could think of nothing but the number of ships which they were sinking." In a document designed to guide the Balfour Mission, the British author noted: the naval "initiative will have to come solely from us. The United States understands little or nothing of the way in which a war is conducted."[17]

The French government sent a delegation headed by René Viviani to Washington to seek American naval assistance. The naval representative, Vice Admiral Paul-Louis-Albert Chocheprat, made proposals for assistance that at times conflicted with requests made by the British. He wanted to develop the ports of Brest and Bordeaux, a plan that Benson favored but that Sims opposed, because he wanted "just one command abroad." Later Sims recognized that he may have erred in this opinion, noting in his memoir: "It was a matter of regret that we could not earlier have made Brest the main naval base for the American naval forces in Europe, for it was in some respects strategically better located for that purpose than was any other port in Europe."[18]

Well before the European delegations arrived in Washington, a critical disparity of views developed between American and British officials. The British wanted the United States to dedicate naval and maritime resources to the supply of the Allies, whereas Benson emphasized preparations not only for the immediate struggle, but also for a continuing war with Germany should the Allies meet defeat. Benson's concern led to a difference of opinion regarding the American building program. British proposals, to which Admiral Sims lent wholehearted and strident support, emphasized the construction of antisubmarine craft and merchant shipping largely to the exclusion of all else, a natural response to the German undersea campaign against shipping. American naval representatives did not immediately accept the British view, leading some historians to cite Benson's presumed Anglophobia as an explanation.[19]

Benson had to weigh several contingencies, including the dangerous prospect of having to wage war later on without allies, which seemed to require the construction of capital ships along with antisubmarine and merchant vessels. As chief of naval operations, Benson had to place his vision of the nation's needs ahead of all other considerations, and he had no doubt concerning what was required of him: "My first thought in the beginning, during and always, was to see that first our coasts and our vessels and our own interests were safeguarded." This hardly surprising nationalist orientation led Benson at times to oppose British recommendations, and some naval historians attribute his behavior to anti-British sentiment. Unlike Sims, Benson had no great confidence in the policies of the British government or great admiration of the British (a not uncommon opinion in the U.S. Navy), but his behavior as chief of naval operations is not explicable simply as an expression of Anglophobia. To his nationalism must be added another vitally important influence: his commitment to the views of Admiral Mahan. Benson never questioned a basic Mahanian precept: to succeed at sea, the nation must build a powerful and balanced battle fleet capable of contesting with any other fleet for general and lasting command of the sea. Such a fleet would become indispensable in the event of an Allied defeat.[20]

Although British conceptions of building policy during the emergency ran directly counter to Benson's interest in continuing to build the balanced battle fleet authorized in 1916, Benson accompanied de Chair to Capitol Hill, where the British admiral urged congressional leaders to support suspension of the battleship building program in favor of constructing antisubmarine craft. Because this approach ignored American long-term concerns, Colonel House advocated a quid pro quo. He suggested that Great Britain demonstrate good will toward the United States by awarding the Americans an option to buy British battleships after the war in sufficient number to compensate for those not built during the war. Given this insurance, House maintained, the United States "could go ahead with [its] destroyers without fear of subsequent events." Benson looked with favor on House's proposal, but he did not take part in the secret discussions that evolved into a complicated consideration of a secret naval treaty. This arrangement would have included Japan and other naval powers as well as the United States and Great Britain. Nothing came of the concept of a secret naval treaty during the war, although the discussions surrounding it were an interesting preliminary to the naval negotiations that took place in Washington during 1921 and 1922. The United States had to make its decision about the building program without benefit of a compensative arrangement with Britain.[21]

At this crucial time the British government made one of its most important decisions of the war by adopting the convoy system, a technique that so often in the past had countered a *guerre de course*—war against commerce. Until it was confronted with the depredations that followed the German resumption of unrestricted submarine warfare, the Admiralty held that in modern conditions ships in convoy presented a more attractive target than individual vessels: convoys could proceed no faster than the slowest vessel in the formation; merchant ship captains lacked the skill to maintain station in the convoy; weather conditions would create undue confusion. Others argued that these difficulties could be overcome, and the Admiralty's view lost credibility as U-boats scored heavily against merchant shipping after February 1917. On 30 April 1917 Lloyd George visited the Admiralty and forced a decision to experiment with convoy. One of the reasons for this move was that American naval vessels would likely be available to serve as escorts. The first convoys were very successful in controlling the German submarines, as convoys proved difficult to attack—their armed escorts formed a dangerous shield. Civilian maritime experts also made important contributions; they developed means of speeding turnaround in port and organizing the available shipping most efficiently. The decision to adopt the convoy system was well received in the United States, given the tremendous success of the German war against commerce.[22]

Admiral Sims in London single-mindedly supported the British decision to adopt convoy, arguing that any other course might lead to a German victory. Admiral Benson at first expressed reservations, as did his assistant, Captain Pratt, who enjoyed the confidence of Sims, but experimentation demonstrated the effectiveness of convoy.[23]

Although the convoy system soon proved itself, Anglo-American differences in emphasis eventually resurfaced. The paramount concern in the Admiralty was to protect merchant shipping that brought sustenance to the Allies. In Washington, however, another consideration assumed increasing importance—the transportation of the American Expeditionary Force to France. Captain Pratt stated this distinction starkly in his unpublished autobiography: "The impelling reason of the British [for adopting convoy] was protection to food and war supplies in transit. Our basic reason was protection to our own military forces in crossing the seas." Sims was informed that the "most important future cross water operations" that would involve American naval forces were those that would ensure "safe transportation of American troops to French soil." Therefore, "it was imperative that these ships should receive the utmost destroyer protection." Sims's continuing support for the British position earned him a sharp injunction from Daniels: "The paramount duty of the destroyers in European waters is principally the proper protection of transports with American troops. Be certain to detail an adequate convoy of destroyers and in making the detail bear in mind that everything is secondary to having a sufficient number to insure protection to American troops."[24]

Transport of American troops to Europe required two forms of naval assistance: sufficient numbers of transports and adequate escorts for convoys. To provide the necessary transports, the United States Shipping Board and the Emergency Fleet Corporation, both led by Edward N. Hurley, adopted many expedients, including seizure of interned enemy vessels, requisition of ships originally built for foreign powers, acquisition of ships in the American service, charter or purchase of foreign ships, and construction of new ships. To coordinate the activities of the army and the navy, interservice cooperation was essential, and Admiral Benson worked effectively with the army's chief of staff, Major General Hugh L. Scott, and his successors to ensure efficiency.[25]

The difficulties that arose between Britain and the United States over whether to assign escorts to protect merchant shipping as against troop transports did not become great until 1918, because only a few American units were readied for service in France during 1917, although a token force went to France soon after American entrance into the war to bolster the morale of the Allied nations. The first troop convoy departed from New York on 14 June 1917 and arrived at St. Nazaire on 2 July, with the loss of "but one horse and that was a mule." An order issued by the chief of the German naval staff, Admiral Henning von Holtzendorff, on 8 May 1917 that enjoined submarines not to attack American warships was still in effect, which could explain why the American convoy arrived in France without incident.[26]

Admiral Benson honored a request from the Marine Corps to send a contingent of Marines with the first troop convoy. Secretary of War Newton D. Baker had notified the Marine commandant, Major General

George Barnett, that it would be "utterly impossible for the War Department to furnish transportation for a Marine regiment," but the CNO provided three naval transports that joined the troop convoy at sea. This action contradicted the impression that Benson was an opponent of the Marine Corps.[27]

Britain's decision to adopt the convoy system, the most important naval initiative taken during the early months of American belligerency, was part of a trend that led ineluctably to the erosion of the American desire, most clearly represented by Admiral Benson and the General Board, to maintain a balanced building program. Despite incipient differences concerning the proper use of the convoy system, the system's immediate success strengthened the argument for building antisubmarine craft and merchant vessels rather than battleships and cruisers. Naval decisions on all sides during 1917 reflected the conviction that the outcome of the German undersea offensive against world commerce would largely determine the winner of the war. In such circumstances it was difficult indeed to continue an American building program that gave attention to postwar considerations as well as to the pressing emergency.

During June and July 1917 the Navy Department moved by degrees to a revised building program that forswore construction of battleships and cruisers in favor of antisubmarine vessels and merchant ships, although the General Board questioned a decision that might cause the "disintegration" of the battle fleet. Like Admiral Benson, the members of the board were uncomfortable with Sims's hopeful view that the United States could rely "on the fact, which I believe to be true that regardless of any future developments we can always count upon the support of the British Navy." The military exigencies of 1917, however, deprived the United States of a choice in the matter. For this reason, Admiral Benson dropped his previous views and supported a policy that postponed construction of battleships and emphasized the building of destroyers, submarines, and merchant ships. A special group, chaired by Captain Pratt, proposed this change in direction. Pratt then wrote to Sims: "Admiral Benson is strong for it [the change in building policy] and every effort of his will be directed towards getting the Secretary to make a decision." The General Board proved recalcitrant, favoring acceleration of the original program, but Pratt informed Sims that the issue was "fought out and the Admiral [Benson] went to the mat on it yesterday." On the same date, 21 July, Daniels ordered a delay of battleship construction and approved construction of 116 destroyers and 150 of a proposed new standardized type, thus providing for a destroyer program of 266 boats overall.[28]

The General Board did not abandon its views on the need for a balanced battle fleet. Making known its ideas about the building program for 1919, the board maintained that, despite the necessity to concentrate for the moment on antisubmarine craft, the "battleship remains as heretofore the principal reliance of the sea power of a nation." The board cautioned that a "new alignment of powers after the present war must not find our fleet in all the types of vessels composing it, unprepared to meet possible enemies in the Atlantic and Pacific at liberty to act singly or jointly with all their naval powers against us." The fate of the balanced battle fleet was left for the postwar era to decide.[29]

Although the United States adjusted its building program to help surmount the naval crisis of 1917, the Navy Department entertained serious reservations about British naval strategy and tactics. The essence of these criticisms was that the British had adopted unduly passive or defensive measures; the Americans believed that a much more aggressive or offensive effort was required to ensure a victory at sea. A controversy over these matters developed during the anxious summer and fall of 1917, as the United States continued to search for an acceptable naval policy. Admiral Benson became deeply involved in this debate.

CHAPTER VII

OPERATIONAL DEBATES

The favorable effects of the convoy system did not become fully apparent during the summer of 1917, a circumstance that encouraged American criticisms of British naval operations. Continuing to worry about Britain's staying power, Admiral Benson coupled support for construction of destroyers with agitation for more aggressive operations against the German U-boats. Admiral Sims, however, remained steadfast in his support of British practices, including operations of the antisubmarine forces that guarded the maritime lines of communication to the Allies.

Benson's special interest in proposals to take the offensive against submarines in their bases irritated the Admiralty. In a letter to Admiral Browning, Admiral Jellicoe bluntly contrasted Sims and Benson: "Sims and I see eye to eye on everything and, as he is absolutely independent and does not care a hang what they say to him from the other side, he strengthens my hand considerably." How was it possible, he questioned, for Sims to hold such "sound" opinions when views on the other side of the ocean were so unsound? "The real truth is that Admiral Benson has an idea in his head that the gun and a sharp pair of eyes are the answer to a submerged submarine: One would hardly believe that such ideas could be held by any naval officer—but there it is." He asked Admiral Browning to help correct the views of the Americans: "The more you can see of the United States Fleet the better, and I am sure that you will take every opportunity of getting incorrect ideas out of their heads and getting correct into them instead."[1]

The presence of Captain Pratt in the Office of Naval Operations provided a means of improving communications between the Washington headquarters and the theater commander in London, because both Benson and Sims trusted the new assistant chief of naval operations. Pratt had assumed the responsibilities of Captain Volney O. Chase, heretofore Benson's most respected subordinate, who died on 24 June 1917. Pratt was quick to signal Washington's discomfort with Sims's closeness to the Admiralty. As early as 27 May he cautioned Sims that, while Britain's naval policy naturally dominated those of the other members of the anti-German coalition, the American interest was "big and growing," and American naval leaders would not accept British direction unquestioningly. Although he explained that he was not criticizing British policy, he wanted to note that "our position, and our weight in this war if it lasts, will be such that our views of policy, etc., in naval matters will have to be listened to, and not necessarily that we should accept theirs unless we too have a voice in the matter."[2]

Pratt, with Benson's concurrence, explained to Sims the Navy Department's view of relations with the Admiralty. The department, he wrote on 2 July, was fully aware of the emergency at sea and was fully prepared to cooperate with its British counterpart. "This office does not have to be scared into sending ships because we do not realize the seriousness of the situation. We do. Every man jack in the Plans Department has laid awake nights." What was needed? Admiral Benson was prepared to do everything that was required, "so long as he knows, and he wants to know not in any critical spirit, but in the spirit of utmost cooperation, what the Admiralty's strategical and tactical conceptions are." Pratt had in mind a series of questions: "Just what is their major plan? Is its fundamental conception offensive or defensive? What are the tactical details in general by which this plan is to be solved?" Why should Britain provide this information? Because the department was "directing every effort, building, concerning shipping, to arrive at a successful conclusion of this war, even to the possible sacrifice of our own individual good later."[3]

Not waiting for a reply from Sims, Pratt cabled a general policy statement drafted by Captain Chase shortly before his death; the statement summarized the Navy Department's conception of proper guidelines for the United States Navy. The first principle of the statement must have been welcomed in London: "The most hearty cooperation with the allies to meet the present submarine situation in European waters or other waters compatible with an adequate defense of our own home waters." The second principle applied the policy of cooperation to "any future situation during the present war." The third was probably less appreciated; it required consideration for the "future position of the United States" while striving for "successful termination of the present war"—the concern Benson had earlier expressed forcefully. The United States had to contemplate both offensive and defensive action in safeguarding the lines of communication to the Allies, and it

Chief of Naval Operations William S. Benson, Washington, D.C., 1917.

was prepared to accept "any joint plan of action the Allies deemed necessary to meet immediate needs." To work toward effective coordination, the Navy Department had in mind three activities: to send over needed antisubmarine forces in numbers consistent with requirements in home waters; to retain the main fleet in home waters until an emergency developed that required its presence elsewhere; and to discuss "more fully plans for joint operations."[4]

As the Navy Department attempted to clarify its position with Sims, the commander in London sought through Ambassador Page to influence the president, but this enterprise produced a negative response. To Secretary Daniels, President Wilson wrote: "As you and I agreed the other day, the British Admiralty had done absolutely nothing con-

Mary Augusta Wyse Benson (Mrs. William S. Benson),
Washington, D.C., 1917.

structive in the use of their navy and I think it is time we were making
and insisting upon plans of our own even if we render some of the more
conservative of our own naval advisers uncomfortable." Not content
to convey this criticism solely to Daniels, Wilson immediately conveyed
the same sentiments directly to Admiral Sims: "From the beginning of
the war I have been greatly surprised at the failure of the British Admiralty to use Great Britain's great naval superiority in an effective way.
In the presence of the present submarine emergency they are helpless
to the point of panic. Every plan we suggest they reject for some reason
of prudence." The president concluded with an observation that must
have been applauded in the Navy Department: "In my view this not a

time for prudence but for boldness, even at the cost of great losses." Sims was asked to report on the Admiralty's activities and accomplishments, and to make his comments and suggestions without regard for opinions of the Admiralty.[5]

The president's strongly worded message did not sway Sims, who responded immediately with a defense of his procedure. He was quick to deny that he was under the thumb of the Admiralty: "I wish to make it perfectly clear that my reports and despatches have been in all cases an independent opinion based on specific facts and data which I have collected in the various Admiralty and other Government Departments. They constitute my own conviction and hence comply with your request for an independent opinion." Still of greatest importance, in his view, was that the "success or failure of the submarine campaign" would decide the war. He wanted "to concentrate all naval construction on destroyers and light craft and postpone construction of heavy craft." He was unconcerned about the long run because, *regardless of any future developments, we can always count upon the support of the British Navy.*" To ensure the most efficient American contributions to operations in European waters, he asked for a staff composed of "the younger and more progressive types," such as Dudley Knox, William Pratt, and Nathan Twining. In these terms Sims dismissed concerns in Washington about defense against enemy operations in American waters, the postwar situation, and the operational premises of the Admiralty.[6]

Washington reacted calmly, but Sims's defense did not strengthen his standing. During a conversation on 13 July with Sir William Wiseman, head of British intelligence operations in the United States, President Wilson roundly criticized his naval commander in London: "Admiral Sims, who is always considered an original man, [has] done nothing since his arrival in London but report views of the British Admiralty." Obviously Secretary Daniels had expressed this opinion to Wilson. In later years Pratt sought an explanation for Sims's belief that the Office of Naval Operations had not provided sufficient support. Sims, he noted, had "never held an administrative job . . . which required that he be on the producing end." He had the impression that "it should only be necessary to ask in order to receive bountifully."[7]

British officers who dealt with the Navy Department understood its attitude. For example, Captain Gaunt sought to educate the Admiralty concerning Admiral Benson, who, Gaunt explained, "does not exactly complain, but points out that all we do is to ask for things as they come along, but there is no settled policy that he can put forward and say we are working along those lines." Commenting on the CNO's state of mind, he accurately concluded: "I think that he has a sort of feeling that he should be taken closer into the general scheme of Allies' sea policy, instead of, as at present, just being asked from time to time to supply units which have no connection with one another." On 26

July, when Browning responded to some suggestions that Benson had transmitted to him, the British admiral observed that the Admiralty had not kept him abreast of various matters. Browning had referred Benson's suggestions to Jellicoe, who had intimated to Ambassador Page in London that "perhaps the best way of attaining close cooperation would be for a certain number of Officers of the United States Navy, in the confidence of the Department, to come over and work at the Admiralty in London; any scheme of operations could then be discussed, and the sooner the better."[8]

Admiral Jellicoe responded to Benson's suggestions by sending a policy paper to President Wilson that defended standing British views. The Royal Navy was committed to four missions: (1) protection of communications to the Allied armies, especially those in France; (2) interdiction of the enemy's trade to handicap his military operations and civilian population; (3) protection of British trade to ensure continuing supply of food to the people and munitions to the armies; (4) defense against invasion or raids. The Royal Navy could accomplish these missions "by defeating and destroying the enemy's fighting fleets, both above and below water," but it must of necessity "wait for favorable opportunities to engage the elusive enemy fleet."[9]

From the Navy Department's perspective, this statement hardly dispelled the suspicion that more offensive-minded operations were in order. Captain Joel R. Poinsett Pringle, returning to the United States from a sojourn in Queenstown with the Destroyer Force, wrote to Sims that the secretary of the navy "appeared to be imbued with the idea that the apparent activity of the British Fleet represented a failure to prosecute the war with all the vigor demanded," and that this sentiment came "not only from civilians but also from Naval officers[,] . . . the implication being that they [the Admiralty] can do more than they are doing." Daniels summarized his reactions to Jellicoe's paper pungently: "No proposition from England for conference to determine upon joint program—we are asked to send and send, but not [to attend] a conference where we have equal voice."[10]

While the Navy Department harbored doubts about the energy of the Admiralty, Sims's circle advanced comparable criticism of Benson's organization. Lieutenant Robert R. M. Emmet of Sims's staff, visiting in Washington, wrote to his chief to report: "Operations can't or won't push." The CNO, Emmet stated, "allowed [the] Secretary to Boo him down on important and vital things." Emmet believed that "Operations [needed] a man with a drive," and that "Admiral Benson [had] his job largely because he [would not] cross the secretary." In this fashion criticism of Benson by the insurgents continued into the period of belligerency.[11]

A more serious difficulty developed from the activities of Assistant Secretary Franklin D. Roosevelt, who aligned himself with the Sims faction, although he avoided acts that could be construed as insubordinate or disloyal. Roosevelt arranged for the American novelist Winston Churchill (related to Mrs. Sims but not to his British namesake) to conduct a number of interviews in the Navy Department. Churchill then published several articles in the daily press that were critical of the Navy Department, and he prepared a report that went to the president. Wilson forwarded it to Daniels with a note: "Here is a suggestion for the new Operation which I am sure you will welcome along with the rest." Churchill was uncomplimentary to Benson, describing him as "perhaps a suitable head, but too prudent, too unimaginative, too early in training to do the necessary bold thinking and planning." Benson, he thought, should associate "with much younger men—men of the new school and training, few of whom have passed and some of whom have not yet reached the rank of Commander."[12]

Benson had his defenders. Captain Pratt wrote to none other than Sims to report that certain officers hoped to succeed Benson as CNO: "I found that there had been a lot of cutting under, of what I call work not on the square," notably "in the case of Benson." He assured Sims that Benson stood "for the most offensive kind of stuff." Another officer, Lieutenant Commander Charles Belknap, Jr., writing to Sims, reflected Benson's doubts about the energy of the Admiralty: "If you live in a mosquito infested country you do not hire five thousand boy scouts to go out and swat mosquitoes for you, but you go where they are bred." Belknap favored an attack on the German fleet, although he recognized that aggressive action would probably entail serious losses. Rear Admiral Ralph Earle, chief of the Bureau of Ordnance, added his voice to those who complained of Britain's failure to send clear information about naval plans and purposes: "We do not know what the British Admiralty wants us to do, or what they are willing to allow us to do, and on that hangs the whole situation."[13]

It was left to President Wilson, during an unpublicized visit to the Atlantic Fleet on 11 August, to summarize the frustrations of the Navy and to propose a course of action. Speaking to more than three hundred officers on Admiral Mayo's flagship, the *Pennsylvania*, he dwelt on the unprecedented nature of the conflict. Because it was unprecedented, he thought it a "war in one sense for amateurs." Then he drew attention to the frustrating circumstances that the British and American navies together outnumbered the enemy "by a very great margin" but were "casting about for a way in which to use our superiority and our strength." Finally he turned to a striking metaphor:

> We are hunting hornets all over the farm and letting the nest alone. None of us knows how to go to the nest and crush it, and yet I despair of hunting for hornets all over the sea when I know that the nest is breeding hornets as fast as I can find them. I am willing for my part, and I know you are willing because I know

the stuff you are made of, I am willing to sacrifice half the navy. Great Britain and we together have to crush that nest, because if we crush it, the war is won.

Here in graphic language was marked presidential support for the Navy Department's view that the Royal Navy lacked offensive spirit and that dramatic deeds were called for to resolve the naval emergency.[14]

Dissatisfaction with British naval policy resulted in a decision to send the commander in chief of the Atlantic Fleet, Admiral Mayo, on a mission to Europe to improve relations with the Entente navies. To Assistant Secretary of State William Phillips, Daniels explained his reasons for favoring an initiative: he was *"getting tired of playing second fiddle to the British by meeting all their demands*[,] *and . . . a definite policy for our Government should be decided upon."* He asked Phillips to inform the British government of the American desire for an early naval conference to discuss naval matters. The project soon blossomed into a full-fledged naval conference, including French and Italian as well as British and American participation.[15]

On 16 August, Admiral Benson, Secretary Daniels, Admiral Mayo, and Captain Richard H. Jackson (who was designated to represent the Navy Department in France) called on President Wilson to discuss naval matters. Once again the president criticized the inactivity of the Allies. He dwelt especially on the "absolute necessity of finding & ending the hornet's nest, & destroying the poison or removing the cork." He wanted offensive action: "We cannot win this war by merely hunting submarines when they have gotten into the great ocean." Admiral Mayo then wondered aloud whether the president might have undue expectations of the forthcoming negotiations. "No," Daniels explained, but the president "expected plans by which America could lead & be the senior partner in a successful naval campaign. He was ready to make great ventures for a chance to win but of course wished no policy that would mean suicide." Wilson's comments on this occasion support the view that he wanted to send Admiral Mayo to Europe to press his case because he assumed that Admiral Sims would not do so effectively.[16]

On his way to Europe, Admiral Mayo developed a list of subjects to take up at the forthcoming naval conference, deriving inspiration from a memorandum Admiral Benson had given him. Mayo hoped to inquire into what had been accomplished, what was underway, and what was planned. Certain specific concerns were included on his list, including antisubmarine measures, the use of aircraft, the merchant shipping situation, troop transports, and political questions. On arriving in Liverpool on 27 August, he delivered a letter from Benson to Admiral de Chair, Britain's naval representative on the Balfour Mission, that stressed the necessity of providing the United States with information on British policy and strategy. In return, de Chair asked for suggestions of items to be included on the agenda of the naval conference. Mayo took an opportunity to explain his purposes to the First Lord of the Admiralty, Sir Eric Geddes, who, as the civilian head of the Royal Navy, was Daniels's counterpart in Great Britain. Mayo sought to "ascertain in what possible way the Americans can more fully come into naval warfare." The president had told him that he should not worry unduly about risk: "You cannot make omelettes without breaking eggs. . . . War is made up of taking risks." Geddes may have misconstrued Mayo's purpose in making these comments, because he informed Prime Minister David Lloyd George: "We hope to be able to get more cooperation from them both now and in the future."[17]

The naval conference met on 4 and 5 September, with Geddes in the chair, and it discussed a large number of naval questions, following an agenda prepared by Admiral Jellicoe. Some prior decisions were reaffirmed, especially antisubmarine measures, and new initiatives were discussed, such as attacks on submarine bases and the construction of barrages in the North Sea and the Strait of Otranto. The net outcome, however, was less than inspiring: Mayo reported that "while the conference was very useful to all concerned, it is extremely difficult to reach any conclusions other than those of a very general nature."[18]

Although the conference did not produce concrete agreements of great significance, it did stimulate improvements in the relations between some of the most important naval personages. Admiral Jellicoe took advantage of the opportunity presented to inaugurate a correspondence with Admiral Benson. Sensitive to the CNO's doubts about the cautious nature of British naval strategy and tactics, he argued: "It takes two to make a fight and our difficulty throughout the war has been that, except on one or two exceedingly rare occasions, the second party to the fight has not been there." At the same time, Sims finally responded to urgings from Pratt to write to the chief of naval operations. Realizing that he had irritated the Washington headquarters, Sims attempted to make amends: "I assure you that I have thoroughly appreciated the difficulties of your position." He was hopeful about the future: "While I may at times have been impatient to get things done as quickly as possible, still, when I look back over what has been accomplished within the last few months I can realize that it is 'some achievement.' All this[,] not to mention what is now going forward in the way of increased forces and increased facilities." Sims detected a distant attitude toward him on Mayo's part, one of the reasons he became concerned about his standing at home. He informed Benson that he was "very anxious that the present relations should not be imperiled by any change in the personnel or in command."[19]

At this time a misunderstanding arose after Admiral Benson complained to Captain Gaunt, the British attaché in Washington, that he was kept "in the dark on important matters." Gaunt suggested that the Admiralty transmit important information to Benson through him rather than through Sims. The force commander immediately questioned this procedure; it obviously would diminish his importance in London. Gaunt was then called to London to discuss the situation. Despite Sims's objections, the Admiralty, no doubt as part of an effort to conciliate the Navy Department and to counter the American notion that Sims simply mouthed the Admiralty's point of view, decided to establish communications between Jellicoe and Benson through Gaunt. The story of this minor affair somehow leaked to the Washington news correspondent David Lawrence, who claimed that serious friction existed between the Admiralty and the Navy Department because of British secretiveness. Daniels sent for Lawrence and denied his allegations. When Gaunt inquired about the source of these contentions, he reported, Benson received him in the most friendly way, stating that the "cooperation between the Admiralty and American Naval officers had been complete since outbreak of the war."[20]

When Admiral Mayo returned to Washington, he volunteered considerable criticism of the Admiralty. He had been unable to obtain historical information about the prior course of the war; "reports of operations are so isolated and scattered and without system that there is not available any comprehensive record of original plans, the governing reasons therefore, and the degree of success or failure in each case." He doubted the existence of a plan; the war had been "carried out from day to day and not according to the effective co-ordination and co-operation of efforts against the enemy." Despite these negative circumstances, Mayo expressed optimism about the future. Some desirable measures had been instituted; for example, there had been improvements in patrolling and minesweeping. His most important recommendation was that the "United States make the earliest possible decision as to what forms and extent the assistance to be given shall take and then proceed to exert every effort to expedite the production, dispatch and employment of such assistance."[21]

Officials in Washington praised the naval conference in communications to London but privately entertained considerable reservations about its outcome. Benson expressed appreciation to Jellicoe for the cordial reception of Mayo and his staff and added a fine statement of his pleasure at the state of Anglo-American relations. He had hoped for closer relations "for the good of mankind," and the time had come. "I can assure you," he concluded, "that it is in harmony with such sentiments as these that I shall try to reply to your most welcome letter and to carry on what I hope shall prove to be a most agreeable and profitable correspondence." More candid was the president's reaction, as reported by Daniels. The British had proposed blocking a German channel to the North Sea by sinking one hundred ships in it. Wilson thought this futile, because dynamite would soon clear a path through the obstacle. Instead, he hoped for "some real offensive."[22]

On the surface Sims seemed more prepared to represent the Navy Department loyally, but appearances were deceiving. Although he established a direct correspondence with Benson, his recommendations continued to reflect questionable Admiralty positions. British Ambassador Cecil Spring Rice informed Balfour of continuing suspicions in Washington: "I have often told you that Mr. Page, like Admiral Sims, and most American officials on your side, are considered to be too much under your influence. It would be dangerous to take their advice as representing the opinion of their Government." Benson apparently found Sims's letters to Pratt so disturbing that he decided not to read them. Sims chose to consider this a sign of Benson's probity, describing it as "one of the biggest and finest things that has happened to me during my naval career."[23]

The summer and fall had generated anxiety and frustration in the Navy Department. Unlike those with lesser areas of responsibility, Admiral Benson had to consider the defense of home waters and the offensive in enemy waters, short-run objectives and long-term interests, the desires of the Wilson administration and the importunities of the beleaguered British government, the strategic maxims of Mahan and the desperate appeals of Sims. Rear Admiral Josiah S. McKean wryly summarized the dilemma of the Navy Department and its leaders:

> Had we listened only to Sims, and we did listen to him hardest, it would have been all destroyers. Had we listened only to Gleaves, it would have been cruisers and transports. Had we listened only to Cone, the whole Navy and Navy Department would have been in the air. Had we listened to Fullam only, the navy yards and appropriations would have been devoted to his old armored cruisers. Had we listened to Grant only it would have been subs at one time and old battleships at another.

Despite the pressures of his office, Benson maintained his poise. Duty was more important than personal gratification. Benson's imperturbability reflected his strong character, which calls to mind the great Civil War commander General Ulysses S. Grant—although this comparison may have embarrassed the son of a Confederate soldier.[24]

Benson could not have realized it, but he was about to take part in an international negotiation that measurably ameliorated European perceptions of his wartime service. This development freed him from relying on others, like Sims and Mayo, to conduct important discussions with his counterparts in Europe. The year 1917 had proven disastrous in many ways for the Allied Powers and the United States. At the beginning of the year the French army had suffered a terrible defeat on the western front, one that led to huge British losses at Passchendaele later on. The submarines continued to wreak extraordinary damage at sea, and, most important of all, revolutionary Russia lost the capacity to continue the war against Germany. Another disaster, the catastrophic defeat of the Italian army at Caporetto, lay in the immediate future. All these circumstances combined to force a comprehensive reappraisal of the inter-Allied war effort. In this connection the United States, without enthusiasm, decided to break significantly with tradition and send a group of high-ranking officials to Europe for extensive consultations. One of these leaders was the chief of naval operations. At this critical juncture, Admiral Benson found himself among those entrusted with political-military responsibilities of the first importance.

CHAPTER VIII

ADMIRAL BENSON AND THE HOUSE MISSION

In September 1917, when Admiral Mayo was still in London, the British War Cabinet broached the possibility of holding a general conference to enhance cooperation among the Allied and Associated Powers. Interest in such a gathering grew with each passing week, as the Entente Powers grasped the full extent of the crisis that lay ahead. The events of 1917 had heightened concern about German intentions in 1918. British and French offensives on the western front had failed miserably, both Russia and Italy had experienced great difficulties, and the actions of the German U-boats had intensified the German threat. In October the British and French governments formally invited the United States to attend a conference designed to concert the plans of the Western coalition for 1918.[1]

Wilson proved unenthusiastic about the conference, but Colonel House felt differently, and he urged the president to send a delegation to Europe. When at length Wilson acquiesced, he proposed that House lead the American mission. The colonel, who was not in robust health, did not want to undertake the assignment, but he eventually agreed to go, on the condition that he be excused from ceremonial duties. Others who took part in the House Mission included officials of the Treasury Department, the War Trade Board, the Shipping Board, the Food Administration, and the War Industries Board. To represent the armed services, the president named the chief of staff of the United States Army, Major General Tasker Howard Bliss, and the chief of naval operations, Admiral Benson. Given the president's desire to stress technical rather than political questions, it was appropriate to send uniformed officers rather than civilian secretaries as representatives of the armed services.[2]

The choice of Benson reflected the wishes of both the British Admiralty and Admiral Sims. Ambassador Page had informed the president in September that Admiral Jellicoe would like the chief of naval operations to pay an official visit to London. Sims was of like mind, writing to Pratt in October: "I think [that] one of the most useful things that could happen would be for Admiral Benson himself to come over and bring with him a number of experts in various lines. I am sure he would go back enlightened to a degree that I have not been able to accomplish." The selection of Benson also reflected widespread recognition in both Washington and London that he was the appropriate choice to provide naval expertise. President Wilson's emphasis on operations rather than on policy is what Daniels referred to when he discussed the forthcoming trip with Benson. Daniels reported the president's position as "All possible cooperation but we must be free." Wilson was prepared to cooperate fully in achieving victory over the Central Powers, but he was unwilling to accept political commitments that might limit his freedom of action at war's end.[3]

The workload in Operations was very heavy, but the CNO left for Europe confident that his assistant, Captain Pratt, was fully prepared to substitute for him. Benson regarded Pratt so highly that he made provision for the captain to succeed to his office should anything befall him during the dangerous trip across the Atlantic. Pratt, in turn, recognized the most compelling reason Benson was being sent to Europe: the CNO had "all the threads in his hand, and was controlling them." In a letter to Benson, Pratt lavished praise on his superior: "I am not much given to saying things, but I want you to know I have learned to admire the character you show in every line of your face: the dignity, poise, fine clear judgement, and above all that sterling rugged integrity which is the soul of honor and which this country needs so much at present." In a letter to Sims, Pratt expressed similar sentiments: "I am glad the Admiral is coming, you will like him as I do, and learn to appreciate that rugged honesty which is the highest compliment I can pay him. God! but we need men like that now-a-days." Pratt obviously hoped to stimulate further improvement in the relations between Benson and Sims.[4]

On 28 October the House Mission left Washington by rail in great secrecy. Mrs. House accompanied the colonel, but neither Mrs. Bliss nor Mrs. Benson knew her husband's destination. Only House, Benson, and the CNO's aide, Lieutenant Commander Carter, knew where or when the party would depart. On 30 October the train arrived at Halifax, Nova Scotia, where three American vessels—the cruisers *Huntington* and *St. Louis* and the destroyer *Bach*—lay at anchor. The vessels made only 10 to 12 knots during the first few days at sea in order to reach the submarine danger zone when there was no moon. The voyagers talked of nothing but submarines. House confided to his diary that the setting reminded him "of the time when people took ships in earlier days and did nothing but discuss pirates and the possibility of being attacked, robbed, and sunk by them."[5]

The passage through the dangerous sea proved exciting. On 4 November the first of the destroyers sent from Queenstown to escort the incoming vessels joined them, and three others arrived later. On the afternoon of 5 November the fog cleared and visibility improved just as the small convoy entered the danger zone. Gun crews took their stations, and other crew members stood by to drop depth charges. This weapon, a novelty in 1917, attracted the attention of General Bliss. "They are said to be fatal to a submarine anywhere within 80 feet by crushing in her sides or starting her rivets," he wrote to his wife. Life preservers were donned and worn until the ships entered port. A strong northwest wind dampened spirits, but there was consolation in the knowledge that it was "bad weather for submarines." Somewhat concerned, Bliss sought the company of Admiral Benson. He entered his colleague's stateroom only to find him "braced in a chair athwartship fast asleep and snoring away."[6]

News that the House Mission had arrived on 7 November at Plymouth brought great relief in official Washington. The State Department then announced that mission members would participate in an inter-Allied war conference aimed at "perfecting a more complete coordination of activities." Admiral Sir John Jellicoe was present with Admiral Sims to welcome the Americans and to accompany them to London. During the train ride, House, Benson, Jellicoe, and Sims held an initial discussion. Sims was favorably impressed, writing to his wife: "You know of course how much I have always thought of Admiral Benson, particularly the extremely valuable quality of absolute honesty in all his dealings." He also commented on Benson's command of the situation. "He really seems to have developed wonderfully in the two or three years he has been in the Navy Department, or else I never appreciated what he was before because he is such a quiet and non-assertive man." He wrote in similar terms to Pratt: "You know how much I have always admired the Admiral, and how much value to the service I think his inflexible honesty is. This has been strikingly exemplified in everything he has said and done in the less than two days he has been here." In another letter to his wife Sims commented again on Benson's absolute honesty, adding that his "entire frankness" was "in such startling contrast with that of others I could mention, that you can imagine how satisfactory it is to meet him. He very highly approves of everything we have done over here."[7]

The House Mission had intended to spend only a few days in Europe, but a series of unexpected and untoward events prolonged its stay. The Italian army had just been defeated at Caporetto, and Italy appeared close to collapse. The Entente prime ministers and their mil-

General Bliss, Colonel House, and Admiral Benson on board the *Huntington* on the way to Europe, 1917.

itary advisers had gone to Rapallo, Italy, for an emergency meeting. On 7 November, just as the House Mission arrived at Plymouth, the Allied representatives at Rapallo signed an agreement establishing an Inter-Allied Supreme War Council to provide an institutional setting for essential cooperation. Shortly thereafter, the French premier, Paul Painlevé, was forced from office. Georges Clemenceau, who succeeded him, could not participate in the planned conference until he had formed a government. The most dramatic and important event of the time, the Bolshevik seizure of power in Russia, also took place just as the House Mission arrived in Britian. Colonel House's son-in-law Gordon Auchincloss, who served as secretary of the mission, summarized the situation starkly: "We have certainly come to a critical time and have found things in a terrible mess: governments falling right and left, and general panic prevailing."[8]

The delay of the formal conference did not leave the House Mission at leisure; rather, members of the mission set to work in London immediately, conferring at length with their counterparts in the British government. Benson tackled his duties with characteristic candor and vigor. Meeting with Admiral Jellicoe and First Lord of the Admiralty Sir Eric Geddes, he assured them that he had come to find out how the United States could be of greatest assistance to the Allies. He was interested in future plans, especially those of the British; he wanted to map out definite courses of action and to determine the role of each member of the coalition in them. The United States was anxious to contribute all of its naval strength, but it wished to do so according to well-defined plans, which he "would be glad of the opportunity to help prepare, and which must be jointly approved by the active participants before being undertaken." However tactfully phrased, this statement communicated some of the Navy Department's sentiment that the Royal Navy had not been sufficiently inventive and aggressive. In further meetings with Jellicoe and Geddes, Benson frankly reported American dissatisfaction with the policies of the Admiralty.[9]

This information came as no surprise to British officials. Their observers in the United States were well aware of the situation. Lord Northcliffe, head of the permanent British Mission in the United States, agreed with the Navy Department. Daniels noted on 29 October that he had talked with Northcliffe, "who was evidently depressed and said he hoped we would build fire under English Navy. Jellicoe had but one thought and that was to preserve the great fleet. Not accustomed to fighting & had had no real engagement since Nelson's day." (Northcliffe neglected the naval battle at Jutland.) An influential naval journalist, Arthur Pollen, wrote to Colonel Arthur Murray (later Lord Elibank), the assistant military attaché in Washington, to report that he had heard expressions of a "very generous admiration" for the British sailor and his fighting spirit, but that he had also heard extensive criticism of the

House Mission in London, 1917. *Front row, left to right:* General Bliss, Ambassador Walter Hines Page, Colonel House, Admiral Benson, and Vice Admiral Sims.

Admiralty. Americans expressed dissatisfaction because of Britain's failure to establish a close blockade of the enemy; to defeat the German High Sea Fleet decisively at Jutland; to make sufficient preparations for the antisubmarine warfare; and to adopt the convoy system. Although American feelings were kept quiet and the nation remained "entirely loyal to the Alliance, and would strain every effort to remain so," Pollen warned that "some day the forces making for reticence would cease to act" and an attack would be leveled on the Admiralty "with apparently the whole authority of the American Navy" behind it. He saw no alternative to a "joint responsibility for the war" and to joint planning—the approach Benson had advocated from the time the United States had entered the war.[10]

Although Benson expressed himself frankly in London, he did so with great consideration for his hosts. Sims reported extensively on this subject to various correspondents. He informed Admiral Bayly that he had the "highest possible respect" for Benson, because he had "the indispensable quality of perfect honesty and as much impartiality as any human being could have." In another communication to Bayly he added: "The more I see of Admiral Benson the more valuable I think his visit is going to prove and the more I admire the man." He was even moved to revise his earlier presumption that Benson was anti-

British, a view that he had expressed as recently as 1 November. To Mrs. Sims he wrote: "I can see no anti-British feeling in anything B[enson] says or does. At all events he is intensely anti-German. He will believe no good of them."[11]

Actions soon followed Benson's consultations at the Admiralty, the first of which was a decision to honor a British request that the United States send a division of four battleships to reinforce the Grand Fleet in the North Sea. The proposal for this measure had reached Washington before Benson's departure, but the proposal had not been accepted because Britain had made no explanation of the rationale for it. When Benson asked why the ships were needed and how they would be maintained, he was informed that their presence would allow Britain to release four battleships from the Grand Fleet for service in the vicinity of the Strait of Dover, where they would help guard against sorties of German cruisers or other surface vessels. The American ships were to be of the coal-burning variety, because Britain lacked fuel oil. Jellicoe also requested eight American destroyers to protect the battleships, because he would have to detach that number from the Grand Fleet to screen the British vessels at the Strait of Dover. When Benson replied that the United States had no destroyers to offer, the British agreed to delay withdrawal of their units. The CNO soon recommended the dispatch of the American battleships. Accordingly, Battleship Division Nine of the Atlantic Fleet, which included the *New York*, the *Florida*, the *Delaware*, and the *Wyoming*, left the United States on 25 November, reaching Britain on 19 December. It soon joined the Grand Fleet, an outcome that proved most satisfactory to British naval leaders. Benson would have preferred to dispatch a more "homogenous" force, one that required less maintenance, but such vessels would not become available until December.[12]

The possibility of deploying the entire American battle fleet to European waters was discussed in London. It was agreed that, "if the logistics situation should be met, and conditions otherwise developed as anticipated," the entire Atlantic Fleet except those vessels required for duty as escorts for convoys would come to the North Sea in the spring. All agreed that the "moral effect alone of such a step would be most beneficial, not only to the naval services, but generally to the Allied cause."[13]

American proposals that Benson wanted to discuss were the closing of the Strait of Dover and the construction of a mine barrage across the North Sea between Aberdeen, Scotland, and Egersund, Norway. The British explanation for the failure to pursue these projects was a lack of adequate equipment. The slope of the seabed made it difficult to keep mine anchors in place. Benson drew on his service with the Light-House Board to suggest a means of surmounting the anchoring problem. Mrs. Benson later responded to an inquiry concerning this suggestion. She reported that Admiral Benson "told them to make large heavy concrete blocks with long sharp spikes extending beneath them which would stick down in the bottom and hold the blocks to which lines for holding the mines could be made fast." A much more serious objection to the barriers was the lack of an effective mine. Benson reminded the Admiralty that the United States had developed a mine that could be produced at the rate of four thousand per week. He recognized the difficulty of locating sufficient tonnage to ship the large quantities of material required for the North Sea barrage, but he nevertheless urged the British to undertake the project. Responding to American pressure, the Admiralty appointed a special commission of engineers to study the feasibility of the American project.

Another favorite American project, one that met the criterion of offensive-mindedness, was an attack on German submarine bases and those points at which submarines exited from German waters. Benson had entertained such plans even before the United States became a belligerent, and he had raised the question during the Hampton Roads conference in April 1917. Among his ideas was to use old battleships to attack such locations, running the calculated risk of losing them. Jellicoe was not encouraging. He pointed out that the Germans had occupied the Belgian coast for three years, ample time in which to develop fortifications. Moreover, the Germans could easily attack a hostile naval force with aircraft, submarines, and destroyers. Once again American pressure, in this case with the support of Lloyd George, was sufficient to force adoption of a plan to undertake such an attack, with the United States supplying the necessary vessels. But the plan was never executed. After the war Benson refused to reveal the details of this abortive project, arguing that he considered the plan conceivably useful to Britain in a possible future war. In 1918 the Royal Navy attempted an attack on the German submarine bases at Ostend and Zeebrugge but did not succeed in interdicting the movements of submarines from either location.[14]

Although Benson managed to dispel rumors about his alleged Anglophobia while in London, his energetic advocacy of various projects that the Admiralty deemed unworkable resulted in continuing skepticism about his abilities. Before the CNO went to Rosyth for a visit to the Grand Fleet, Jellicoe informed the commander in chief of the fleet, Admiral Sir David Beatty, that he would "find Benson very willing to help, but very ignorant of sea warfare. He has never had his flag up afloat and has odd ideas." Jellicoe cautioned Beatty not to reveal information about the secret intelligence methods for reading encrypted German messages that had been developed to track the movements of German ships. Benson did not *"know anything about our secret information and he will not be told,* so please don't mention it. All he knows is that our Secret Service is very good."[15]

During Benson's visit to the Grand Fleet he once again urged bombardment of German submarine bases, but Admiral Beatty supported Jellicoe, stressing the importance of achieving command of the air in connection with any such assault. Benson accepted this view: he cabled Daniels that a "sufficient number of vessels carrying aircraft [were required] to permit the extensive bombing operations absolutely indispensable to the successful attack on German Fleet, munitions, and shore batteries." He also reported that the British suffered from a "decided inferiority of destroyers with main fleet compared to the number that could be sent out by Germany." For this reason he urged that "every possible effort should be made to speed up" construction of American destroyers. Beatty was disinclined to initiate an offensive policy until spring 1918, when he anticipated the delivery of many American destroyers.[16]

Although Benson conducted independent investigations in Europe, he maintained regular contact with Admiral Sims. If Sims suspected that Benson had come to Europe with the thought of removing him or limiting his authority, he was soon disabused of any such notion. Sims informed his wife that Benson was making inquiries on an independent basis, but he was "sure this is because he wants to be able to say that he formed his own opinion." Sims believed that this tactic "should remove from W. W[ilson's] mind the idea that I am hopelessly British— so much so that I can form no independent judgement." Similar letters went to Bayly and some of Sims's subordinates in Europe. He noted that Benson had approved actions that Sims had recommended since April but that had not been acted on. Unmentioned was Sims's frequent failure to provide justification for his support of Admiralty views, one of the reasons for delay in Washington.[17]

Of all the controversies that divided the American naval representatives and their British counterparts, the most difficult was a considerable disagreement on the proper employment of naval forces afloat. Britain gave first priority to the preservation of the Grand Fleet and second priority to the protection of merchant shipping. Jellicoe's memorandum for the War Cabinet on 18 November 1917 noted that the Grand Fleet should avoid offensive operations until it acquired an adequate destroyer screen. Benson and members of the General Board entertained two concerns about the British priorities. First, they were unwilling to support the Grand Fleet to the extent of weakening the American fleet so severely that it was rendered incapable of challenging the German fleet. Second, they opposed diverting destroyers to escort merchant convoys if this policy deprived American troop and supply transports of adequate protection.[18]

Differences of this nature might have been mitigated or even resolved had cooperative Anglo-American naval planning been possible. Benson sensed this problem, informing Daniels that the British were "not prepared now to offer definite plans of their own for our consideration." To eliminate this difficulty, he recommended the establishment of a "strict Planning Section for joint operations" in London, so that American naval personnel could place themselves "in a position to obtain latest British and allied information and to urge as joint plans such plans as our estimates and policies may indicate." This form of coordination was necessary because "any offensive operations which we may undertake must be in conjunction with British forces and must be from bases established or occupied within British territorial waters." Benson was quick to warn against appointing officers to this organization who would kowtow to the Admiralty: "The officers detailed for this duty should come here fully imbued with our national and naval policy and ideas." When in possession of detailed information from Europe, such men could place themselves "in a position to urge upon British any plans that promise satisfactory results." Benson suggested two officers for the planning section, Captain Frank H. Schofield and Commander Dudley W. Knox, and he proposed to select a third person on his return to Washington. Commander Harry E. Yarnell was designated for this duty, leaving only one officer, Captain Luke McNamee, in the Washington planning section.[19] On 26 December an American planning section was set up in accordance with Benson's recommendation.

Sims had earlier urged a similar arrangement. In October he had been able to influence the content of a letter recommending certain naval practices that the American author Winston Churchill had sent to President Wilson. Among other things, Churchill called for a "combined staff of American and British strategists and materiel officers to sit constantly together and exert their entire energies upon making plans for the future conduct of war." The American officers would form a part of Sims's London headquarters. When President Wilson received this letter, he referred it to Daniels, who reacted cautiously. The secretary discussed Churchill's suggestion with Captain Pratt, who considered Sims a great leader of men but not a gifted strategist. He did not believe that Sims needed additional staff officers. Daniels asked Benson and Churchill to confer with each other, but no such meeting took place, because Churchill had gone to Paris.[20]

While in London, Benson made Sims the naval attaché, much to the force commander's satisfaction. Sims and the incumbent attaché, Captain William D. MacDougall, had clashed because of their differing assessments of British naval policy. Their reports often either duplicated or contradicted each other, a cause of annoyance in the Admiralty and confusion in the Navy Department. Sims, of course, became subordinate to the American ambassador "only in such matters as would ordinarily in peace come under the Naval Attaché."[21]

Another arrangement that Sims very much desired was unacceptable to Washington—honorary membership on the Board of Admiralty. To obtain much-needed information, Benson proposed that Sims be allowed to attend the daily meetings of this group. First Lord of the Admiralty Geddes suggested that Sims not only attend meetings, but also become an honorary member of the Admiralty. He wanted also to "extend the same privilege to the Chief of Naval Operations." When this proposition was forwarded to Washington, it encountered "an emphatic *no.*" There were limits to the president's willingness to associate American officers with other governments. Ambassador Page attempted to reverse the president's decision, but he did not succeed. Wilson's response stated definitively why he could not approve: the "English persist in thinking of the United States as an English people, but of course they are not and I am afraid that our people would resent and misunderstand what they would interpret as a digestion of Sims into the British official organization." "I appreciate fully the spirit in which this honor is offered Sims," the president wrote, "and I wish he could accept it: but I am afraid it would be a mistake for him to do so." Benson agreed with the decision, maintaining that such a designation would injure Sims. "Officers were saying he was looking too much to English approval."[22]

Colonel House's disinclination to participate in ceremonial functions while in Europe meant that Admiral Benson, the next senior member of the mission, on occasion served as spokesman for the mission at formal gatherings. On 13 November he acted in this role at a dinner given by the British foreign secretary, Arthur Balfour. Three days later he and the other members of the mission were guests of the royal family at Buckingham Palace. As the ranking American present, Benson sat to the right of King George V. A final affair of this character took place on 20 November, a luncheon at 10 Downing Street, residence of the British prime minister, David Lloyd George. The participants gathered in the room where Lord North had taken action against the American colonies; this time, representatives of the former contenders were gathered "to concert common action [for] the liberties of the world." Lloyd George spoke of his desire to assist the United States in every possible way, but he did not dwell on detailed plans for the future.[23]

Despite the deep sense of shared danger and the camaraderie of the London meetings, Benson refused to accept Sims's view that the national interests of the United States and Great Britain were identical or inseparable. He recognized that the British were reluctant to treat the Americans as equal partners because doing so would mean the end of British predominance in world affairs. Like President Wilson, Benson thought of the United States not as simply a source of reinforcement for the Entente war effort, but as a full partner in policy making. Responding to Lloyd George's remarks at the meeting of 20 November, Benson thanked his hosts for their kindnesses during the visit and made the obligatory statement of support for the common effort: "With all the strength and vigour of the young and matured manhood, and with the experience reaped from the development of our own great country, we come to you with a strong feeling and desire to do all that is possible for the freedom of the world so that everyone may experience the right of life, liberty, and pursuit of happiness." Giving assurance to his auditors that the United States was "heart and soul" in the war and would spare no resources in waging war, he nevertheless made reference to the sorest point in the relations of the two countries—their differing views on the question of the freedom of the seas. "We particularly appreciate the necessity for the freedom of the seas," he began. "In order that the various countries of the world may carry on their trade and may be of real assistance to each other, there must be free communication, and that communication can only be carried on through freedom of the seas."

These sentiments reflected American interest, not only in a strongly held national policy, but in a just and lasting peace after the defeat of the Central Powers. However indirectly, Benson's statement challenged British imperialism, which was based largely on the ability of the Royal Navy to establish general and lasting command of the sea along the sea lines of communication to its various dependencies. Having expressed his views on freedom of the seas, Benson closed with words intended to encourage his hosts at a time of great danger: "I would like you to feel, and I would like to impress upon you as earnestly as I can, the sincere and earnest feeling there is in our country and the unanimity and the firm resolution to hold on until the very last."

There followed a discussion in which certain differences came to the surface. Each side doubted that the other had contributed all the merchant shipping that was available for war service, an indication of underlying trade competition. The British shipping controller, Sir Joseph P. Maclay, detected "some mutual suspicion" about decisions that divided shipping between war services and trading, but he and Lloyd George argued that it was possible to adjust these matters.[24]

One subject of considerable importance had not yet been resolved in London—provision for effective inter-Allied naval planning. The arrangements for a Supreme War Council included a group of Permanent Military Representatives to advise the heads of government who sat on the council, but there was no comparable group of naval representatives. Daniels noted this omission in a message to the president, who responded: "Undoubtedly House [Wilson's representative on the Supreme War Council] ought to have a naval adviser as well as a military adviser when he takes part in the proposed new council." He was puzzled because none had been designated. Neither Daniels nor Wilson was as yet aware of discussions about this very question then ongoing in London. On the evening of 20 November, Benson and Sims dined with Geddes and Jellicoe to discuss a proposed naval council whose representatives would have functions comparable to those of the Permanent Military Representatives. The British favored creation of an inter-Allied planning group but wanted to separate it from the Supreme War Council and locate it in London—a means of protecting British naval interests. The discussion of 20 November led to a preliminary agreement on the organization of an inter-Allied naval council. It was immediately sent to Wilson for his approval.[25]

The time had come to travel to Paris for the formal inter-Allied conference and a session of the Supreme War Council. Benson left London much more highly regarded than he had been previously. Colonel House observed: "Someone told me the other day that the British thought Admiral Sims a first rate man until Admiral Benson appeared upon the scene." The Admiralty felt that "very great benefit" had been derived from the exchanges with the CNO and that cooperation was now "far easier and more complete." After Benson held a farewell conference with Jellicoe on 21 November, House noted in his diary that the First Sea Lord "spoke highly of Benson, for whom I have warm regard. It is Benson who has insisted on their making a further attempt to close the Straits of Dover." With these accomplishments behind him, Benson joined other members of the mission in a journey to Paris, where the inter-Allied conference was to meet on 29 November and the Supreme War Council on 1 December.[26]

While awaiting the formal meetings, the members of the House Mission, including Benson, conferred with various American and French officials. On 23 November, Benson visited the American ambassador, William Graves Sharp, to express once again concern about the lack of offensive naval plans. On the same day he met the French chief of the naval staff, Admiral Ferdinand-Jean-Jacques de Bon, and the French minister of marine, Georges Leygues, who had just come from a naval conference in Rome in the company of the Deputy First Sea Lord of the Admiralty, Vice Admiral Sir Wester Wemyss. Both de Bon and Wemyss complained that the Italian fleet was not being utilized fully; its principal ships were located in a base "so situated that a strong enemy force could prevent their exit." Benson considered traveling to Rome for meetings with Italian naval leaders, but Colonel House did not think that he could excuse Benson from preparations for the forthcoming conferences. The CNO nevertheless sought independent information on the situation in Italy, which he obtained from Commander Charles R. Train, the naval attaché in Rome.[27]

The serious situation in Italy gave impetus to consideration of the proposed joint naval council. De Bon and Wemyss thought that the creation of such an institution might "induce the Italians to use their vessels to the best possible advantage for the common cause." Benson sent the formal plan for an Allied naval council to Washington with a favorable recommendation. The council was to be composed of the chiefs of the several naval staffs, including those of the American and Japanese navies, or their representatives, to meet whenever a need arose.

President Wilson proved agreeable. Daniels soon cabled that Wilson would agree to membership if the council was "organized on the same lines as the Inter-Allied Military Council [Supreme War Council] formerly agreed on."[28]

The Allied Naval Council sat for the first time in Paris on 29–30 November 1917. Since the organization had yet to gain formal approval, initial discussions clarified its purpose. Sir Eric Geddes obtained acceptance of his view that the naval chiefs of staff of Britain, France, and Italy, joined by admirals appointed by the United States and Japan, should meet "with the object of making their agreement more complete and in order to follow naval warfare in a joint study and to decide together on the manner and conditions of making the best use of all the Allied resources." The formal constitution of the Allied Naval Council stated its missions concisely: "to watch generally over the policy connected with the naval conduct of the war, [and to] ensure the coordination of naval action . . . and [the] development of scientific means for waging war." The United States soon accepted the arrangement; on 8 January 1918 Sims was officially designated the American member of the council in the absence of Admiral Benson.[29]

On 29 November Benson was present at the opening session of the formal inter-Allied conference, which took place in the Salon de l'Horloge at the Ministry of Foreign Affairs. The session lasted only eight minutes. Georges Clemenceau, in the chair as the head of the host government, addressed the conference briefly, closing with a cogent injunction: "The noble spirit which animates us must be translated into action. The order of the day is work. Let us get to work." After committees were named to conduct the principal work of the conference, the session came to an abrupt end.[30]

Because Benson was not a part of the Supreme War Council, he spent much of his remaining time in France conducting discussions with other naval officials and taking field trips. With de Bon, Benson went over problems of naval aviation, the need for tugs on the Atlantic and Mediterranean coasts of France, and the methods of communication between the French naval attaché in Washington and the Navy Department. With Italian leaders he reviewed the general situation confronting Italy. With Cone he deliberated on the development of American naval aviation in Europe, with Sims the disposition of American naval vessels, and with General Bliss certain problems connected with the transportation of troops and their accommodations.

Perhaps the most memorable of Benson's trips was a visit in the company of General Bliss to the headquarters of the French commander in chief, General Henry Philippe B. O. J. Pétain, at Compiègne. The high point of the trip was a visit to the front line of the French Third Army. Its commander, General Georges Louis Humbert, guided the

Admiral William Shepherd Benson and Vice Admiral William Sowden Sims, Paris, France, 1917.

American party through the ruined city of Chauny and the medieval Chateau de Coucy, which the Germans had almost totally destroyed. From the ruins of this chateau Humbert and his staff pointed out the German line, plainly visible on a ridge about three thousand yards distant. A French battery was firing shells into the German position. Sims, who accompanied Benson, doubted the wisdom of such trips, because he considered them an "unjustifiable risk," but he did not say so until he had returned from the front. He later wrote Mrs. Sims: "I could not decline to go out when he invited me."[31]

Benson also visited naval installations. During a stop at the port of Paullic, he saw German prisoners unloading a large American tramp steamer, which had been there for ten days. He was stunned at the "slow and inefficient method" of unloading; appropriate facilities would have permitted a much more expeditious turnaround. He also visited a site chosen by Cone to be the location of a plant for assembling naval aircraft shipped to Europe. He noted "evidence of great zeal, earnestness, and intelligence on the part of both officers and men," but little progress—a function of limited resources.

These experiences led Benson to compose a memorandum titled simply "Doctrine," in which he discussed some of the means of ensuring efficiency in the conduct of naval warfare in modern conditions. To begin with, the CNO noted the difficulty of ensuring effective coordination of effort in operations involving large numbers of units in wartime conditions. The pressures of time, the separation of units, and the difficulty of maintaining communications would normally preclude effective coordination if commanders depended on instructions just recently issued to them and on signals and radio messages exchanged while operations were in progress. To ensure mutual support it was essential that commanders possess a "bond of mutual understanding, or doctrine, to coordinate decisions and to promote prompt and united actions." The rest of the memorandum took up the basis of doctrine and its germination and promulgation, loyalty to plan, discretion of subordinates, initiative of subordinates, command doctrine, action doctrine, and special doctrines. This document stands as impressive evidence of the degree to which the difficulties of contemporary warfare, particularly on an inter-Allied basis, had impressed Benson during his European sojourn.[32]

After attending the closing session of the international conference on 3 December, Benson undertook several more field trips. The next day, accompanied by Colonel House and General Bliss, he visited General John J. Pershing at army installations located in Chaumont and Contrecourt. His last visits were to the port of St. Nazaire, where American troops and supplies were scheduled to arrive, to the naval aviation station at Croisic, and to the American naval base and hospital at Brest.

Although Benson recognized that great efforts were being made, he left Brest aboard the *Mount Vernon* on 7 December with a number of concerns. Chief among these was his conviction that an American naval command should have been established in France. Rear Admiral Henry B. Wilson had assumed command of the United States Patrol Squadron on 1 November, but he did not control other naval organizations and installations in the vicinity. Benson planned to discuss this question with Sims, but the force commander left the *Mount Vernon* without learning of Benson's desire to confer on this subject. Benson drew attention to this episode as a preliminary to stating his views on the need for a reorganization of the naval establishment in France. The CNO did not drop the issue. He wrote to Admiral Wilson about his concerns as soon as he returned to the United States.[33]

During the return voyage to the United States, the members of the House Mission exchanged information and observations. All agreed with Paul D. Cravath that there was a "ghastly lack of cooperation

General John J. Pershing, USA, Admiral W. S. Benson, USN, and an unidentified officer, United States Army headquarters in France, 4 December 1917.

between the Allies" in both political and military dimensions. The three principals—House, Benson, and Bliss—shared the view that disunity stemmed from "military jealousy and suspicion as to ultimate national aim." The American presence in Europe ensured that actions were taken to arrange for effective coordination of national efforts. The greatest achievement of the House Mission was to bring about the creation of institutional machinery designed to stimulate improvements in inter-Allied coordination during the critical year of 1918.[34]

Nevertheless, Admiral Benson recognized that important goals had been accomplished in connection with inter-Allied naval cooperation. Among specific gains were the founding of the Allied Naval Council, the decision to send a division of American battleships to the North Sea, the agreement to send the entire Atlantic Fleet later if necessary, and plans to complete the Dover and North Sea barrages. Of comparable significance in Benson's view were the decision to formulate a comprehensive plan of offensive operations in which the United States would play an important role, arrangements for Sims to attend the daily Admiralty conference, and the establishment of an American planning section in London to improve cooperation between the Admiralty and the Navy Department.[35]

Benson's activities in Europe were among his most important contributions to the victory of 1918. His agitation for energetic action, if sometimes misplaced, contributed a great deal to the burst of naval activity that followed the conferences of November and December. Moreover, his visit to Europe equipped him with first-hand information that proved invaluable on his return to Washington. Colonel House recognized the extent of Benson's achievement. To the president he remarked that for some time he had realized that "there was a man in the Navy who was doing things," and he had now discovered that "that man was Benson."[36]

CHAPTER IX

THE DRIVE TOWARD VICTORY

Admiral Benson returned from Europe with a mature conception of the role the United States Navy must play during the rest of the war. He recognized that a crisis existed in Europe, but the attitude of the Allied naval leaders had encouraged him. Daniels noted that the CNO "found the situation grave but was pleased with the spirit of the English and French navies." In his report on the House Mission, Benson began with the observation that the United States could "expect no additional naval assistance whatever from the continental European Allies." Noting that the Allies were "jealous and suspicious of one another," he saw hope in their views of America: "They believe, however, in the sincerity and unselfishness of the United States; and feeling thus, they are not only willing for the United States to take the lead in matters which affect our common cause; but they are entirely anxious that we should dominate the entire Allied situation both as regards active belligerent operations against the enemy and economically." One reason for Benson's favorable prognosis for 1918 was his newly established relationship with Admiral Jellicoe. He had succeeded in obtaining British consent to some of his proposals, even if this outcome reflected American pressure on the Admiralty rather than real agreement. Soon after Benson returned to Washington, however, Jellicoe was removed from office, and Admiral Wester Wemyss became First Sea Lord.[1]

During 1918 Benson subjected himself to an extraordinarily grueling schedule, in accordance with his lifelong conception of duty. When a subordinate complained about an inconvenient command arrangement, Benson responded tartly that he could not understand how any naval officer in wartime could give a thought to personal convenience or to any consideration other than "efficient administration." He also observed that he himself had "no [government] servants, . . . no [government] automobile; nor have I anything else which the Government provides for the Chief of Naval Operations except my flat rate of pay." He could devote no time to personal matters: "The country needs every minute of my time and thought, and my time and thought will be in vain unless I can depend upon others in your position to devote an equal amount of time and thought to the efficient administration of the functions of the Navy Department which come under your cognizance." The offending officer immediately changed his mind. To a Sunday school class in Geneva, New York, Benson summarized his views cogently: "Every man who is a man—whatever the degree of his material prosperity, wherever he may labor—in factory, office, farm, or mine, is eagerly grasping today the opportunity to rise above all temptation towards sordid self-seeking and put forth now his supreme unselfish effort to the end that he may stand with honor and without shame before his conscience, his countrymen, and God."[2]

Benson's credo found expression in the work of the officers in the Navy Department. Captain Pratt starkly summarized the hectic situation that prevailed in 1918: "There was no glory in it—only work. Work seven days of the week, some days almost 24 hours of it. . . . I entered upon my work without a grey hair on my head or a nerve in my body. I left with both." The assistant CNO stressed the need to ensure the well-being of his chief. Benson was the "*one* strong man" in the war effort. "We watch him like hawks to see his health stands up. . . . The Navy is safe in his hands, but God help us if it ever got out of them, for the strong men are not to be found, who are willing to stand public abuse and still pursue a steadfast course."[3]

The navy generally escaped public criticism during the war, although the army underwent an extensive congressional inquiry early in 1918 for its alleged failure to mobilize efficiently. On one occasion Congressman Fred A. Britten (R-Ill.) sought copies of complaints that supposedly had emanated from Admiral Sims. Both Daniels and Benson asked Sims to comment on this question, Benson noting that an attempt was underway "to create [the] impression you have been hampered by failure of the Navy Department to meet your request for various things[,] particularly personnel. I feel that a strong positive statement on this subject from you is highly desirable." Sims's reply was somewhat qualified, although he began firmly: "I strongly deprecate any effort to create an impression that our Naval Forces in European Waters have been avoidably hampered by failure of the Navy Department to comply with my recommendations for various things[,] particularly personnel." He then reiterated his continuing desire for additional destroyers and "certain classes of personnel," but he noted that the task of deciding the allocation of scarce resources was clearly a matter for the Navy Department: "I consider it the first duty of those at the Front loyally to accept such decisions and make the best of conditions which are at present admittedly unsatisfactory and must remain so until the energetic measures now being taken to increase our antisubmarine forces produce the necessary reinforcements." Early in 1918 Admiral Benson appeared before a closed meeting of a House subcommittee. The chairman of this group, Congressman William B. Oliver (D-Ala.), later stated that "every member of the committee who heard Admiral Benson's statement was gratified with the operations of the fleet, the co-operation on the part of the department with request[s] made for supplies, and with the unity that prevailed between the American fleet and those of the Allies."[4]

Benson clearly enjoyed the confidence of his political superiors. There seems to have been no serious criticism of him by the president or any other of Benson's civilian superiors. Indeed, Colonel House believed that the navy had "pretty well righted itself under the direction of such men as Benson." After a conversation with the president's adviser early in 1918, Daniels recorded the colonel's view that the "good condition of the Navy had saved the day" and that no one was happier about this outcome than President Wilson. Reporting on his sojourn in Europe, House told Daniels that "everybody abroad praised the alertness of the men of the Navy" and that "Benson was easily the first man of the military men in the Council—towered over Jellico [*sic*] & told them what to do, & put them to doing it."[5]

Benson also received the praise of his naval colleagues. Admiral William B. Caperton, commanding naval forces in the South Atlantic, wrote after Benson's trip to Europe: "Well, we are all proud of you, old man, and appreciate the manner in which you pulled off everything on the other side. . . . I hope you are not overtaxing yourself; take care of your health[,] as we need you." The commander of the Asiatic Fleet, Admiral Austin M. Knight, wrote from his flagship, the *Brooklyn:* "I think of you many times and always with highest admiration for the way in which you are carrying your burden and with warmest affection for you personally." A naval constructor close to Admiral Sims wrote that, after visiting the Navy Department, he agreed with the "general verdict one hears around Washington that as compared with other departments, the Navy knows pretty well what it wants to do, and is going ahead with its job."[6]

The exceptions to this rule were the disgruntled naval reformer, Admiral Bradley Fiske, and Sims's aide, Lieutenant Commander Babcock. Fiske mounted public criticism of such intensity that Benson was compelled to warn him that continued behavior of this nature might lead to a court-martial. During a brief visit to the United States, Babcock wrote to Sims that Benson was unduly preoccupied with detail and unwilling to delegate authority, as had been done in London. It was satisfying "to see the extent of everyone's knowledge of the real situation abroad," but depressing to observe Benson poring "over a pile of despatches fully four inches thick [the department's cable traffic for the preceding twenty-four hours]."[7]

This kind of criticism aroused the ire of some of Benson's staff officers. Commander Charles Belknap, Jr., an associate of Sims, wrote heatedly: "There is too damned much criticism. . . . I can state that it is the desire of the gang here to further the gang over there heart and soul. We put across an awful lot that neither you nor anyone under you know of and it is discouraging to hear only that we are PUNK and the organization is rotten." Captain Harris Laning, the acting chief of the Bureau of Navigation, wrote in similar terms to Sims much later: "Criticism is easy, and just criticism beneficial[,] but there is nothing more lowering to the morale than unjust criticism, and criticism made without full knowledge and thought is apt to be unjust." Benson's associates in the Navy Department thus demonstrated their confidence in him, despite the barrage of complaints from Sims's headquarters.[8]

Benson's first order of business on returning from Europe was to fulfill commitments that he had made to the Allies and to Sims. As soon as he was able, Benson dispatched the officers to London whom he had recommended for assignment to the American naval planning section. Admiral Wemyss wanted to treat these men as individual liaison officers and to assign them to various material branches, but this suggestion was entirely contrary to the American intention, and the members of the planning section immediately reported this fact to the First Sea Lord. The planning section must "work as a unit[,] with the privileges of the Admiralty" but "with complete freedom of action." Accordingly, Captain Twining, Sims's chief of staff, who had become ex officio head of the planning section, agreed that it could serve best if it was "held together as a unit and work[ed] in close cooperation and conjunction with the Plans Division of the Admiralty." Wemyss concurred in this view, and the planning section went to work in quarters set aside for it both in Sims's headquarters and in the Admiralty. One or more members of the section attended the force commander at meetings of the Allied Naval Council. Sims soon reported that the members of the American group "had a very much more thorough training in this kind of work [planning] than the corresponding British officers have had," and that they exerted a "very marked influence upon policy-making."[9]

British interest in employing additional U.S. destroyers emerged shortly after the House Mission returned to the United States. While in London, Benson had ruled that no more U.S. destroyers were to be sent to the British until new ones then under construction became available. The CNO remained true to this position in responding to a British request for destroyers to serve with the Grand Fleet. He informed Sims: "No destroyers can be diverted from present occupation of guarding merchant tonnage and antisubmarine efforts, for purpose of acting as screening vessels of capital ships of Grand Fleet."[10]

Benson remained concerned about coastal defense, given the detachment of destroyers and other patrol craft for duty as escorts for convoys, and he took steps to ensure adequate provisions against enemy operations in American waters. At length the group appointed to make recommendations, the Special Board to Formulate a Plan of Defense in Home Waters, issued a statement. The board favored sending "maximum possible force abroad for offensive operations in the active theater of war" but maintained that the American navy should concentrate on protecting troop transports rather than on escorting merchant shipping that carried supplies to the Allied nations. This emphasis reflected the great increase in the number of American troops being sent to Europe during the early months of 1918. The board speculated that Germany might send submarines to American waters and that, if any ships carrying troops and supplies to Europe were sunk, or if submarines succeeded in interfering with coastal shipping, it might become necessary to recall some American naval vessels to home waters. Thus, it was important to maintain the minimum force required to parry a submarine campaign off the American coast, despite "repeated urgings to send all forces abroad, cf individuals who have not fully considered the situation as a whole." The board also recommended secret routing measures; local defenses, such as submarine nets and mines; steps to control outgoing and incoming shipping; and provision of necessary personnel. Admiral Benson approved these recommendations on 6 March 1918.[11]

The observations Benson made in Europe strengthened his earlier view that Sims had erred in concentrating most of the American destroyers at Queenstown on the Irish coast rather than at Brest, a French port in Brittany. This difference in strategic emphasis reflected Benson's and Sims's divergent views of the primary naval mission. As early as 2 December 1917 General Pershing had indicated that the United States must make a major contribution to the land war in 1918, because Germany planned to force a decision on the western front during that year. This concern led the War Department to accelerate the transfer of American troops to Europe. Responding to this circumstance, on 18 January 1918 Admiral Benson created the Naval Overseas Transportation Service. He assigned seventy-four ships to transport men and supplies. These developments confirmed Benson's belief that an important force of destroyers should operate from Brest to protect incoming troop transports and supply ships.[12]

Admiral Sims from the beginning of his service in London had maintained that it would be a "radical mistake" for the United States to ship troops in such numbers as to interfere with the supply of the Allies. He continued to believe that the primary task for American destroyers was to protect merchant ships sailing to and from the British

Isles. He did not send any ships to Brest until after an American merchant ship, the *Antilles*, was sunk on a return voyage from France. Eight yachts were then based on Brest to provide needed escorts. Even as late as 8 January 1918 Sims requested more destroyers for Queenstown. On the same day, Benson sent him an extract from a cable Pershing had recently sent to the War Department calling for additional destroyers to escort troopships: "Nothing could possibly be more important than the rapid movements of our transports under proper protection[,] and Navy destroyers should be taken from service with British fleet or elsewhere without delay to serve fully our own needs." Benson, of course, was already on record with Sims regarding the need to transfer ships from Queenstown, where they were used principally to protect merchant shipping, to Brest, where they could help escort troopships. On 8 December 1917, for example, he wrote to Sims: "As our activities or necessities have so materially increased on the French coast, due to the bringing in of the Army and the supplies and equipment incident thereto, the importance of the French coast and the attention to be paid to it is rapidly surpassing that of the English Channel or the waters of the United Kingdom."[13]

The decision to strengthen the naval forces on the French coast led to a change in command arrangements. On 3 January 1918 Benson sent a ten-point directive to Sims that reorganized the naval command in France. All naval activities in France were placed under the command of a "Senior U.S. Navy Officer in France." This officer, Rear Admiral Henry B. Wilson, would serve under Sims, the "Commander U.S. Navy Forces in European Waters." Sims modified this directive only to the extent of making Wilson "Commander, U.S. Naval Forces in France." Wilson assumed his command on 18 January and made the destroyer tender *Prometheus* his flagship.[14]

The vastly increased transportation of American troops to France posed many difficult problems. Shipping was in desperately short supply, given the depredations of the U-boats and the tremendous demand for vessels to carry supplies to the Allies and American troops and equipment to Europe. One means of easing the traffic problem to France was to send some troop units to Britain, whence they could eventually cross the English Channel to the Continent. Benson favored the direct route, but he recognized the pressing need to enlarge French ports so that they could deal with the expanded volume. Only the United States could undertake the task of port development. Secretary of War Newton D. Baker concurred in this view. Before the Senate Committee on Military Affairs, he reported that all manner of items—locomotives, railroad cars, rails, bridging material, crossties, spikes, fishplates, and even nails—must be transported to France. Eventually the shipping problem was effectively settled. Britain agreed to provide the necessary additional shipping, provided the United States sent only combat troops during the emergency, a step that delayed formation of an independent American army but brought essential reinforcements expeditiously to France. In addition, it was agreed that half of the American troops would be sent to Britain and the other half directly to France, thereby spreading the burden of troop reception to a number of ports.[15]

Throughout 1918 Admiral Benson had to respond to various complaints from Admiral Sims in London. The force commander continually worried that another officer might supersede him. When Sims heard rumors that Admiral Mayo, the commander in chief of the Atlantic Fleet, had requested orders for overseas service, he wrote anxiously to Benson: "I do not know what there might be in these rumors, but I think you will realize that in case Admiral Mayo should be sent over here that my position would become impossible." Sims also reacted to a news report that Rear Admiral Edward W. Eberle might assume command of the American destroyers at Queenstown. When Benson firmly opposed the dispatch of Mayo to Europe and President Wilson concurred in this view, Sims became worried that Benson intended to replace Mayo as commander in chief of the Atlantic Fleet and come to Europe himself. Captain Pratt informed Sims that Benson had no such plans: "About *Benson* don't you believe it for a minute. He will stay CNO. He will not go C-in-C." Perhaps, he surmised, the rumor began because Secretary Daniels had once said that the "real *C-in-C of the fleet in this war was the CNO.*" Pratt insisted that there was no plan to replace him with Mayo, Eberle, or anyone else: "I talked often to CNO about it. He feels you are the only man on the Admiral's list with the grasp of big things." Benson also felt the need to calm the agitated Sims. He cabled forcefully: "Department perfectly satisfied with your administration of destroyers as well as of other forces." This message apparently mollified Sims, who wrote to his wife elatedly: "You can readily understand how gratifying this was." To Pratt he communicated similarly, stating that Benson's cable was a "great comfort" to him, although he added a rather irritating comment: "If they will only let things alone as they are now I will have no complaint to make." A few weeks later Sims became excited when he learned that Admiral Albert Gleaves wanted to come to Europe. To Benson he argued that he could not detect "any possible utility" in such a trip. The CNO steadfastly supported Sims, avoiding any actions that might have compromised the authority of the force commander.[16]

During May 1918 a German U-boat finally appeared off the American East Coast, again raising the concerns that had earlier troubled the Navy Department. Secretary Daniels then informed Sims that he was to "put extra emphasis upon escorting troop convoys both in number of destroyers and distance to which they operate." He concluded forthrightly: "If necessary in order to ensure safe landing of troops, fewer destroyers shall be assigned to the protection of ships carrying merchandise." Sims proved fractious, responding that he recognized the importance of protecting troop transports, but that the "safety of vessels carrying merchandise to Europe is hardly less essential to the successful prosecution of the war than is safety of troop transports and we might conceivably lose the war through making excessive demands upon our escort forces for the protection of troops." Because it was impossible to guarantee safe conduct for troopships, he suggested that the "public mind should be prepared for possible loss of transport." Sims did not deploy additional destroyers to the base at Brest until a troopship, the *President Lincoln*, was sunk while returning to the United States on 31 May. Thereafter, transfers of vessels to Brest eventually resulted in the destroyer flotilla there being larger than the one at Queenstown.[17]

When additional German U-boats came to American waters, Benson resisted measures that might have slowed the transportation of troops to Europe. To improve antisubmarine warfare, he ordered the commanders of the naval districts to assume control of coastal shipping. He also established the Coastwise Routing Office in the Office of Naval Operations to direct offensive operations against the U-boats. Benson summarized his attitude toward this problem in a letter to his son Howard, then commanding the yacht *Noma* as part of the United States Patrol Squadron in France: "Of course since the German submarine came over I am terribly hard put to as we are short of the many things we should have. It is certainly making bricks without straw." Nevertheless, despite the extent of American coastal waters, he had "no doubt we will come out all right in the end." An increase in the size of the navy to 131,485 men gave him comfort. To his son he remarked: "They give me credit for the increase and I suppose if it had not been for me the measure would not have gone through. We will need them and more too before the world finally settles down to normal conditions."[18]

As always in wartime, Benson was anxious to preserve secrecy about important naval movements. On one occasion he attended a dinner at which his dining partner proved to be a "charming lady of the Washington social set." To his astonishment, she reported to him detailed information about the sailing of a certain vessel to Europe. The next morning a furious Benson called in all officers in Operations and warned them about the danger of loose talk, ending plainly: "Keep your mouths shut!"[19]

After his European trip, Benson's interest in naval aviation became very apparent. Rear Admiral David W. Taylor reported to Sims that there had been a "flurry on the aeroplane situation." Benson had doubled Commander Cone's proposal for the construction of single-engine flying boats and had quadrupled his proposal for twin-engine flying boats. He also attempted to improve command arrangements for naval aviation in France, and he directed Captain Noble E. Irwin, head of the Office of Naval Aviation in Washington, to man and equip naval air stations in France at the earliest possible date. Sims was impressed; he wrote to Captain Bristol that he was doing everything possible to improve the naval air effort. "As far as I can see," he stated, "the principal dignitaries at home are absolutely alive to the necessity of giving us all practicable assistance, and I believe that they are doing this to the extreme extent of their power. This is a pretty strong statement, but I believe it to be true."[20]

Despite the short time it had to develop its air service, the United States Navy made an impressive contribution to the war in the air. The first land-based naval aircraft reached France in May 1918, supplanting seaplanes and kite balloons towed by destroyers as the principal means of operating against submarines. At war's end the naval aviation effort encompassed 1,300 officers, 15,000 men, 500 airplanes, 50 kite balloons, and 3 dirigibles based on twenty-seven air stations in England, Ireland, France, and Italy.

Benson had returned from Europe with a British commitment to support the construction of a great mine barrage across the North Sea between the British Isles and Norway, a means of interfering with the passage of German submarines into the North Atlantic. The planning section in London gave particular attention to this project. Rear Admiral Joseph Strauss took command of the Atlantic Fleet's Mine Force, and he spearheaded construction of the barrage, which was completed shortly before the war came to an end. This remarkable project reflected the ingenuity and energy that the navy under Admiral Benson brought to innovative antisubmarine measures.[21]

One of the most persistent questions of policy during 1918 was whether the Allies should sponsor large projects for intervention in Russia to restore a second front in that troubled country, and Admiral Benson on occasion became involved in discussions relating to this matter. The CNO saw proposals for intervention as a means of engaging Japan more actively in the maritime struggle against the Central Powers. On 14 February 1918 Benson prepared a memorandum for Secretary Daniels titled "Use of Japanese Shipping." This document served as the basis of a recommendation from Daniels to Secretary of State Robert Lansing that proposed arrangements for constructing two or three hundred thousand tons of new merchant shipping in Japan, for chartering existing Japanese-owned vessels on liberal terms, and for using Japanese vessels to transport the Australian wheat crop to the United States. Benson suspected that Japan might abandon the Allies and join the Central Powers. The means of avoiding this outcome was to give Japan "a free foot to throw the might of her power into the balance against Germany." Otherwise Germany might make an attractive offer that the Japanese could not refuse. Nevertheless, Benson was opposed to any agreements that might affect China adversely. He favored negotiations with Japan concerning Siberia, proposing to inform Japan frankly "that we want her to be in a position to dominate and if necessary to control Eastern or all Siberia," but to come to the "distinct understanding that the integrity of Chinese territory be assured." Japan and China together would preclude European aggression in East Asia. He considered "Japan's firm friendship in addition to that of China" of greater importance than that of any European power or combination of powers.[22]

When the Inter-Allied Supreme War Council prepared to discuss possible intervention in Siberia during its sessions in March 1918, Benson forwarded a plan to Admiral Sims for consideration. He suggested a joint expedition composed of American, British, French, and Italian forces to occupy Vladivostok and to hold the Amur Railroad to its junction with the main line of the Trans-Siberian Railroad at Karimska. China was to hold the China Eastern Railroad through Manchuria. The role of the Japanese would be to operate west from Karimska, basing themselves on their own railroad through Harbin. Recognizing the political sensitivity of intervention in Siberia, Benson called for a solemn proclamation stating that "no territory or privileges of any kind" would be retained beyond the emergency. It was important, he concluded, that the advance into Siberia penetrate as far as the Ural Mountains in order to raise a barrier against further German advances.[23]

Nothing came of Benson's proposal during the March meetings of the Supreme War Council, but it proved to be a precursor of the ultimate decision of the Supreme War Council to send an inter-Allied expedition to Siberia in July 1918. Units of both the army and the navy participated in the expedition, which eventually occupied Vladivostok and penetrated deeply into the Siberian hinterland. Despite efforts such as those proposed by Benson to inhibit Japanese imperialism, the troops of that nation remained in Siberia until arrangements were made at the Washington naval conference of 1921–22 to remove them.

The tremendous burdens that Admiral Benson and his staff carried during the spring and summer of 1918 took a terrible physical toll. Captain Pratt came close to a complete physical collapse and was forced to convalesce at his home in Maine. Concerned for his loyal subordinate, Benson extended the leave to a period of almost four weeks. Finally, in August, Admiral Benson himself yielded to the entreaties of his staff and went to Saranac Lake in the Adirondak Mountains in New York for a respite. He maintained contact with his office through Captain Pratt, who had returned to duty, but he was able to refresh himself. One of Benson's aides reported to Pratt that the "C.N.O. was feeling wonderfully well this morning and every foot he went into those woods made him feel better. . . . His whole countenance looks freer from care than I have seen it in many moons. . . . I am sure this quiet spot is going to do C.N.O. lots of good." When Benson returned to Washington,

Daniels noticed that "his face shone, his health was strengthened, and he came back to his duties refreshed and invigorated in every way."[24]

During the anxious winter, spring, and summer of 1918 Admiral Benson labored unstintingly if almost anonymously to ensure that the navy sustained its indispensable contribution to the total war against the Central Powers. Given his self-effacing nature, it was no surprise that Benson was called by one journalist "The Mysterious Admiral Who Quietly Dominates the Navy." The naval effort in countering the submarine permitted an enormous reinforcement of the western front that unexpectedly produced a turn of the tide in the Allies' favor during July. Despite Admiral Sims's suspicions, the CNO and his staff established a high degree of cooperation with the force commander's headquarters in London; this was not the least of the navy's contributions to the unexpected victory in 1918.[25]

A more public task lay dead ahead for Benson. The approaching end of the war ineluctably led him to contemplate the naval aspects of the armistice and the postwar peace settlement. Very soon he found himself directly engaged in the negotiations that settled these exceedingly complicated matters.

CHAPTER X

ON THE EVE OF PEACE

Beginning on 21 March 1918 and continuing to the third week in July, the German army in France launched five powerful offensives, seeking to end the war before massive American reinforcements could determine the outcome. The Allies struggled to prevent a German breakthrough. Their lines bent considerably under enormous pressure, but they did not break. As soon as the last German offensive was contained, General Ferdinand Foch, the Allied generalissimo, assumed the offensive. His forces made sufficient progress during August and September to make victory a prospect in 1918, at least one year and possibly two years sooner than anticipated in the United States.

Despite the desperate situation that developed in France during 1918, the British government undertook a number of initiatives that looked ahead to the postwar years and the resumption of normal economic competition. These early attempts to strengthen Britain's competitive position in world markets after the war aroused considerable concern among a number of American leaders, including Admiral Benson.

A particularly intriguing stimulus to such sentiment among American leaders was a British effort to capture Latin American markets that had been lost to the United States during the war. The foreign secretary, Arthur Balfour, clearly signaled British intentions in a confidential cable to Sir William Wiseman. He noted that Britain had no political aspirations in Latin America, but that British commercial interests there were "of the highest importance." Latin American investments amounted to half of Britain's total investments overseas. "We need now, and shall need after the war, all the return that we can draw from this source.

Suspicion, however, exists here and causes some anxiety that the United States are inclined to use their political influence in these countries to further their own intersts at our expense." To prevent any such development, a special trade mission departed from England on 21 April 1918 for an extended stay in Latin America. Britain did not give prior notice of this enterprise to the United States. The leader of this mission, Sir Maurice de Bunsen, enjoyed the assistance of experts on Latin American trade. Balfour announced that the purpose of the de Bunsen Mission was to "offer congratulations to those countries that had definitely shown their sympathy with the Allied cause," to "indicate to them the principles" for which the war was being fought, and to point out the ideals that Britain sought to preserve by waging war. De Bunsen, however, communicated to Balfour a different conception of his activity. It was to "maintain and even largely to develop both politically and economically" Britain's position in Latin America.

When de Bunsen appeared in Brazil, he tried to convey the impression that his mission was planned with the knowledge of the United States and that it had the full support of the U.S. government. Roy Howard of the United States Press, reporting on the mission's activities from Brazil, emphasized the potential Anglo-American conflict inherent in the situation, stressing the "undisguised animosity between British and American commercial interests in South America," which was "untempered and unmodified by the common purpose on French battlefields." Brazilian censors intercepted Howard's dispatch, and the Department of State suppressed it to "avoid a very possible controversy with Great Britain."[1]

Admiral Benson learned of the de Bunsen Mission when he received a report of its activities in Brazil from the American naval attaché stationed in Rio de Janeiro. This intelligence included a copy of a contract prepared in Great Britain that would have interfered with American commercial activity in South America after the war. Benson gave the document careful attention. His reaction, one of "terrible outrage," led him to report the matter to Secretary Daniels. He and Daniels concluded that such a contract would keep businessmen from the United States out of shipbuilding and the manufacture of munitions. It would also confer exclusive control of the Brazilian iron and steel industry on Britain—specifically, the firm of Vickers and Armstrong. Daniels wrote to Secretary Lansing that "secret trade agreements were fraught at this time with the greatest danger," especially if it became known that while the war was still being waged "our loans to the British Government were making it possible for that government to undertake commercial developments against our trade interests in the Western Hemisphere."[2]

A less flagrant but persistent aspect of Britain's interest in postwar trade was the British practice of questioning passengers on their return from visits to foreign countries. The Office of Naval Intelligence thought that British naval officers stationed in New York ostensibly for intelligence appeared most interested in gathering information of commercial significance. Sir Arthur Willert, a British journalist attached to the British Mission in Washington, wrote to Geoffrey Dawson, the editor of the *Times* of London, that there was "genuine distrust" in America of Britain's plans for postwar economic activity, even in "surprising places" such as the "higher altitudes of Government. There is a suspicion that we are finding time to prepare to nobble the sunnier markets of the world while demanding that the United States put everything into the war."[3]

A British attempt to acquire merchant ships built in the United States during the war added to growing distrust of British postwar intentions. The Admiralty contended that it was entitled to options on such vessels because it was repairing American destroyers in British shipyards, an activity that prevented construction of merchant ships at home during the war. The Wilson administration, which made prompt payment for repairs of American vessels in Britain, delayed its response to this unwelcome proposition. Sims was unhappy, writing to his wife: "It seemed to me an astonishing piece of blindness that the principal dignitaries could not understand the psychological effect of the proposal that was made by the First Lord."

Sims then urged the Navy Department to act, but Admiral Benson drafted a cable for Daniels's signature that sharply criticized Sims: "Department feels that in initiating policy decidedly contrary to the wishes and intentions of this government you have committed an error in judgment. In future do not initiate general policies of international character without first communicating with the Department, giving your recommendations and obtaining views of this government, through the Department, before taking up with foreign official matters affecting international policy." Sims naturally resented this message. He replied that he had not initiated policy but had merely made a "tentative suggestion of a possible method by which the difficulties in which we were involved in the matter of repair facilities for our naval vessels could be met." He denied having made any commitments, and he insisted that having to obtain prior clearance regarding such matters would create a very difficult situation for him.[4]

To clarify the situation and to soothe Sims, Benson sent another message that explained the Navy Department's views forthrightly but in temperate language. Sims was informed that he had full authority to discuss "all matters dealing directly with naval policy" but that he must refer decisions on questions of national policy to the department. As to the British purchase of American merchant ships, Benson took an entirely defensible position. The matter was in the jurisdiction of another department of the government. Moreover, the "need of ships here is so great that [the United States] cannot agree to release for any purpose the ownership of any tonnage. Repair of ships is comity that must prevail among Allied nations." Reminding Sims that the United States paid Britain for making repairs to American destroyers, he concluded: "When it is remembered that we are making very great loans and that our sorest need is ships you will understand more clearly the unwillingness of the Government to accede to the suggestions." Sims, then, was forced to report the American position to the Admiralty, but he persisted in his belief that the United States should have permitted the proposed transaction. Benson continued to oppose Sims's view, reminding him that for some time to come the United States had to devote all production to the needs of the army and explaining that a "considerable portion of the duty of our [American] vessels is in the protection of British shipping as well as our own."[5]

This contretemps led the First Lord of the Admiralty, Sir Eric Geddes, to pursue British purposes by another means. He informed the Board of Admiralty on 1 August 1918 that he intended to negotiate a joint shipbuilding program for the year 1920 that would improve the British position, and he reiterated this idea to a congressional delegation from the United States the very next day. On 16 August he proposed to a meeting at the Foreign Office that Great Britain not seek American vessels to replace those that Britain could not build; rather, Britain should ensure that the proportion of warships and merchant ships built in the two nations be the same. Sims echoed Geddes's views at a luncheon given for a group of American editors by Lord Beaverbrook, the minister of information. Geddes even sought through an American visitor, Assistant Secretary of the Navy Franklin D. Roosevelt, to persuade Daniels to visit Europe. The secretary politely declined, giving as his excuse pressing duties at home.[6]

Undaunted by his early failure, Geddes decided to pay a visit to the United States, and an invitation from Secretary Daniels was soon forthcoming. Sims informed Captain Pratt that the British ambassador to the United States, Lord Reading, and some of the sea lords would accompany Geddes. They might present a proposition "concerning the question of reciprocity in building." He thought the visit the "best possible opportunity for the United States to show that [it is] willing to cooperate in a way which will promote good relations."[7]

When Geddes arrived in Washington, however, he introduced an issue of quite a different character: the threat of an intensified German undersea campaign in 1919. Basing his views on intelligence information, he stated: "We know they are building many of the most powerful submarines and will be ready for a killing on incomparably the largest scale ever dreamed of and will carry out their plans as soon as their great building program is completed. Unless we can have an adequate number of destroyers and weapons and devices to defeat them, the war will go against us."[8]

This contention did not take into account the possibility that the war might end very soon. Just as Geddes arrived in Washington on 6 October, Germany initiated discussions with President Wilson that looked toward an agreement to negotiate peace based on the Fourteen Points and associated pronouncements. Almost immediately Geddes informed the press that he did not believe Germany was beaten; it would be "worse than folly to allow the people of the allied nations to believe the Kaiser is on his knees." He wanted peace, but one that assured "no next time." "My business," he concluded, "is not to make peace, but to get on with the war." The next day the *New York Times* carried a story reporting that Geddes insisted that the "Great Final Effort of Hun U-Boats is Coming." Even as the Germans cried for peace, Geddes believed, they were preparing a last desperate fight at sea.[9]

President Wilson immediately took umbrage at these comments, referring to them as a "piece of impertinence," and he decided not to see Geddes before the First Lord departed for England. Wilson feared that Geddes's activities might compromise his diplomatic exchanges with Germany. However lacking in tact, Geddes reflected the views of the British government. Lloyd George instructed the First Lord to "be careful to express no approval or disapproval" of Wilson's dealings with the Germans: "You can of course say that the British Empire is resolute that there shall be no sham or humbugging peace." He was concerned especially about the American views on the freedom of the seas, which ran directly counter to those of Britain.[10]

Relenting when Mrs. Wilson made representations to him at the urging of Colonel House, President Wilson consented to see Geddes. Their discussion did not intensify friction. Geddes reported that Wilson seemed "fully alive to the need for continuing the prosecution of the war and retaining the national will for war." He also recognized that the time had come to consult the Allies about the American diplomatic exchanges with Germany. Concerning freedom of the seas, the First Lord thought the president's views "obviously unformed." Apparently Wilson proposed to secure this part of his peace program "in generalities." He would press for "acceptance of the principle that no one Power in the League of Nations shall exercise its Naval strength to crush a belligerent power without the consent of the League, leaving until the occasion arises any decision as to the nationality of Naval Police force."[11]

What came of Geddes's interest in merchant shipbuilding? While concentrating on obtaining an agreement on a building program to counter the predicted German U-boat campaign and on the pressing postwar question of the freedom of the seas, the First Lord retained an active interest in the future of the British merchant marine and overseas trade generally. Geddes was to obtain an increase in the American naval presence in European waters; a specific plan of naval construction to

include "mine sweepers, offensive minelayers, and possibly the new
type of ocean escort ship"; and compensation for British assistance in
the repair of American vessels. He wanted five oilers by the end of the
year, and he sought decisions on the types of other vessels to be transferred, these to be determined "on a basis of man-power involved, and
payment to be made for the actual vessels provided and for the actual
work done in refits." Discussions with the members of the British delegation led Captain Pratt to conclude that "one of the things Sir Eric
was most interested in was our merchant shipping. Naturally, that will
be a matter of greatest interest with them after this war is over." Clearly
the Geddes Mission strengthened suspicions in the United States about
British postwar intentions. Although the First Lord emphasized the
general building program while he was in Washington, he retained his
earlier concerns about merchant shipping.[12]

When it became evident that Germany was prepared to end the
war provided the Allies agreed to negotiate a peace settlement based
on the Wilsonian pronouncements of 1918, President Wilson dispatched
Colonel House to Paris to participate in pre-armistice negotiations with
Entente leaders. These talks would decide the content of the armistice
as well as the political basis for the ensuing peace negotiations. House
arranged for Admiral Benson to accompany him so that the CNO could
provide expert naval advice on the "steps that should be taken, from
a naval standpoint, with the enemy fleet during the armistice." Before
he left the United States, Benson requested the London planning section
to state its views on the naval terms to be included in both the armistice
and the peace treaty. He also wanted advice on "what should be our
attitude and what action should be taken to secure reasonably long
peace."[13]

To update his superiors in London on President Wilson's position,
the English intelligence officer Sir William Wiseman reported on two
interviews with the president. Wilson believed that "many nations, great
and small, chafed under the feeling" that their "sea-borne trade and
maritime development proceeded only with the permission and under
the shadow of the British Navy." After the war came to an end, it would
be necessary "to have a Conference to revise international law, and
particularly International Maritime Laws." The president had no specific remedy in mind, but he entertained the idea that the "great power
of the British Navy ought in some way be used in connection with the
League of Nations and thereby cease to be a cause of jealousy and
irritation." This report was accurate. When Captain Pratt briefed Admiral Benson about the president's views on naval matters, he stated
that equal American and British contributions to a League of Nations
navy would allow Britain to "yield gracefully" to the American concept
of Anglo-American naval parity and permit a "general decrease in Naval
Armament."[14]

The views of the London planning section awaited Admiral Benson when he arrived in Paris. Mostly of a technical nature, the section's proposals were based on a list of armistice terms drafted earlier by the British, French, and Italian prime ministers that General Tasker H. Bliss, the American Permanent Military Representative at the Inter-Allied Supreme War Council, had refused to approve in the absence of instructions from his government. The planning section, however, differed from the prime ministers on some important questions. It recommended internment of the enemy fleet rather than its surrender, and it also opposed the requirement that the enemy surrender Heligoland.[15]

Initial discussions between Colonel House and representatives of Great Britain revealed wide disparities. When Lord Reading told the colonel that Britain rebelled against the doctrine of freedom of the seas and sought "reparations for losses at sea," House responded coldly: "If the British were not careful they would bring upon themselves the dislike of the world." He compared the British navy to the German army. The United States would not "willingly submit to Great Britain's domination of the seas any more than to Germany's domination of the land, and the sooner the British recognized this fact, the better it would be for them." If challenged, the American people would "build a navy and maintain an army greater than [that of the British people]." This exchange suggested that considerable controversy would attend further discussion of naval questions.[16]

On 29 October, House and Benson received presidential instructions concerning naval questions. In general, Wilson favored moderate terms that would prevent Germany from resuming naval warfare but that would avoid unnecessarily punitive requirements. He wanted to defer the problem of deciding the future of the German fleet to the peace conference, proposing merely to intern submarines in neutral ports. He continued to favor freedom of the seas. On the two most important items of discussion in Paris—disposition of the German fleet and freedom of the seas—Wilson staked out positions in direct opposition to those of the leading sea power.[17]

The naval terms of the armistice were first discussed in the Allied Naval Council and then presented to the political leaders gathered in the Supreme War Council. Earlier Sims had represented the United States in the Allied Naval Council, but, at the insistence of Colonel House, Benson supplanted Sims during the armistice negotiations. Benson suggested that Sims "might as well return to London." To his wife Sims wrote on returning to his headquarters: "So here I am." The difficulties that Benson and House were to encounter quickly became apparent. Britain dominated the Allied Naval Council, a circumstance that forced Admiral Benson into frequent conflicts with his British counterpart, Admiral Wemyss, who enjoyed political support from his civilian superiors.

Given broad public support in Great Britain for the Royal Navy, the First Sea Lord's views carried great weight with Lloyd George. When the prime minister made various objections to several of the Fourteen Points, including freedom of the seas, House indicated that the United States might have to suspend its participation in the Paris discussions and take up negotiations with the Central Powers separately. Clemenceau said that any such course "would amount to a separate peace between the United States and the Central Powers." House responded significantly: "It might." Lloyd George replied that the British would regret such a separate peace, but, he continued, "we could not give up the blockade, the power which enabled us to live; as far as the British public is concerned, we will fight on." Clemenceau concurred: "Yes, war would not be war if there was freedom of the seas." This exchange indicated that, while the Allies were prepared generally to accept the Wilsonian program because they could not afford separate American negotiations with the Central Powers, they were intent on obtaining certain concessions regarding questions of vital national concern, among them freedom of the seas.[18]

After his initial experiences in Paris, Admiral Benson conveyed his observations regarding naval terms to Colonel House. Recognizing that neither Britain nor France was very interested in a Wilsonian peace, Benson held that the American position on naval terms for the armistice would "fully protect the interests of the people involved and insure to the Associated governments the unrestricted power to safeguard and enforce the details of the peace to which the German Government has agreed." Benson favored surrender of German vessels, the best means of preventing Germany from resuming naval warfare, but he was adamantly opposed to any distribution of these vessels to the victorious powers. For this reason he had reserved his views on the disposition of surrendered vessels during a discussion in the Allied Naval Council.[19]

Secretary Daniels now intervened; he evaluated the proposed naval terms with a view to sending instructions to Benson. Captain Pratt offered counsel: "Unless we can find some way to give Admiral Benson more definite approval, his position will be somewhat negative, unless he takes matters in his own hands, which he has no instructions to do that I am aware of." Daniels cabled Benson: "In advising Colonel House with regard to the terms of armistice, you are authorized to use your judgment, but the President's judgment is clear that it ought to be distinctly understood that all armed vessels taken should be held in trust and that it is quite possible to go too far in demanding excessive security."[20]

Meanwhile, President Wilson took up the larger political question—freedom of the seas. In a message to Colonel House, he insisted that "England cannot dispense with our friendship in the future and the other Allies cannot without our assistance get their rights as against

England." What should be done? "If it is the purpose of the statesmen to nullify my influence let me speak of it boldly to all the world as I shall." The next day he provided House with a systematic statement of his position:

> I feel it is my solemn duty to authorize you to say that I cannot consent to take part in the negotiations of a peace that does not include Freedom of the Seas, because we are pledged to fight not only Prussian militarism but militarism everywhere.
>
> Neither could I participate in a settlement which does not include a League of Nations because such a peace would result within a period of years in there being no guarantee except universal armaments, which would be disastrous. I hope I shall not be obligated to make this decision public.

The American president had no intention of modifying his views on these important questions, regardless of pressure brought to bear in Paris.[21]

The controversy over the naval terms now moved toward a denouement. On 30 October Lloyd George sent House a message that announced Britain's willingness to make peace on the basis of President Wilson's points, although the prime minister reserved his views on freedom of the seas. That principle could be interpreted in various ways, some of which were unacceptable; British negotiators must therefore retain "complete freedom on this subject when they enter the Peace Conference." By this device Britain neither repudiated the principle nor accepted it. Lord Reading pointed out to Admiral Wemyss the difficulty of taking such a position. The British had never intended to accept Wilson's freedom of the seas, but they had not said so earlier. "Now, of course we cannot enter into Armistice without saying so, or giving the enemy the chance of saying that we are breaking faith and got them to accept terms of Armistice under false pretenses." It is difficult, however, to imagine that Lloyd George could have favored freedom of the seas, given the general insistence of his nation on the fullest possible freedom of action for the Royal Navy.[22]

Meanwhile Benson continued to press the British for clarification of their views on the disposition of the German High Sea Fleet. Sir Eric Geddes responded in a meeting of the Allied Naval Council that in his opinion all of the enemy's naval units should be destroyed. So far as he knew, everyone agreed with this view. Benson, however, retained the suspicion that the Allies favored some form of distribution. He remained faithful to the president's view that the naval terms "should neither be humiliating in expression nor impossible of acceptance because of their severity." After a conversation with the president, Captain Pratt was convinced that the chief executive was correct in opposing the terms that had been developed in Europe and that Sims had endorsed: Wilson's terms were "far more just and easier to accomplish than the original terms submitted by Sims. . . . His policy is creative, not destructive." Sims naturally thought differently. Sims wrote to his wife that Benson believed he must adopt the views of his civilian superiors. "Of course the wishes of the superior should be carried out, but in my opinion the military officer should express his opinion for the guidance of his superior and should express his own personal, technical opinion in the discussions in council, otherwise the discussions in council would be of little value as a guide as to what safe terms of an armistice should be."[23]

Attempting to find a solution to the question of the disposition of the German fleet, Lloyd George offered a compromise. He proposed the surrender of submarines, cruisers, and destroyers and the internment of ten dreadnoughts. The Allied Naval Council, however, held to its view that Germany should surrender all its vessels. Benson then stated his support for Lloyd George in a formal reservation: "10 battleships could, without danger, be required under the Armistice to be interned in Neutral Ports during the Armistice, their final disposition to be settled at the Peace Conference." The likelihood of a compromise along this line increased when Foch, now promoted to marshal, held that the military terms would guarantee victory on land; the naval terms should be sufficiently moderate to ensure Germany's acceptance of the armistice.[24]

At this time there was the beginning of a shift in the inflexible American stance toward freedom of the seas when President Wilson decided to alter his position somewhat. Although reiterating his support for freedom of the seas in unambiguous terms, he gave House the authority to "insist at the right time and in the right way" on freedom of the seas along with three other "essentially American terms": open covenants, leveling of trade barriers, and the League of Nations. He also opted for a redefinition of the blockade, given the new conditions of warfare, but he was willing to assure the British that "there was no danger of [the blockade] being abolished." He noted that the victors would not have to discuss the question of freedom of the seas with the Central Powers if they agreed among themselves beforehand. On 3 November, Wilson's views were presented to the European political leaders. House held that Britain's position placed the United States in a position toward Britain like that of Germany during the war. If there was a contest, the United States, possessed of superior resources, would emerge the victor. Lloyd George, defiant, replied that Britain "would spend her last guinea to keep a navy superior to that of the United States or any other power, and that no cabinet officer could continue in the Government in England who took a different position." However, he was prepared to discuss freedom of seas at the peace conference. Also, he suggested that "instead of confiscating cruisers and battleships we intern the whole lot." Colonel House responded immediately: "That is what I think, and leave the ultimate disposition of ships to the Peace Conference."[25]

This breakthrough led immediately to a formal agreement on the naval terms of armistice. Forced to accept the political decision of the Supreme War Council, the Allied Naval Council convened on 4 November and hastily drafted armistice terms that provided for internment and disarmament of the German surface fleet—seventy-six vessels—in neutral ports with the proviso that "this is an Armistice term only and . . . these ships will not, under any circumstances, be returned to Germany on the conclusion of the Armistice, or at any time." The Supreme War Council adopted the formula prepared by the Allied Naval Council.[26]

The pre-armistice agreement that emerged from the Supreme War Council on 4 November stated the political foundation for the forthcoming peace negotiations. The Entente Powers agreed to treat with the Central Powers on the basis of President Wilson's Fourteen Points and associated pronouncements, except for a reservation permitting Britain to discuss freedom of the seas at the peace conference and a provision permitting assessment of reparations for injuries to civilians and their property. The American bargaining position at Paris was very strong, ensuring almost complete success in the negotiations. House could not resist cabling Wilson: "I consider that we have won a great diplomatic victory. . . . I doubt whether any of the heads of the governments with whom we have been dealing quite recognize how far they are now committed to the American peace program."[27]

Thus, President Wilson obtained all that he sought during the pre-armistice discussions except commitment to freedom of the seas. He could argue that he had not surrendered the principle, he had merely agreed to settle the matter during the peace conference. It was a considerable concession, but one that in retrospect appears to have been unavoidable, given the importance Britain attached to the right of blockade. The Wilsonian desire for moderation, ably advocated in the Allied Naval Council by Admiral Benson, prevailed in the end.

Nevertheless, the outcome in Paris caused measurable concern in the navy, a reaction that was reflected in an important memorandum from the London planning section titled "United States Naval Interests in the Armistice Terms," dated 4 November 1918. The planners assumed a distribution of the German navy. Given this distribution, the "United States with 17 modern capital ships would be faced at once with an alliance between Great Britain and Japan controlling a total of 67 capital ships." Even alone, the British fleet would have three times as many capital ships as that of the United States. Referring to naval history, the planners observed that four great powers had challenged Britain on the sea—Spain, Holland, France, and Germany—and all had been defeated. There were signs already of naval jealousy between the United States and Great Britain. Given these considerations, there was need for "some constraining influence on British naval power." The United States must assure that Great Britain would not come to occupy "so commanding a naval position that she may regulate the high seas through the world in accordance with her will."[28]

As the war sped to an end, Admiral Benson expressed pride in victory but concern for the future. Writing to Secretary Daniels, he explained that the position he had taken during the meetings of the Allied Naval Council had practically isolated him from the other members. There followed a troubled passage:

> We came to these people in their hour of need and almost darkest despair, and unquestionably have saved them from ruin and all the horrors that would have followed German subjugation. Now, however, as the danger is past and the wonderful wealth and power of our country is made more apparent to them by the tremendous efforts we have made, and the success which has attended our efforts, some are alarmed at our power and wealth; others are envious and jealous of it.

Benson had in mind the British naval authorities. Their desire for recognition might obscure the American naval contribution, but Benson adopted a philosophic attitude toward that possibility: "Whether or not the European governments appreciate our efforts in saving them really matters little. We have . . . impressed them with the magnitude of our power and our resources and our willingness to utilize them in a just cause, and we have unquestionably impressed them with the fact that there is no task so great that we will not undertake, and once undertaken will carry through to a successful termination." Admiral Benson carried these considerations with him into the peace negotiations.[29]

CHAPTER XI

THE NAVAL BATTLE OF PARIS: THE PRELIMINARIES

Representatives of the German government signed the armistice on 11 November 1918 in the presence of French and British officials. Marshal Foch presided. In attendance also was Admiral Wemyss, in recognition, as Sims put it, of the "prominence of the British Navy in the war." Neither General Pershing nor Admiral Benson was invited to witness this historic event.

At war's end there was time for the American naval effort to be praised. Admiral Benson cabled Secretary Daniels: "Accept congratulations on successful part Navy has played under your administration in this greatest war of all times." For his part, Daniels emphasized the "excellent team work" of the CNO. Benson must have been pleased by a letter from Admiral Caperton that said, in part, "While the whole world is rejoicing over the end of the war, I want to write a few lines to tell you how much I personally appreciate the great part you have had in achieving this result. The work of our Navy, no less than of our Army, has been the determining factor in this success, [and] as the Navy knows and the country should know, its successful administration is due more to you than to any other person." Although he was not well known to most of his fellow Americans, Benson had served his country with great distinction during the war. He was soon to have an opportunity to make a contribution of comparable importance to peace.[1]

As soon as the armistice began, Admiral Benson directed his attention to an especially pressing question—the execution of the naval terms. He also became preoccupied with an even more important issue—the naval terms to be included in the definitive treaties of peace. In both of these contexts he found it necessary to grapple with the many divergent plans and purposes that materialized among the victors. Naval rivalries were not the least of the motives influencing the victorious Allied Powers.

A letter sent on 12 November 1918 by the commander of the British Grand Fleet, Admiral Sir David Beatty, to the First Sea Lord, Admiral Wemyss, would have amply substantiated Benson's belief that British leaders were likely to minimize the American part in the naval triumph. Beatty showed little appreciation of American support. He attributed the victory at sea almost entirely to British operations and neglected the consideration that Captain Pratt expressed cogently: the American contribution "lay not in the fighting ships which we would throw to the front, but in our ability to mobilize and transport America's great reserve power quickly to the European war front." Beatty feared that, because there had been no "dramatic episode such as would appeal to popular imagination," the public would not appreciate the part naval warfare played in the defeat of the Central Powers. Beatty, incidentally, advocated a humiliating surrender of the German High Sea Fleet to emphasize the significance of the naval war: "It would be for our good, and for the good of all that we as a race stand for, it will consolidate our position at the Peace conference, serve as a recompense to seamen who have suffered at the enemy's hands, and be a tribute in some measure to those who have fallen." Attitudes of this nature ensured extensive, heated negotiations concerning naval matters at the end of the war.[2]

Arrangements to execute the naval terms of the armistice were made on the day of the armistice. During a meeting of the naval leaders, Admiral Wemyss recommended internment of the German fleet at Scapa Flow (the northern anchorage of the Royal Navy), rather than in neutral locations (presumably the fjords of Norway), and Admiral Beatty was assigned responsibility for the High Sea Fleet. The Allied Naval Armistice Commission, which included British, French, and American representatives, was created to administer the internment. Vice Admiral Browning chaired the commission; the American representative to it, as designated by Admiral Benson, was Rear Admiral Samuel S. Robison. When the French admiral de Grasset, like Browning a wartime associate of Admiral Benson, questioned the broad authority conferred on Admiral Beatty, Wemyss cautioned Browning to proceed judiciously. On 13 November an emergency meeting of the Allied Naval Council was held in London. Sims sat in for Benson, who was in Paris. The session was called to "confirm or amend" the arrangements made in Paris, a purpose that irritated Benson, who thought the agreement reached in Paris was final rather than provisional and therefore not subject to review. In either event, the London gathering substantially ratified the earlier agreement.[3]

On 18 November, Sims and Robison attended a meeting of the Allied Naval Armistice Commission in which certain arrangements were made that irritated Admiral Benson. Admiral Browning stated at this gathering that Beatty would manage the internment of the German fleet at Scapa Flow. He suggested that his flagship, the *Hercules*, take the commission to Kiel and Wilhelmshaven to ensure full execution of the naval armistice terms. Robison proposed that the American flag should appear on this occasion, a statement that led to similar proposals by the French and Italians on behalf of their navies. The point was left unresolved, because Sims thought that such a procedure "would be distasteful to the British." The next day Sims informed Benson that the commission would inspect the German ports on the *Hercules*. He added an apparently innocent sentence: "Request to be informed whether American representative may join the rest of the commission or whether he should proceed in an American ship." Benson replied: "If all other representatives are going in British ship with Vice Admiral Browning and it is entirely convenient, U.S. Naval Representatives may go with Party." In this fashion Benson unsuspectingly agreed to a procedure that appeared to allow a surrender of the Germans to the British alone.[4]

The internment of the German High Sea Fleet at Scapa Flow took place on 21 November 1918, following the arrangements that had been made earlier. The *Hercules* led the German vessels into the North Sea, and then the High Sea Fleet passed between 229 ships of the Grand Fleet, which included the American battleships, arranged in two columns. Sims observed the event from the *New York*. The German ships anchored in Scapa Flow and lowered their national flags for the last time. Sims was elated with the outcome. He lunched with the British admirals and the royal family on the *Queen Elizabeth* and afterward received the group on the *New York*.[5]

Admiral Benson did not share Sims's enthusiasm. He believed that the ceremony had not given adequate recognition to the United States Navy. When the CNO received Captain Twining's report of the affair, he penciled in two comments on it. Why were no American battle flags present? Why did no American officer take part in the inspection of the German ships? "How did you satisfy yourself on this point?" On 17 December he expressed himself sharply on these matters directly to Sims: "As the situation has developed I am constrained to believe that our force and our representatives who were to participate in this particular part of the armistice have been used by the British Admiralty for their own purpose, insofar as their prestige was concerned, and by failing to anticipate this action, we have unwittingly assisted them in using the French in the same way." Noting that his comments were for Sims only, he added: "I trust that they will be used throughout the remainder of the armistice tactfully and positively for the best interests of the prestige of our own flag and service, and for insuring a fair discharge of our obligations as signatory parties to the terms of the armistice." Sims, stung, replied angrily: "If you had desired a United

States vessel to go it is to be presumed that you would have so instructed me. The fact that you did not so instruct me furnishes a fair basis for the assumption that you did not consider it necessary that a United States Naval vessel should go[,] in which opinion I fully concur." He judged his behavior to be fully in accordance with Benson's instructions and neglected his failure to inform the CNO that Britain might attempt to exploit the situation for its own purposes.[6]

Benson was concerned about what he considered undue concessions to the British naval leaders, but he displayed a comparable attitude toward other naval leaders of the Entente. He was especially concerned about the naval attaché in Rome, Charles R. Train, who had discussed sensitive aspects of the peace treaty with Italian naval leaders. He wrote: "You are too much influenced by the atmosphere in which you are living and too readily accept the views presented to you by the representatives of the Government where you are." Train was reminded that, whereas he should seek information and for this purpose must consult the Italian chief of the naval staff, he should recognize that "most of the subjects which you have discussed with him are all of a diplomatic nature and must be left for final consideration by the Peace Conference." Train's responsibility, Benson concluded, was simply to see that the armistice was "strictly and properly carried out."[7]

Perhaps Benson's suspicions of Entente motives were strongest regarding the possible distribution of the German fleet. The CNO reacted strongly to an Admiralty proposal concerning the use of the German merchant fleet after the war. This initiative seemed to Benson a possible means of preparing the way for distribution of the German ships of war. On 26 November he informed Secretary Daniels that the armistice terms left Great Britain with the only navy stronger than that of the United States. Distribution might worsen this situation. If a distribution took place, it would reflect the relative participation of various navies in the blockade of the German ships. "According to these figures," Benson wrote, "our proportion of German men-of-war would be very little whereas British proportion would be such that practically the entire strength of German captured vessels would go to British." Benson remained convinced that a failure to limit armaments in the peace treaty would force the United States to build a navy "equal to or superior to that of any other country." If an unfair distribution took place, it would increase the cost of building a navy second to none: "We have fought for the avowed purpose of destroying a military autocracy. To use or to consent to the use of captured instruments of this autocracy would weaken our purpose while to insist upon their destruction would greatly strengthen it."[8]

Sims did not share Benson's views. He suggested that, when such vessels became available, the United States man five German submarines and bring them to the United States. When Benson learned of this proposition, he made his views known to Secretary Daniels, who cabled a firm "NO" to the acquisition of the U-boats. The CNO expanded his views to argue that enemy ships and ships under construction be restored to the defeated powers as part of the peace settlement. He and his advisory staff opposed restrictions on German naval construction in the future. Any such provision in the peace treaty would cause "bitter feeling" to no purpose, because, in any case, Germany's financial situation would "induce her for the time being to maintain a Navy of a minimum."[9]

Benson's suspicions of British intentions were not without foundation; influential sectors in Britain were profoundly opposed to making concessions on naval matters to the United States. The head of the British Board of Agriculture and Fisheries, N. E. Prothero, drew Lloyd George's attention to the fact that the Democratic party had lost control of Congress during the recent election and that President Wilson, therefore, lacked political support; an appeal might be made over his head directly to the American people. To counter the Fourteen Points and especially the provision for freedom of the seas, Prothero thought it "imperatively necessary that the Press, in some guarded way, should be set to work to make it abundantly clear that the retention of seapower is, to us, a matter of life and death; and that we cannot put our hands to any treaty which, at this moment of complete victory, will lead to our ultimate extinction!"[10]

Admiral Benson was committed fully to the view that the most effective means of influencing the peace settlement would be for the United States to build the strongest navy in the world. As Congress prepared to consider the naval bill of 1919, Benson expressed himself forthrightly in support of President Wilson's peace plans and a great navy, manifesting strong suspicion of the Allies: "Further knowledge of situation over here [has] convinced me that unless peace is secured in accordance with principles laid down by President, this war will have been fought in vain. Allied propaganda amongst our people [is] more dangerous than German. Apparent efforts being made at home to have peace terms in accordance with views and wishes [of] Great Britain, France and Italy [are] most injurious and dangerous." He did not hesitate to offer his prescription for diplomatic success: "No one thing will serve more to help in carrying through President's views, particularly freedom of the seas, than decided evidence that we are going to build up our Navy as soon as possible."[11]

President Wilson decided to head the American Commission to Negotiate Peace himself; he named as other members Colonel House, Secretary Lansing, General Bliss (the Permanent Military Representative at the Supreme War Council), and a nominal Republican, the diplomat Henry White. Admiral Benson remained in Paris as the "technical adviser for naval affairs." If some observers, including Mrs. Benson, were surprised that the CNO was not made a plenipotentiary, others were irritated at his advisory role. Admiral Bayly, Sims's close friend at Queenstown, wrote that a sound arrangement would have placed Sims in Paris and Benson in Washington. Admiral Fullam also thought that Sims should have been detailed to the peace conference: "My friend Benson is a fine fellow, but he never did anything brilliant, can't speak French, has never been to the war college, and is one of the last men who should have been selected for such a job. It is probable that this was the reason he *was* selected!" In response, Sims betrayed his disappointment: "Of course you are aware that it is not customary to appoint one of the 'blood-stained' participants as a member of the judicial council that is to decide the terms of peace. Pershing might just as well complain of not being a delegate as I could." He then allowed his feelings about Benson to surface: "As for our naval advisor with the peace delegates he is exactly the kind of man they want; of course you know why!"[12]

Before sailing to Europe, President Wilson indicated his position on the resumption of the naval building program that had been authorized in 1916 but suspended during the war. Addressing a joint session of Congress, he noted that the plans submitted by Secretary Daniels called for authority to complete the next three years of the plan. "These plans have been prepared along the lines and in accordance with the policy which the Congress established, not under the exceptional conditions of the war, but with the intention of adhering to a definite period of development for the navy," the president said, and he recommended "uninterrupted pursuit" of this goal: "It would clearly be unwise for us to attempt to adjust our program to a future world policy as yet undetermined." Probably this statement was purposefully ambiguous. The president may have hoped that negotiations in Paris would make it unnecessary to complete the program of 1916, but it seems apparent that he had no intention of abandoning the goal of a navy second to none; which meant at least attaining parity with Great Britain. In other words, the president probably intended to use the naval building program as leverage during negotiations in Paris.[13]

Secretary Daniels soon proposed to Congress not only the completion of the 1916 program but also a second three-year program that included the construction of 156 naval vessels at a cost of $600 million. He testified before the House Naval Affairs Committee in support of his proposition, stating that the president supported naval construction because "nothing would so aid him in [the] peace conference" as an authorization by Congress of a big navy. The United States, Daniels maintained, had no designs on the trade or territory of other nations, but the nation was "pledged to support . . . the Monroe Doctrine; she is pledged to the protection of the weak wherever they may suffer threats; she is incomparably rich, incomparably strong in natural resources . . . incomparably strong in defense against aggressors and in offense against evildoers." In these words Daniels certainly intended to indicate to the Allies, however indirectly, that failure to accept President Wilson's peace plans, including freedom of the seas, would force them into a naval race with the United States in which the United States would surely emerge the winner.[14]

Great Britain, the principal naval power, lacked the resources required to outbuild the United States. On 6 December 1918 the Lord Commissioner of the Admiralty wrote to the Lord Commissioner of His Majesty's Treasury to propose that Parliament be asked to vote a general credit for the year 1919–20 without stipulating policy, standards, or estimates. This request for a blank check was too much for the treasury, which recommended a drastic reduction in naval contracts: "The resources of the Country in capital, labour, and material should be devoted at as early a date as possible to the revival of industry and commerce instead of being dissipated upon the production of engines of war." A blank check for the Royal Navy, "beyond the proved requirements of the Fleet after the war (or any possible assumption as to its size in addition to the vast war accumulations), would be a capital error of economic policy which would react most seriously upon the general trade of the country and upon the position of the already heavily burdened taxpayer." This treasury statement proved that the American threat to outbuild other navies should other nations refuse to accept the Wilsonian design for the postwar world was not an idle one. There was open to Great Britain, however, the possibility of striking a bargain on naval questions with the United States in return for general support of the American peace proposals.[15]

On 4 December 1918, President and Mrs. Wilson boarded the *George Washington* for the voyage to Europe. Two other peace commissioners, Secretary Lansing and Henry White, accompanied them. Others on board included members of the Inquiry—a group of scholars who had collected data for use during the peace negotiations—and various other advisers, including Captain Pratt, who wanted to consult with the CNO. Mrs. Benson was also aboard; she intended to be with her husband during the rest of his stay in Europe. Admiral Mayo, the commander in chief of the North Atlantic Fleet, escorted the *George Washington* on his flagship, the *Pennsylvania*.[16]

As President Wilson approached a landfall at Brest, the navy prepared offices for him in Paris. Of his staff, the chief executive had brought along only his brilliant stenographer, Charles Swem, who had served him since the campaign of 1912. When House and Benson discovered this situation, they set up additional support. In response to House's preference for naval personnel, Sims provided six stenographers, and Benson ordered Commander Royal E. Ingersoll to establish a communications center. Assisting Ingersoll was Commander Charles

A. Blakely, Sims's communications officer. Ingersoll carried with him ciphers for communications between Paris and Washington. Benson later praised the work of the communications center. It was only the first of the Navy's contributions to the American Commission to Negotiate Peace.[17]

On 13 December 1918, President Wilson steamed into Brest. Salvos of welcome boomed from land batteries and welcoming warships. The French minister of foreign affairs, Stephen J. Pichon, accompanied by an escort of admirals and generals, including General Pershing, Admiral Benson, and Admiral Sims, boarded the *George Washington* to greet the president. Wilson traveled to Paris, viewed an elaborate parade in his honor, and then took up residence in the Murate Palace. No British statesmen were present when the American president arrived in Brest or in Paris. Lloyd George was waging a general election campaign in Great Britain, and Balfour was enjoying a vacation. Lloyd George soon received a rousing vote of confidence from the electorate, who responded to the slogan stating that Germany should be squeezed during the peace negotiations "until the pips squeak." Meanwhile, Clemenceau engaged in a successful effort to strengthen his political position. These developments delayed the start of the peace conference, despite the president's desire for a speedy settlement.

Admiral Benson set up an efficient organization to support his work during the Paris conference. His personal staff consisted of his aide, Commander Carter, a liaison officer, Commander John C. Fremont, and his secretary, Lieutenant (j.g.) John R. Pratt. His offices were located in room 316 at the Crillon Hotel, where the plenipotentiaries also occupied space. His daily routine was exhausting. Seeking to keep the peace commissioners fully informed about naval matters, he met with the Naval Advisory Staff daily to prepare materials for this purpose. He conferred regularly with Colonel House, Secretary Lansing, General Bliss, and with the American naval attaché in Paris, Rear Admiral Andrew T. Long; Commander Ingersoll; the chairman of the United States Shipping Board, Edward N. Hurley; and the food commissioner for the Food Relief Program for Former Enemy Countries, Herbert Hoover.[18]

As the peace conference got underway, Admiral Benson settled into a routine that included a varied schedule. On 25 January 1919, for example, he began the day with the Naval Advisory Staff. In the afternoon he considered a letter from General Pershing asking him to designate naval officers to cooperate with the army's Services of Supply in arranging for the transport of American troops. He then deciphered a message from Secretary Daniels for President Wilson that requested the president's views on the necessity of obtaining congressional authorization of the three-year program of naval construction, later delivering the message to the president with a covering note. He also sent

General Tasker H. Bliss and Admiral W. S. Benson leaving the first session of the Peace Conference in the French Ministry of Foreign Affairs, 13 January 1919.

Secretary Daniels two documents, one a fitness report on Rear Admiral William H. G. Bullard and the other a report on the behavior of an Italian officer aboard an Austrian merchant ship that had been requisitioned by the Allies. Finally, he dispatched a memorandum to Captain John K. Robison concerning an extension of the armistice with Germany that had been concluded at a conference held in Trèves.[19]

Mrs. Benson's presence in Paris eased Benson's wearing schedule. In a warm letter to his daughter, Mary Krafft, the admiral expressed pleasure in his wife's company: "I cannot tell you how grateful I am that you all helped to get mama off to me. I simply could not have stood this loneliness and gloomy weather very much longer." Ever concerned for Mrs. Benson's well-being, he concluded: "I hope and believe [the visit to Paris] will be a life saver for mama. She will be able to have a rest and I hope some diversion. So far she thoroughly enjoys it and is very well."[20]

As the various plenipotentiaries prepared for negotiations, indications from Great Britain suggested that the forthcoming discussion of naval questions would prove difficult. British statesmen, aware that economic constraints might preclude an extensive program of postwar naval construction, clearly indicated complete opposition to any outcome in Paris that would undermine their country's primacy at sea. They also showed themselves unwilling to accept a league that did not confer control of naval matters on Great Britain. On 26 November 1918 the minister of munitions, Winston Churchill, expressed this outlook with utter frankness to a British audience:

> Nothing in the world, nothing that you may think of, or dream of, or anyone may tell you, no arguments, however specious, no appeals, however seductive, must lead you to abandon that naval supremacy on which the life of our country depends. . . . I am a hopeful and sincere advocate of the League of Nations. I will do everything in my power to make such an instrument a reality, a practical reality and a powerful reality. But a League of Nations is no substitute for the supremacy of the British Fleet.

This speech attracted broad attention at home and abroad. The following day a headline in the *Times* of London proclaimed: "British Navy Must Be Supreme," while one in the *New York Times* stated: "Churchill Favors League But It Will Not Affect British Supremacy at Sea." Sir Eric Geddes manifested lukewarm interest in a League of Nations while speaking at an opening of an exhibition on "Sea Power" in London: "There are those who look forward to a League of Nations as a sort of Utopia. Even if we got that Utopia we should have a police force. The British Navy had performed the policing of the seas with impartiality and faithfulness, as all rightminded nations publicly recognized." In a secret memorandum circulated earlier to his colleagues in the British government, he was more candid: "British Naval requirements should be prepared on the assumption that no League of Nations is established, such modifications being indicated as are considered possible in the event of an effective League of Nations being formed." In any case, the new international organization would pose serious difficulties: "In any League of Nations we shall almost certainly be in a minority in matters affecting sea power. . . . Any limitation of sea power is clearly to our disadvantage and should be strongly opposed." Given one of Wilson's Fourteen Points, a provision for disarmament, Sir Eric's attitude portended serious clashes in Paris.[21]

For quite different reasons, Admiral Benson also dismissed the proposed navy of the League of Nations. When the planning section in the Office of Naval Operations, a counterpart of the London group, developed a plan for such a navy—suggesting a force twice as large as that of any nation, with contributions of not more than 25 percent each from the United States and Great Britain, 10 percent each from France, Italy, and Japan, and 20 percent from all other states—Benson categorically rejected it. On his copy of the document, he wrote: "A so-called League Navy is absolutely impractical." When one of the planners, Admiral Robert E. Coontz, transmitted another such scheme, Benson wrote on it: "Time Wasted."[22]

To Benson the principal concern was the size of the British fleet, especially because of the Anglo-Japanese alliance. During the war, Britain had engaged to support Japanese claims to the German concession in the Shantung Province of China and to German-held islands in the Pacific Ocean in exchange for naval assistance in the Mediterranean Sea. This arrangement raised the possibility, however remote, of an Anglo-Japanese coalition to endanger American interests in the Pacific Ocean. The proposal for an international navy brought back into play the naval considerations that had led Benson in 1917 to question the decision to suspend the American naval building program. In his mind, the first naval objective at Paris was to ensure against measures that perpetuated British supremacy at sea. For this reason he consistently advocated a navy second to none and freedom of the seas, his means of countering a future threat at sea from Britain or an Anglo-Japanese combine. He believed that superiority in naval strength was the only true guarantee of future national security because, given the outcome of the war, the principal naval danger emanated from Great Britain, especially in combination with Japan.

Difficult negotiations lay ahead. The British and French prime ministers, Lloyd George and Clemenceau, had received strong support from their respective nations as they approached the peace table, whereas Wilson had suffered an embarrassing electoral setback because of the election of a Republican Congress in November 1918. This disparity should not be overemphasized. Wilson held a strong hand, given the great and growing strength of the United States at war's end in contrast to the plenary exhaustion evident throughout Europe. The victors were hardly less prostrate than the vanquished.

The president's general strategy in naval negotiations was to use the proposal to restart the construction of a U.S. Navy second to none as a means of compelling Great Britain to accept extensive disarmament. He hoped by this device to avoid a great naval armaments program;

to him the congressional program was primarily a bargaining chip, whereas to Benson it was a necessity. The president assumed that the principal means of enforcing the obligations of the league covenant would be the use of an international navy, in which the British and the Americans would dominate. Wilson's chief congressional opponent, Senator Henry Cabot Lodge (R-Mass.), thought it "unbelievable" that the American Commission to Negotiate Peace would try to establish peace by proposing a U.S. Navy that would equal that of Great Britain in seven years.

On 27 January 1919 the Entente Powers honored the pre-armistice agreement when the peace conference adopted a set of resolutions that authorized a League of Nations. This action looked toward a way out of the difficulty that resulted from the British reservation on freedom of the seas. Much later, Wilson explained why freedom of the seas did not stimulate heated debate during the negotiations in Paris: "One of the principles that I went to Paris most insisting on was the freedom of the seas. Now, the freedom of the seas means the definition of the right of neutrals to use the seas when other nations are at war, but under the League of Nations there are no neutrals, and, therefore, what I have called the practical joke on myself was that by the very thing that I was advocating it became unnecessary to define the freedom of the seas." This convenient rationale did not assuage the advocates of American naval parity with or naval superiority over Great Britain (such as Admiral Benson).[23]

The president's intention to make use of naval construction as a bargaining chip became apparent before the end of January, when Secretary Daniels asked for Wilson's opinion on whether to continue with the three-year program. First, Wilson repeated his earlier position: "I can say with very deliberate conviction that it is necessary to the accomplishment of our objects here that the Three-Year Building Program should be adopted as recommended." Then he added a significant qualification: "I am quite willing that the proviso should be included that if by international agreement a reduction of armaments is arranged, . . . I will be authorized to withhold further contracts until Congress is consulted, but it would be fatal to go beyond that at this juncture." When Secretary Daniels conveyed this message to the House Committee on Naval Affairs, the naval appropriation bill received unanimous approval.[24]

President Wilson, meanwhile, agreed to a proposal for the disposal of German submarines that brought a quick reaction from Admiral Benson. On 21 January 1919 Lloyd George successfully proposed that the Allies dismantle all but eighty of the German U-boats and divide the parts among the Allies. Benson sensed in this arrangement a step toward distribution of the enemy fleets, against which he had campaigned vigorously during the pre-armistice negotiations. To the president he wrote worriedly: "Behind this apparently simple agreement may lie larger questions which those who made the suggestion may hope to have decided in accordance with the precedent thus established." He ended with cautionary advice: "In view of the great maritime interest of the British in all questions now before the Peace conference I consider that all proposals they put forward should be very carefully scrutinized." The president responded graciously, promising to be vigilant thereafter and to consult with the CNO when questions involving maritime issues arose during the deliberations of the peacemakers.[25]

In Paris at this point, serious negotiations began to determine the naval terms of the peace treaty with Germany. The preliminaries of the naval battle of Paris were over. A long tug of war had begun; now the naval leaders and their political superiors would seek to resolve the principal issues that had surfaced during the initial stages of the discussions in Paris.

CHAPTER XII

THE NAVAL BATTLE OF PARIS: THE DENOUEMENT

To prepare final naval terms for the definitive treaties of peace, the naval leaders in Paris set up an unofficial committee as a drafting group. Admirals Benson, de Bon, and Wemyss made this arrangement on 27 January, subject to the approval of their governments. At Benson's suggestion, Vice Admiral Count Thaon di Revel of Italy and Vice Admiral Toyoji Takeshita of Japan were added to the group.

The drafting committee, known as the Admirals of the Allied and Associated Powers, encountered immediate difficulties. All concurred that an early agreement was imperative, but there were differences regarding procedure. Benson wanted to "confine the discussion to the actual [naval] terms of peace." Wemyss, however, sought also to consider a territorial issue that went beyond strictly naval matters: the ultimate disposition of Heligoland. Control of Heligoland was essential to the defense of the German naval bases at Kiel and elsewhere. De Bon and Benson favored discussing naval air matters, but Wemyss objected because the Royal Navy did not have jurisdiction in this area. Wemyss and de Bon wanted to consider the future of the Kiel Canal, but, again, Benson resisted any such debate. Differences materialized on many other important questions, including the surrender of additional German vessels, the disposition of German vessels already interned, the destruction of German fortifications that covered the sea route to the Baltic Sea, the fate of the German overseas colonies, the future of the Bosphorus, the question of who would sweep mines laid during the war, the return of Allied merchant ships that had fallen into the hands of Germany, the future of wireless communications, and the disposition of German auxiliary cruisers. Throughout this period Admiral Benson maintained that the group was meeting "purely and simply for the handling of the naval armament of the German Government, the limit to which we wish to reduce it, and the time in which this is to be done." All other points "had something of a political character and would be handled by the Peace Commissioners."[1]

While the peace conference debated the terms of the definitive treaties, the armistice of 11 November 1918 came up for renewal, a development that revealed further differences between the intentions of the United States and those of the Allies. The British wanted to stiffen the terms of the armistice. Accordingly, instead of at the Supreme War Council, Admiral Wemyss appeared at a session of the peace conference, where he conveyed the impression that the admirals thought the preliminary naval terms should also become the terms of the armistice renewal. Benson, opposed to this course, protested to President Wilson and suggested a different approach: "If the Supreme War Council decides that a further extension of the armistice is advisable, the Naval Advisers [should] be directed to follow the usual procedure and submit the results of their deliberations for approval of the Supreme Body." Benson's suspicion of British motives increased as Wemyss continued his vigorous defense of British naval interests.[2]

The question of distribution continued to be a prime source of Anglo-American friction. Initially the British Admiralty circulated a draft of the naval terms that called for what Benson had consistently advocated—sinking of all interned and surrendered German vessels. On 7 February, however, Benson informed President Wilson that the French showed a "marked tendency" to favor distribution and that the British did not manifest "marked opposition." Benson had some ground for concern. On 15 February, Captain Cyril T. M. Fuller of the Royal Navy met with the French minister of marine, Georges Leygues, and Admiral de Bon to discuss distribution. The Frenchmen maintained that their country should receive some of the interned vessels as compensation for ships not built during the war. Fuller noted that a "general decrease of the world's Navies, with the French force as a comparison, would be more in accordance with the general spirit of limitation of armaments," but he nevertheless described "four bases on which the distribution of the enemy vessels might be made." British action on this question "depended upon the action of the United States[,] especially with regard to their future building programme." If the United States insisted on completing its huge program of naval construction, the British might have to "reconsider" their position.[3]

When Admiral de Bon formally objected to the destruction of the German vessels, Admiral Benson reported the French position to the president and the other members of the peace commission. Benson continued to insist on destruction: "No argument which may take place in the Supreme War Council or elsewhere should be allowed to prevail in omitting its provision."[4]

At this time President Wilson was forced to return to the United States to fulfill his constitutional responsibilities at the adjournment of Congress, leaving Colonel House in charge of the American Commission to Negotiate Peace, but the conference continued to discuss naval terms of peace as well as military and air terms. Benson insisted that the adoption of the draft covenant of the league had not eliminated the need for an American naval building program that ensured at least naval parity with Great Britain. To Secretary Daniels he forwarded a statement he had made to the American commissioners: "In order to stabilize [the] League of Nations, it is vitally necessary that no one power included in it should dominate in military or naval strength. There should be at least two powers of equal Naval strength. If this principle is accepted, it should be the deciding factor in our present Naval building program, as Great Britain and the United States are the only two present powers to be considered in this connection at the present time." Benson concluded: "I strongly urge you to take this up with the President immediately upon his arrival."[5]

This question became pressing because the proposed naval, military, and air terms were submitted to the Supreme War Council on 3 March. They included provision for the dismemberment or sinking of the German ships, although the French registered their reservation in favor of distribution. President Wilson had informed Secretary Daniels that he did not "quite understand" Admiral Benson's position, to which Daniels replied that he was also confused. Daniels agreed that "no nation ought to have a force either on land or sea, to dominate," and that the United States "ought to be ready and willing to furnish in proportion to its strength and commercial importance the necessary force to maintain the world's peace," but he questioned whether the administration could obtain from Congress huge sums of money to build American ships while at the same time it supported "sinking so many [German] ships." Like the president, Daniels thought that this matter should be discussed with Benson.[6]

On 7 March an attempt was made in Paris to resolve the naval question; Lloyd George, Clemenceau, and House met to explore the possibility of reaching an agreement. Lloyd George recognized that the French navy was lacking in certain classes of modern ships. Why not supply this deficiency out of the German navy? The United States, Japan, and Britain would permit their shares to be destroyed. Further, he suggested that the United States agree to avoid entering into a building competition with Great Britain. House assented to this arrangement. When he told Benson of the agreement, he neglected to indicate the price, a source of future misunderstanding. Sir Maurice Hankey informed Admiral Wemyss that the British and American shares were to be sunk "as a part of an Anglo-American understanding about new construction." A copy of this document went to Colonel House's private secretary, Gordon Auchincloss, for his "personal information," with the request that it not be shown to Admiral Benson.[7]

When President Wilson returned to the peace conference on 14 March 1919 after an absence of more than a month, Admiral Benson immediately attempted to press his views. That very evening he delivered a memorandum titled "Disposition of German and Austrian Vessels of War," dated 13 March, over his signature and those of Harry S. Knapp, Frank H. Schofield, and Luke McNamee. In a covering letter, Benson urged the president to read the entire paper. He asked for an interview to discuss the contents of the memorandum should the president have any "doubts" in his mind or should he "wish to ascertain what I believe to be professional opinions of the officers of the foreign Navies with whom I have been associated in the various conferences in Paris." The document began with the argument that "no international navy made up of ships of heterogeneous types, training, language, custom and command could hope to cope with the British fleet" unless the international force included at least one navy equal to that of Britain. The United States must therefore build to parity with Britain. A large American navy posed no threat to anyone. The United States was a "satisfied" power and could be depended on to support the league. In any event, the league navy, with the help of the Royal Navy, could "apply the remedy." Further, the navies of other nations should be kept at a minimum to protect against a situation that would allow Britain to add those forces to its own and thus gain an advantage. The United States should not accept any spoils of war; if the treaty did not preclude distribution, the issue would be settled according to the desires of the strongest power—Great Britain. That nation would receive between ten and twenty German ships as a consequence of distribution, an outcome that would force the United States to build a comparable number plus twenty-six more in order to achieve equality.[8]

On 17 March the Council of Ten, a group that included the foreign ministers and heads of government of the five principal nations at the peace conference (Great Britain, France, Italy, Japan, and the United States), met to consider the naval terms of the treaty, and Benson once again sought to influence the American position. To the peace commissioners he sent a memorandum supporting the destruction of German ships and material. In particular he objected to Article 35 of the proposed treaty of Versailles, which dealt with Heligoland; Article 38, which dealt with the Kiel Canal; and Article 40, which disposed of the German cable systems. He also opposed placing an indefinite limitation on German armaments and the establishment of an inter-Allied commission of undefined duration.[9]

The Council of Ten decided to place strict limitations on the size of Germany's postwar navy, but it made no mention of sinking vessels. Benson then renewed his pressure on the president, complaining about the indefinite nature of the limitations. Acceptance of this approach would make the nation a "member of continuing alliance to curtail the sovereignty of Germany, and [would hamper] the application of the principle of the League of Nations to Germany later on."[10]

On 25 March, when Secretary Daniels arrived in Paris, Benson met him at the railroad station and briefed him on the situation. This effort did not prevent the secretary from making a public statement that undercut Benson's opposition to distribution of the German fleet. The United States, he said, did not "wish to participate in any division of the German ships," but if the European nations who were first in the war wanted them, they could "divide them as they see fit." A shocked Benson discovered that the bureau chiefs in the Navy Department had advised the secretary that the German ships would be as much a liability as an asset because they were not built along the same lines as American ships. Realizing that Daniels did not grasp the reason he had opposed distribution, Benson read the Naval Advisory Staff's memorandum of 13 March 1919 to the secretary, hoping to change his mind.[11]

The situation now approached a climax. The day after Daniels arrived in Paris, Benson was called to the secretary's quarters, where, to his surprise, he found Admiral Wemyss (who was supposed to be in London) conducting an "earnest" conversation with Benson's civilian superior. He considered Wemyss's call on Daniels without an appointment to be a "complete breach of diplomatic etiquette." As Benson entered Daniels's room, he heard Wemyss confront Daniels with urgent questions: "Why are you so intent on increasing your Navy, and to what extent do you propose to carry it out?" Benson vehemently objected to this "unorthodox procedure" and what he deemed Wemyss's "impertinence." To Daniels he said: "Mr. Secretary, please do not answer this question." Describing this exchange years later, Daniels wrote: "I never saw two men in their high standing so infuriated as Admiral Benson and Admiral Wemyss in that conversation. They exchanged such bitter comments that at one time I feared they would pass the bounds and have an altercation."[12]

Later that day Daniels and Benson held a long conference with Colonel House on the subject of the naval terms. House agreed in principle with Benson about the need for naval parity, but he believed that the United States could safely discontinue the naval building program provided Great Britain made certain concessions. In other words, House shared the president's conception of the building program as primarily a diplomatic bargaining chip, whereas Benson wanted to construct the ships.[13]

Secretary Daniels and Admiral Benson, Paris, France, 1919.

The principal navy dignitaries of Great Britain and the United States met on 29 March in the hope, as President Wilson put it, that they could "reach some right understanding." After exchanging formal pleasantries, the participants concentrated their discussion on the American naval building program and on the extensive construction of merchant ships. Wemyss expressed "alarm" lest the American enterprise place the British fleet in second place, an "unthinkable" outcome. He was prepared to sink the German fleet, but he asked the Americans to accept British supremacy at sea, which would require curtailment of the American building program. Benson retorted that assent on his part

Left to right: Admiral Benson, Rear Admiral William A. Moffett, Mrs.
Benson, and Commander Carter, France, 1919.

would amount to "treason to his own country." Further, the United
States would "never agree to any nation having supremacy of the seas
or the biggest navy in the world. The Navy of the United States must
have equality with the British Navy."[14]

This impasse was based on the fact that Benson had not been
informed of the agreement that had been reached on 7 March in which
House had appeared to accept limits on American naval construction
in return for a British agreement to destroy the German fleet. Wemyss
must have been very disconcerted. Perhaps he did not know that the
failure to notify Benson was in part a result of Hankey's request to
Auchincloss that the understanding be kept from Benson. On 29 March,
the First Sea Lord and the CNO both firmly maintained their positions.
"You forget," said Wemyss, "that ours is an island nation with colonies
all over the globe, making the greatest navy essential to Great Britain's
existence." Benson answered: "You must remember that the United
States possessions extend from the Philippines to the Virgin Islands;
from Alaska to the protection of the farthest portion of South America,
because the Monroe Doctrine imposes a duty upon us we must always
be ready to perform."

Daniels and Long had an exchange that further demarcated the
gulf between the two sides. The secretary of the navy assured his auditors that the Americans did not want to precipitate a naval armaments

race. Seeking only to safeguard the peace of the world, the United States was convinced that "no single nation ought to demand superiority of naval strength." In other words, the United States sought naval parity with Great Britain. Long replied that, given Britain's enormous sacrifices during the war, he could not accept a settlement that demoted his nation to a second-class sea power. Lloyd George would not support the League of Nations if the United States persisted in a great naval building program: "Great Britain could not consent for any other nation to have superiority."

This exchange led to the firing of final salvos on both sides. Benson said: "Mr. Long, I gather from what you said what you mean in plain English is that Great Britain always has been supreme on the sea, both from a naval standpoint and commercially, and that she intends to continue so at all hazards." Long replied: "Well, Admiral, that is about the size of it." Benson could not contain himself at this comment. "Well, Mr. Long, if you and the other members of your Government continue to argue along the lines you are proceeding this morning, I can assure you that it will mean but one thing, and that is war between Great Britain and the United States." Long then noted: "Admiral, that is a very strong statement." Benson continued: "Mr. Long, we are discussing a very serious subject, and further, if the people of the United States only knew that such a conference as this was going on in Paris, it would start a flame that nothing under Heaven could quench."[15]

The meeting came to a conclusion without an agreement. Long said to Daniels: "Mr. Secretary, I am very much impressed with what the Admiral says, and the way in which he says it." Daniels did not think that Benson had "stated the case any too strongly." "In that case," Long concluded, "you had better talk to your President, and I will talk to my Prime Minister."[16]

This meeting greatly disturbed Secretary Daniels, who feared that the controversy over the American building program might delay formation of the League of Nations. After carefully considering the possibility of obtaining British support for the league by scrapping the proposed increase in the American fleet, he supported Benson's position on the distribution of the German fleet and informed President Wilson: "The more I think of it, the more I am impressed by the conviction that it would be a mistake to divide the ships between the nations and for Great Britain to sink the portion that comes to her and for the other nations to keep their portion."[17]

Long's report to Lloyd George reflected comparable concern about the prospects for a settlement. The discussions, he emphasized, had been conducted "with utmost frankness on either side for it was realized that no good was likely to accrue from it unless we thoroughly appreciate each other's position." Although he had the "greatest respect" for Benson's "honesty and straightforwardness," he thought the CNO a "man of mulish character and not very quick at grasping any ideas other than his own." The First Lord of the Admiralty thought that Daniels's views were less firm than those of Benson. For this reason he recommended another meeting, which neither he nor Benson would attend; then there might be a "better chance at arriving at some conclusion satisfactory to both sides."[18]

Admiral Benson shared Long's opinion of Daniels's position. The secretary had scheduled a visit to Rome; Benson proposed that he make this visit and not come back to Paris. President Wilson, however, asked Daniels to confer with Lloyd George and then go to Italy, whence he was to return to Paris.[19]

On 1 April, Daniels breakfasted with the prime minister to discuss naval issues. Contrary to the earlier arrangement to exclude both Benson and Long, the First Lord accompanied Lloyd George, but Benson was not present. The British prime minister proved inflexible. Daniels reported to the president that Lloyd George "would not give a snap of his finger for the League of Nations" if the United States continued its construction program, even though Daniels had explained that the program adopted in 1916 could not be abandoned and had insisted that "when the League of Nations is a going concern, a large reduction in armament will be safe and certain."[20]

Daniels went to Rome a worried man. Before departing, he arranged for Benson to see Colonel House, hoping that the persuasive Texan could help to moderate the CNO's inflexible position. This approach proved ineffective. Benson continued to insist on naval parity with Great Britain, characterizing the British position that the United States "should agree never to build a navy as large as [that of] Great Britain" as "perfectly preposterous." He asked House to arrange with the president to keep Daniels away from Paris.[21]

Wemyss and Long were no less concerned about the impasse than was Benson. Admiral Wemyss was convinced that Wilson and Daniels were using Benson, an "honest man," as a political tool. The CNO's superiors would repudiate him and the navy whenever it served their purpose to do so. Writing to Long, the First Sea Lord maintained: "It is a pity that this crisis should have arisen before Daniels's visit to England instead of afterwards." This statement referred to a plan for Daniels to follow his trip to Rome with one to London. When Daniels returned to Paris on 7 April, Benson learned that Wemyss had tried to arrange a meeting with the secretary at the railroad station. Benson described this attempt to bypass him as "cheeky," and he opposed any meeting between Daniels and either Wemyss or Long until the secretary had seen the president, citing the danger that Daniels might be "misunderstood or misquoted."[22]

Despite Benson's apprehensions, Daniels met with Long on 7 April, but their conversation did not take them beyond their previous positions. Long argued that only a small reduction in American naval construction—a mere three ships—would result in naval strength equivalent to 60 percent of Great Britain's and 40 percent of France's. Daniels replied that President Wilson had no intention of reducing the American program by a single ship until a peace treaty had been signed. He knew that Lloyd George had publicly declared that he would not sign a treaty until he had reached a naval understanding with the United States. Long recognized the deadlock; the "matter being in the hands of our chiefs," he said, "we have no other duty in connection with it."[23]

At just this moment the Naval Advisory Staff issued a statement on "United States Naval Policy" that provided a mature statement of Benson's views. This document reflected the ideas of the principal American naval thinker, Admiral Alfred Thayer Mahan, concerning the relationship between sea power and overseas commerce. It went beyond Mahan, however, in its treatment of the probable naval rivalry between Great Britain and the United States, a topic that had come to the fore during the negotiations in Paris. The bright promise of the American future was "bound to excite enmity and to cause unjust opposition to our expanding world interests," the statement said. The present danger was Britain; "every commercial rival of the British Empire has eventually found itself at war with Great Britain—and has been defeated." It was evident that America's international position hinged on sea communications and other maritime issues. The Royal Navy, no longer concerned about a German fleet, possessed sufficient strength to control the seas everywhere, a circumstance that threatened the "just interests" of the United States and "the general welfare of the world." A self-evident solution to this problem existed: "With two navies of equal strength, the world would breathe free from the fear of a naval domination that has power at any moment of threatening the economic life of any nation."[24]

Benson, a convinced nationalist, did not trust any other state. He rejected the opinion held by others, notably Admiral Sims, that American and British interests were identical or complementary. The course of events in Paris amply illustrated that Benson's British antagonists shared his views rather than those of Sims. In the heat of the peace conference, Benson returned to the general outlook that had led him to oppose suspension of the building program at the outset of American belligerency in 1917. These views cannot be dismissed as simply a function of Anglophobia.[25]

At this point in the conference President Wilson faced a major crisis. Difficulty with the British over naval questions was only one of a number of disputes that threatened the integrity of the American peace plan. Italian claims in the Mediterranean area and Japanese territorial demands in the Pacific region challenged the central principle of self-determination that dictated Wilson's attitudes toward boundary settlements and related matters. On 6 April, President Wilson replayed an important diplomatic card, the same one that had settled the dispute over the pre-armistice agreement early in November—he threatened to leave Paris. He asked his physician, Rear Admiral Cary T. Grayson, to arrange with Admiral Benson to order the *George Washington* to Brest. To Grayson he said: "I do not want to say that I am going as soon as I can get a boat; I want the boat to be there." The arrangement was leaked to journalists the next day. When Clemenceau asked Grayson whether the president meant to depart, the doctor replied: "If he ever starts for Brest to go aboard *George Washington*, you and your entire French army cannot turn him back." Benson made the arrangements to bring the *George Washington* to Europe.[26]

The president's threat to leave Europe had a measurable effect on the naval dispute, because it helped precipitate discussions between Lord Robert Cecil and Colonel House on this question. Cecil entered the negotiations at the suggestion of Lloyd George. He immediately wrote to House, reiterating the familiar British desire to retain supremacy at sea but asking that the United States "abandon or modify" its naval building program after the establishment of the league. This proposal represented a change in the British position. Long and Wemyss earlier had insisted on American action *before* British agreement to support the league.[27]

House's reply indicated "cordial agreement" with the "spirit" of Cecil's letter and noted that the United States would surely "abandon or modify" the new naval program should the peace conference approve a Wilsonian settlement. He explained that he believed Cecil referred not to the completion of the program legislated in 1916, but to the program for additional construction that had been proposed earlier in 1919 and had not yet been enacted into law. This distinction proved to be of great importance. House's statement shifted responsibility to the British, because it was the second program that concerned them rather than the program already in legislative effect. House described his initiative cogently: "*It is to be noted that I promise nothing whatsoever. It is merely the spirit of his suggestion that I am accepting. I am particularly reserved and insist upon the completion of our past naval program. It is only the future with which we deal.*" He feared that the prime minister might "catch the point and disapprove."[28]

Lloyd George found House's letter unsatisfactory because it did not prevent the United States from building a fleet nearly equal in numbers to the British fleet and superior in armament, a view that led him to a further initiative: support for recognition of the Monroe Doctrine in the covenant of the league in return for American concessions on the building program. Cecil opposed this linkage, describing it as "very harassing and provoking," but Lloyd George proved obdurate. When Cecil discussed this gambit with House, the American was un-

Dinner given by Admiral Benson in Paris on 3 June 1919 in honor of first trans-Atlantic flight.

responsive. The United States intended to proceed independently in dealing with recognition of the Monroe Doctrine. Cecil then requested House's permission to communicate the substance of their conversation to the prime minister.[29]

Cecil's memorandum to Lloyd George brought the naval battle of Paris to an end. He reported that the United States was determined to maintain the building program authorized in 1916. He emphasized that Colonel House had "repeated more than once that there was no idea in the mind of the President of building a fleet in competition with that of Great Britain, and that was entirely foreign to his purpose, that he did not believe that anyone, save possibly some high American naval officers, harbour any such idea." This statement was enough to convince Lloyd George that he must act. That evening he attended a meeting of the League of Nations Commission and supported the American position on the Monroe Doctrine. He felt unable to accept responsibility for the defeat of the United States on this question, even if he had failed to extract a naval agreement from the United States.[30]

The fundamental naval questions discussed in Paris were not resolved at the time. Lloyd George did not obtain American consent to continuing British supremacy at sea, but the United States did not achieve its goal of naval parity with the British fleet. The exchange between Colonel House and Lord Cecil constituted a tacit modus vivendi—the British would support the league and, in particular, acceptance of the Monroe Doctrine in return for an understanding that the Amer-

Admiral Benson and Herbert Hoover, Paris, France, 1919.

icans would postpone the proposed naval program for 1919 and beyond.[31]

Although Admiral Benson did not take part in the Cecil-House discussions, his views guided Colonel House to his position. The issues debated at Paris were finally resolved during the Washington naval conference of 1921–22, when Great Britain accepted naval parity with the United States, an outcome that confirmed the ultimate soundness of the CNO's views. Years later Josephus Daniels wrote: "Wilson was fortunate in having so level-headed a Naval adviser in Paris as Benson, one whose Americanism was undiluted." Perhaps Captain Pratt best summarized the opinion of most men in the United States Navy, writing to Benson in 1927 in praise of the admiral's activity in Paris as "one of the most important works of your entire career." He believed that "very few people realize how many sound decisions originated with you and I feel the Service and the country at large ought to be very thankful that they had a man of your outstanding character, determination and vision to act as an adviser to our President during the particular times which faced us before and during the making of the Versailles Treaty."[32]

Admiral Benson returned to the United States secure in the knowledge that he had at least helped to avoid having limitations placed on the navy; he deemed such limitations most injurious to his country. Some historians believe that he overestimated the threat to the United States posed by the British fleet, but the same scholars also consider the British fears of the American building program to have been entirely illusory. In the end, the "naval battle of Paris" proved to be an important step toward the naval settlement reached in Washington less than three years later—one that provided not only for naval parity between the United States and Great Britain, but also for significant naval disarmament.

CHAPTER XIII

DIRECTING THE NAVY DEPARTMENT 1919

Despite the demands of peacemaking in Paris, Admiral Benson maintained control of his normal advisory and policy-making functions as chief of naval operations. He acted through able assistants, initially Captain Pratt, and was in constant contact with the Navy Department by means of letters and cables between October 1918 and June 1919. His instructions to Pratt left no doubt of his desires: "In future please refer any question of policy to me before sending them elsewhere or before taking action. I cannot too strongly insist that all questions involving policy must be referred to me before taking final action." To Secretary Daniels he wrote that he did not know how long he would remain in Europe but that he was "keeping all the points of the Service well in hand" and was "directing them." As Pratt emphasized later, the responsibility for Operations lay not with him but with Benson, even if some looked askance at Benson's dual role as CNO and naval adviser in Paris.[1]

However interesting the course of the peace conference, Benson was anxious to go home. On 19 December 1918 he informed Daniels that he was pursuing naval questions energetically so that he could return to the United States: "I feel that at a time like this you, as Secretary of the Navy, are entitled to the service of those whom you have selected as your advisors, and I am anxious to be at my desk and fulfilling the duties of my office." When he realized he would have to remain in Paris for some time, he accepted the situation dutifully, writing to Daniels: "I feel that I can say with due modesty that I am performing a most important work here in Paris and one that should add prestige to the Naval Service in the eyes of all Americans who are engaged in this all-important work for negotiating the world's peace." He added that the combination of talented personnel in the Navy Department and the arrangements he had made for maintaining close contact would prevent serious difficulties.[2]

Benson was quick to act when he sensed any challenges to his authority or neglect of his instructions. After Captain Pratt ignored direct orders to reprimand Admiral Rodman for having, contrary to instructions, escorted a convoy of merchant ships across the North Sea, Pratt was "combed down" in no uncertain terms. At times even the loyal Pratt showed irritation. To his wife he confided his hurt feelings: "I do try to consult and refer things to him. But he is a long way off. . . . When I feel sure of his attitude I do act at times because things were so fine that one can't very well wait. . . . God knows I haven't got one single thing out of this and I don't expect or want to." Fortunately Benson was later able to demonstrate his regard for Pratt, whom he described as "always wise" and a "tower of strength." As soon as possible after the war he arranged Pratt's transfer to the fleet, an act intended to further his loyal assistant's naval career. Rear Admiral Josiah S. McKean took Pratt's place.[3]

Benson showed his desire to maintain authority in his reaction to an unauthorized initiative by the commander in chief of the North Atlantic Fleet. When Admiral Mayo went directly to Daniels in order to protest the use of naval vessels as troop transports, Benson pointed out that the subject fell within the domain of the CNO: "I think you will agree that [the] purpose of creating office of Naval Operations is to provide [a] technical advisor for the Secretary in matters of this kind. In my opinion [it is] highly improper for such matters to be presented to Secretary in person before they have been presented to me." Mayo responded politely but defended his action. He had no intention of ignoring Benson: "I think you will admit that my loyalty to you as Chief of Naval Operations has, heretofore, been unquestioned." He implied that Benson sought to muzzle him. To this accusation, the CNO replied that he had "complete confidence and . . . warm personal regard" for Mayo; his prime concern in this instance was to maintain the authority of his office. "It is needless for me to tell you (for you know from our professional relations) that I always encourage officers of the service to talk frankly to the Secretary and express their own views regardless of those which may be held by others."[4]

Benson's efforts to maintain control of the Navy Department while he was in Paris did not escape Sims's attention. As usual, Admiral Sims proved critical of Benson, especially after Sims was excluded from the naval discussions in Paris. To Pratt he wrote: "You must expect a certain amount of confusion in operations, and even administration, for Admiral Benson seems to be running the Navy Dept. from over here with the Navy Dept. itself taking a hand and mixing things up to a certain extent." Sims soon became restless; he asked Daniels through Benson to reassign him to duty as president of the Naval War College. Benson quickly endorsed this request: "I know of no better Officer for this duty than Admiral Sims and therefore recommend approval of his detail for this duty when he is eventually relieved from present duty." On a copy of this letter, which Benson forwarded to Sims, the force commander noted: "I rather think the Department will be glad to approve this, as it will relieve them of some embarrassment as to what to do with me." Sims soon returned to Newport, where he busied himself with the composition of his memoir, *The Victory at Sea.*[5]

The first important question from Washington that Benson handled in Paris was the building program for 1919. Commenting on proposals of the General Board prepared before the armistice, he indicated that he strongly favored constructing "Type C Battleships," which were capable of 30 knots: "We should if possible inaugurate the policy of building one complete, homogeneous division of whatever type of vessels we decided to build." If a division of these ships was built, the United States Navy would leap ahead of all others, and no nation could "overtake such a lead." Benson was ahead of his time; battleships of this type did not join the fleet until 1941. The General Board favored construction of scout destroyers and submarines. Benson opposed the destroyers, thinking it unwise to place big guns on such inadequate platforms. He supported construction of submarines because of their utility as scouts: "Aircraft and submarines can and will do this service much better than any other type of vessels."

Like Secretary Daniels, Admiral Benson wanted to complete the building program in three years rather than seven, offering as a reason what he called the "inherent prejudice of Congress." He thought it "important, with our policy of government, not to have one administration of Congress mortgage the country too far ahead. By asking for things that might do violence to the Congress we lessen our chances of securing what we believe we need for the best interests of our country."[6]

Daniels asked Benson to study the building program and make recommendations on his return from Europe. Meanwhile, the secretary proposed a second three-year program that called for construction of 10 battleships, 6 battle cruisers, and 140 smaller vessels at a total cost of $600 million. Pratt correctly guessed that this initiative would "throw a bombshell into the British camp." Later, when Daniels proposed to build 10 scout cruisers and 6 battle cruisers in addition to 10 battleships, Benson took strong exception. The issue and the legislative initiative both fell by the wayside, however, at the conclusion of the Paris peace conference.[7]

When Captain Pratt returned to Washington from Paris late in December 1918, he carried with him important recommendations from Benson concerning the organization of the fleet. The CNO wanted to retire three old battleships (*Iowa, Massachusetts,* and *Indiana*) and put the next eight battleships constructed into commission with crews at two-thirds of normal strength for training purposes. More important, he proposed to divide the remaining thirty-five battleships to constitute an Atlantic Fleet and a Pacific Fleet, each with four squadrons and eight divisions. Squadron One and Squadron Four, the weakest and the strongest, would operate in the Pacific, and the two others in the Atlantic. This disposition kept almost all the battleships then in the Atlantic where they were and added six ships of the *Connecticut* class, as well as the battleships *Michigan* and *South Carolina.*

New oil-burning destroyers of approximately one thousand tons displacement were to serve in the Pacific, close to adequate supplies of fuel. To command the destroyers, Benson supported the selection of officers with "long experience and mature judgment," so that the younger men aboard with "good intentions and splendid zeal may be shaped so as to bring about the results which have in the past, and we hope will in the future, give the Navy a good name, and keep the esprit de corps up to the point which brings about real cooperation and efficient results." Benson was especially interested in the organization of the Destroyer Force. When sufficient numbers of the new oil-burning ships became available, he proposed to form two or more flotillas of about fifty-four vessels each under a flag officer. Each flotilla would outnumber the total destroyer force available in 1917.

The CNO paid less attention to cruisers and submarines. The disposition of cruisers, he thought, would depend on situations in Central America and elsewhere that might require the presence of American vessels. Cruisers would serve as a "sort of stabilizer in places where the evidence of a little power will have a salutary effect upon disturbers of the peace." Submarines would navigate in designated spheres either singly or in relatively small units such as divisions. Because they would operate on a largely independent basis, division commanders would perform purely administrative duties.[8]

Secretary Daniels welcomed Benson's proposal; given potential difficulties with Japan, it was wise to strengthen naval forces in the Pacific. He approved Benson's plans for the two fleets and supported the CNO's choice of Vice Admiral Wilson to take one of the commands. On 25 June 1919 Secretary Daniels announced the creation of the two fleets. Admiral Wilson assumed command of the Atlantic Fleet, and Admiral Rodman took charge of the Pacific Fleet. Some officers, notably Sims and Fullam, did not approve of this arrangement. Sims disliked Wilson, and Fullam was disappointed at not obtaining the Pacific command to cap his career.[9]

Numerous lesser issues came to Admiral Benson's attention as he continued on in Paris. These matters received due attention; views and decisions, couched in characteristically forthright terms, went back to

Washington. For example, when McKean suggested an increase in the size of the Board of Inspection and Survey to speed up the process of examining ships returning from European service, Benson took strong exception. He believed that sufficient data concerning the condition of the vessels already existed in the department. He wanted to break away from undue dependence on boards and "practical algebraic formulae" to keep the ships in condition, preferring to establish a "practical operating Navy" and minimize long stays in navy yards by putting machine shops on board ships and trained mechanics on board repair vessels. In another instance that once again demonstrated his interest in merchant shipping, Benson supported a system of shipping control proposed by Rear Admiral Philip Andrews that was intended to reduce the number of maritime disasters. To McKean he wrote: "I hope this very important subject has not been pigeonholed, for by following it up along sound seaman like lines, we can accomplish a great deal and we can by starting some such scheme add one more service which the Navy is performing for the general good of all shipping, whether naval or commercial."[10]

While he was in Paris, Benson devoted a good deal of attention to communications. Great Britain, which controlled many cable systems, had refused to relax censorship, giving as a reason the need to maintain inter-Allied control of foodstuffs and raw materials. American traders, seeking to resume normal operations, suspected that the British were inhibiting message traffic in order to benefit their firms. On 17 February 1919 Benson forwarded an intelligence report to Vance McCormick, the chairman of the War Trade Board, that discussed Danish complaints of interference with communications to American merchants: "Danish merchants realize that peace is not yet here, that England must protect itself against Bolshevism etc. but they fail to realize why their telegrams are on the average held up five days in England before they go through, and why many never go through at all." Complaints of this character strengthened Benson's usual tendency to look suspiciously on British commercial measures.[11]

Prior to the war, commercial companies in the United States were unable to establish reliable radio communications across the Atlantic Ocean, but some progress occurred after the United States became a belligerent. The navy assumed control of transmitters at Tuckerton, New Jersey, and Sayville, New York, and succeeded in improving their efficiency. Around February 1919 American officials began to consider establishing an American wireless system to bypass British interference with cable messages. While returning from Europe for the first time in 1919, the president had conversed with Secretary Daniels from nine hundred miles east of New York by radio telephone. Already several radio circuits were in operation: five in the Atlantic and two in the Pacific.

Soon after the war the British Marconi interests attempted to gain exclusive use of the Alexanderson alternator, which had been developed at the General Electric Company and was an important advance in radio technology. Rear Admiral Bullard, on reassuming his duties as director of Naval Communications, managed to halt the negotiations between Marconi and General Electric. This accomplishment led to a plan whereby General Electric would establish a system of international communications making use of the alternator; in return, the company would be allowed to hold a monopoly on the device.

Secretary Daniels sent a proposal for this plan to Admiral Benson, who suggested delay. The CNO favored "Congressional support for Government control of radio" rather than private development. In Paris he had become aware of the extent to which the British and the French sought to control communications: "It is with this in mind that I have consistently contested the British and French demands in the Peace Terms with regard to the German cables and German radio. . . . The British are making a determined fight to get control of the major portion on the cables, whereas the French hope to make considerable gain in controlling radio." When he received a draft contract for General Electric that provided for a "High Power Radio Service," he counseled Daniels again: no private company could hope to compete successfully with the British. "I am satisfied that the only safe course to follow is to continue government control of high power stations and to trust to Congress finally giving the Navy complete government control of radio." As always, Benson was wary of British machinations and asked McKean to change Bullard's view should Bullard favor the General Electric scheme: "Strongly suspect foreign influence at bottom of scheme."[12]

At this point the Italians and the Japanese pressed extreme territorial demands that President Wilson felt unable to condone. This led Benson to conclude that, having obtained acceptance of the League of Nations, Wilson should force a break with the Allies: "If they were to refuse, even on the eve of signing peace, to stick by their agreement, he could go back home, saying that he had yielded all that he could in order to serve the League of Nations but that, on securing it, the principal Allies were unwilling to give it practical application even before the final peace was signed." To back Wilson's diplomacy, Benson believed the "strongest card [Wilson] could possibly play" was the expansion of American naval strength. The CNO's suspicion of European intentions, especially those of Great Britain, reached its zenith at this moment in the Paris negotiations.[13]

Admiral Benson's term as chief of naval operations was scheduled to expire on 10 May 1919, but with the disposition of the enemy fleets still unsettled, the German peace treaty yet unsigned, and postwar naval policy undetermined, Secretary Daniels wished to retain Benson. He informed President Wilson that it would be a mistake to change the existing arrangement, proposing a recess appointment that would extend the CNO's service until he was sixty-four—the specified age for compulsory retirement. When Wilson concurred, Daniels jubilantly informed Benson: "I was glad of privilege of signing your commission before sailing."[14]

Admiral Benson's last controversy in Paris concerned the familiar issue of distribution, which remained unsettled as the conferees neared the end of their discussions concerning peace terms for Germany. He hoped to specify the disposition of the German fleet in the treaty of peace. Lloyd George opposed this course because it would require extensive discussion and therefore cause delay. The prime minister wanted simply to note in the peace treaty that the ships had been surrendered; presumably the victors would consider the disposition of the ships at a later time. Benson retorted that "any decision, except to sink the ships," meant an "increase in armaments." Lloyd George demurred: "The British did not want these ships, and were ready to discuss even the decrease of Navies provided all would agree." Wilson then intervened; he proposed to postpone further consideration of distribution. If Germany raised the issue, the peacemakers would have to reach a decision before completing the terms of peace.[15]

Sorely disappointed, Benson wrote to Wilson in the hope of forcing a reconsideration. Given Britain's sea power, he insisted, the failure to resolve the question of distribution would threaten the League of Nations. Once again reverting to a quasi-Mahanian stance, Benson argued that commercial interests guided the foreign policy of every great power, a circumstance that the United States had to recognize. "This is particularly true," he wrote, "in the case of Great Britain; she has ever maintained her commercial supremacy by superior naval strength. In turn she has crushed Spain, Holland and Germany because they threatened her supremacy on the sea." British objections to the American building program stemmed from a "belief that we are now threatening that supremacy." He remained convinced that "if the final disposition of the surrendered German and Austrian war vessels is not stated in the Peace Terms, they will not be destroyed, but in time will be employed against our interests in some way."[16]

When this argument failed to move the president, Benson wrote again, detailing arguments that had been advanced previously. After listing the vessels that would go to the several naval powers, Benson claimed that additions to the French and Japanese navies were in effect supplements to the Royal Navy because of the intimate connections between the three nations. Britain's leverage at the peace conference, he continued, derived from "her tremendous naval superiority." Therefore, if Britain retained its dominance at sea, the league would simply ensure a stronger British Empire. Wilson replied sympathetically but firmly. "I recognize the high sense of duty from which you are acting, and take very much the same view of the matter that you do," he began. "While it was impossible to get the words that you and I desired into the Treaty, I do not yet at all despair of bringing about the same result, chiefly because I do not believe that the taxpayers of these countries will consent to bear the burden of a larger naval establishment."[17]

Benson persisted in his strong reservations about British intent. To Secretary Daniels he wrote in great perturbation about the impending threat from Great Britain. He hesitated to comment on this issue, however, because he recognized that he might be accused of prejudice. He wrote: "It may be that my fears are ungrounded, but I do not believe so, and I believe it my solemn duty to warn those who are in positions of responsibility that our country is in great danger and it is our duty to be prepared for the worst." Events did not bear out Benson's alarm. A few years later Britain proved willing to accept naval parity for reasons that President Wilson had anticipated, but it was impossible to wring this concession from Lloyd George during the immediate aftermath of the war.[18]

Admiral Benson's concern about the prospect of extensive trade rivalry between Great Britain and the United States elicited a sympathetic response from the president. The CNO had in mind the de Bunsen Mission's effort to make secret trade arrangements with certain Latin American nations during 1918. He stated: "We are on the threshold of the keenest and most active commercial competition that the world has ever seen." For his part, President Wilson welcomed this outcome, assuming that the United States was in a strong position. On 20 May 1919 he informed the Sixty-sixth Congress: "Peculiar and very stimulating conditions await our commerce and industrial enterprise in the immediate future. Unusual opportunities will presently present themselves to our merchants, and producers in foreign markets, and large fields for profitable investments will be opened to our free capital." Secretary Daniels echoed these sentiments, stating later that month: "Never again will the United States be guilty of the folly of trusting our foreign commerce to foreign bottoms."[19]

Benson now determined to return to Washington. The president agreed to this course, provided competent naval representatives were appointed to act in Benson's stead. Rear Admiral Harry S. Knapp and Captain Luke McNamee were given this assignment. Notifying Wilson of his choices, Benson expressed great confidence in them. He explained that he was returning to Washington so that he could "carry out the duties of the Navy Department with which I am charged by law and for which I am responsible to you and the Secretary of the Navy." Both Wilson and House were lavish in praise of the admiral. The president replied: "You have my entire approval in your plan to go home, hard as it is to let you go and much as I am sure I shall feel the lack of your advice on many a matter. We all have to choose which side of the water it is most important that we should be on." House said that he understood Benson's reasons for departing, and he expressed appreciation of his colleague's "courage and wise counsel" during the peace negotiations: "I hope your fellow countrymen may someday know how well you have served them."[20]

Before leaving Paris, Benson undertook a final labor, one that reflected his religious fervor. Article 122 of the peace treaty required "repatriation, without any distinction, of all Germans in former colonies," a provision that would have forced German missionaries to leave their posts and abandon their property. Article 438 provided for the administration and disposition of German holdings. Spokesmen for the Roman Catholic Church objected to these arrangements on two grounds: first, the missions were the property of the Holy See rather than of the German government; second, application of the articles would be unjust, a disservice to humanity. After discussing this question with the Chinese foreign minister and with British representatives, Benson wrote to the president: "It is with extreme hesitancy that I presume to address you on a purely political subject but due to my intimate knowledge of the situation, [I] feel that it would be neglecting a duty not to do so." Explaining the consequences of Articles 122 and 438, Benson concluded that, should these provisions remain unmodified, "an appeal to the conscience of the entire Christian World will be made, and I fear your good intentions might be impugned." Undoubtedly Benson's intervention helped to resolve the issue; the articles were modified so that missionaries could remain on their properties.[21]

On 11 June 1919 Admiral Benson departed Brest on the *Arkansas* full of honors and best wishes. His own nation had decorated him with the Distinguished Service Medal for "Exceptionally Meritorious and Distinguished Service as Chief of Naval Operations through the war with the Central Powers," and President Raymond Poincaré of France had awarded him the Grand Cross of the Legion of Honor. A letter of appreciation arrived from the American peace commissioners. Admiral Beatty sent a telegram expressing regret at his inability to bid farewell personally and thanking Benson for "cordial cooperation and kindly friendship." Captain Pratt emphasized the importance of his return to the Navy Department: "You will arrive to find that if ever a steady hand was needed at the helm of the Navy, now is the time. I think the Service looks to you to steady things as no other naval man can. . . . I have a safer feeling for the Navy when I feel you are at the helm."[22]

Pratt's estimate of the situation was not an exaggeration; Admiral Benson returned to the United States to face important naval questions, especially demobilization and reorganization of the Office of Naval Operations, at a time when congressional opposition to the peace treaty raised serious questions about the future. As the *Arkansas* neared the

East Coast, Admiral Mayo sent four destroyers to escort her. When the battleship anchored in New York harbor, Mayo's flagship, the *Pennsylvania*, fired a salute of seventeen guns. Admirals Mayo, Rodman, Coontz, and Eberle S. Wood, the commandant of the First Naval District, went aboard the *Arkansas* to welcome their chief. On landing, the CNO spoke guardedly to reporters on two subjects that he thought overshadowed all others: the League of Nations and aviation. In his mind was the threat of Anglo-American naval and commercial competition, the subject that had dominated his participation in the peace conference. In reference to the league, he said: "Now, if the League of Nations becomes a fact, it will automatically reduce armaments; but you must remember the 'if,' and that is about all I can say about the League of Nations or future policies of the American or other Navies of the world." His comments on aviation reflected public interest in the recent flight of a naval airplane, the NC-4, to Europe. The navy, he thought, should develop its aviation "seriously and cautiously," because operations in the air would play a large role in future wars. "Naval policy as it affects aviation is bound to go ahead on lines of proven knowledge," Benson said. "There may be nothing spectacular in the way naval aviation develops, but we shall be constantly at it."[23]

On the very day that Benson resumed his work in Washington, 21 June 1919, a sensational development definitively resolved the question that had aroused so much controversy during the discussion of naval terms. Forty-eight hours before the Allies were to assume control of the German ships interned at Scapa Flow, the crews hoisted the national colors and scuttled their vessels. A British writer commented that the "Royal Navy had been made to look a trifle foolish by the ships being scuttled under its nose," but Colonel House recorded a more important observation: "It is all to the liking of Benson and myself who wanted the boats sunk." One week later Rear Admirals Knapp and Long and Captain McNamee attended the signing of the Treaty of Versailles. McNamee wrote to Benson: "I am sorry you were not here. It was very business like and had nothing of the spectacular, but I couldn't help feeling the significance of it and was deeply impressed."[24]

One of the high points of Admiral Benson's service was a thoroughgoing reorganization of the Office of Naval Operations. On 1 August 1919 he issued the *Revised Organization Orders of the Office of Naval Operations*. In his introduction to this document, the CNO cited the wartime experience as the basis for the reform. He hoped that naval officers would "realize the tremendous value to the service and the country of the Office of Naval Operations" and would "use their best efforts to increase its efficiency and its effectiveness." The revised orders provided for two main entities within the Office of Naval Operations, the Planning Division and the Division of Operating Forces,

Admiral W. S. Benson and Assistant Secretary of the Navy F. D. Roosevelt
on 22 June 1919 at Mt. Vernon, where they accompanied the Brazilian
president and his party in the presidential yacht *Mayflower*.

which were formed to cover the primary functions of the office. These
were the study and preparation of policies and plans and the operation
and administration of naval forces in accordance with approved plans.

The Planning Division took responsibility for war plans and plans
for current administrative work. Assigned personnel were not designated by rank, but they were expected to "command the confidence of
the department and of the naval service." Sections within the division
assumed responsibility for Policy, Strategy, Tactics, Education, Submarines, Aviation, Logistics, and Administrative Plans. Recommendations from the Planning Division were to be "submitted to the Chief
of Naval Operations for his action." One officer was designated to
provide the liaison with the Naval War College. The Division of Operating Forces accepted responsibility for "movements of all naval craft,
whether surface, subsurface, or air, not specifically designated for training and experimental purposes exclusively." Officers in the division
assigned to supervise the movements of ships reported to the CNO or
his assistant. This arrangement strengthened the role of naval operations
as a centralized command post.

A number of administrative divisions dealt with naval affairs other
than those involving planning or movements of ships. Among them

Left to right: Assistant Secretary of the Navy F. D. Roosevelt, Secretary of the Navy Josephus Daniels, and Chief of Naval Operations William S. Benson pose with Marine Reservists and Yeomen at their final review in 1919. National Archives, RG 127-G-530164A.

were Intelligence, Communications, Material, Naval Districts, Inspections, Gunnery Exercises and Engineering Performances, and Files and Records. Through these divisions, the CNO and his assistant monitored all aspects of naval administration. The assistant chief of naval operations assumed direct charge of Navy Regulations, Naval Instructions, and General Orders. His relationship with the CNO was described as being the same as an "executive officer of a ship holds to the heads of departments on board ship."[25]

Admiral Benson immediately put the revised organization orders into practice. He issued a directive that provided for a daily conference between the chief of naval operations, the heads of all divisions, the director of submarines, the director of aviation, and "such others as may be designated." Each participant other than the CNO was expected to prepare a daily memorandum in two parts, providing information intended to keep the CNO abreast of activities and asking questions that required the attention of the CNO.[26]

One other administrative matter required attention: permanent status for the Naval Overseas Transportation Service. It began as an ad hoc organization set up to administer vessels placed under naval control, such as naval auxiliaries, troop transports, and army cargo ships. Some 73 ships fell into this category as of the end of 1917; on 9 January 1918 Benson created NOTS, which eventually operated 450 vessels. After the war Admiral Benson moved to make provisions for the ships that remained in the hands of the navy. On 19 June 1919 the Planning Committee offered suggestions that Benson quickly endorsed; he then formed a special joint board to make recommendations concerning the vessels acquired during the war.[27]

The future of naval aviation also required attention. When the United States entered the war, the nation's minuscule naval air service was made up of 48 officers, including 34 aviators; 239 enlisted men; 54 airplanes; a single airship; 3 balloons; and a naval air station at Pensacola. During the war, the air service expanded greatly, and at war's end, 6,716 officers and 30,693 enlisted men served in naval air units, and 282 officers and 2,180 enlisted men served in the Marine air service. Material on hand included 2,107 aircraft, 15 dirigibles, and 215 balloons. Some 18,000 men served overseas, operating from twenty-seven bases in France, England, Ireland, and Italy. American aviators flew as many as 30 million nautical miles during the war, of which about half were flown as part of the Royal Air Force and other Allied units.[28]

Admiral Benson lost no time in developing plans to continue the expansion of the navy's air arm. Before leaving Paris, he arranged for Captain Thomas T. Craven to become director of Naval Aviation. Craven took up this responsibility on 8 April 1919 and quickly presented comprehensive views on "The Immediate Needs of U.S. Naval Aviation." Meanwhile the General Board also developed a plan, one that would "enable the United States Navy to meet on at least equal terms any possible enemy."[29]

These ambitious programs encountered a serious setback on Capitol Hill. After Secretary Daniels withdrew the program calling for a second three years of naval construction, Congress reduced the appropriation for naval aviation from $225 million to $25 million, $20 million less than the sum requested by Craven. The appropriated funds were intended to finance experimental work, conversion of the collier *Jupiter* to an aircraft carrier, purchase of two dirigibles, and operation of only six naval air stations. Benson and Daniels eventually put a modest program into effect that did not match the desires of the fledgling air service but that provided a basis for later postwar development, although modest appropriations continued to inhibit progress.[30]

Admiral Benson became interested in another aspect of the aviation question, a proposal to place all aviation in a separate department of aeronautics. On 28 July 1919 Congressman Charles F. Curry (R-Calif.) introduced a bill that would have created an American counterpart to the Royal Air Force, merging army and naval aviation into a single service. Naval proponents of aviation, Admiral Benson among them, believed that the Royal Navy had suffered greatly from the loss of its own air arm. The CNO ordered Rear Admiral James H. Oliver to study the Curry bill from a naval standpoint, presenting the reasons why "such action is not practical and should not become law." Oliver maintained that aviation was a "major arm of the Fleet" and that "it would hardly seem advisable to create a new department to develop and operate a weapon which in the future will be a major arm of the Navy." This point of view prevailed; Congress did not enact the Curry bill.[31]

Benson continued to contemplate two fundamental questions: Would the nation persist in creating a navy second to none by 1925, the commitment made in 1916? and Should the United States build a navy as strong as the combined forces of Great Britain and Japan? The CNO was unable to obtain satisfactory answers to these questions before his departure from the Navy Department. During 1917–18 the building program of 1916 had been deferred, and during 1919 the program became an element in the diplomacy of President Wilson, used to ensure British support for the League of Nations. During this time Secretary Daniels had proposed a second three-year program of construction (the first three-year program had received congressional authorization earlier), but he withdrew it after House and Cecil arrived at a modus vivendi on naval questions: British support for the league in return for suspension of the second three-year program. During the debate over whether the Senate should give consent to the Treaty of Versailles, the Wilson administration adopted as its battle cry "Ratification of the Treaty or a huge naval construction program." The questions that Benson raised at the end of his tenure in the Office of Naval Operations were not addressed until the great naval disarmament negotiations that took place in Washington in 1921 and 1922.

On 15 September 1919 Acting Secretary of the Navy Roosevelt announced that Admiral Benson would go on the retired list on 25 September, the CNO's sixty-fourth birthday. On 24 September Daniels summarized the admiral's service as chief of naval operations in glowing terms:

> On April 6, 1917, the United States declared war against Germany, and until the armistice was signed on November 11, 1918, the United States Navy was largely responsible for the final and overwhelming defeat of the enemy. During the Peace Negotiations in Paris you were the principal Naval Advisor to the President of the United States, and in this duty your advice and counsel were of inestimable value.
>
> For more than four years during the most momentous period in the history of the Navy, you have performed the duties of the most important office under the Navy Department with an efficiency and loyalty that commands the respect and admiration not only of the Navy but of the nation.

Benson must have taken pleasure also in these words of praise from Secretary of War Newton D. Baker: "Your retirement completes a great service to your country, rendered at a most trying time of our history and rendered with [a] combination of ability, zeal and courtesy quite rare even in the great annals of our military services." He also praised Benson's support of cooperation between the War Department and the Navy Department.[32]

No message came from Woodrow Wilson. Tragically, the president, then in the western states making speeches in support of the Treaty of Versailles, collapsed on Admiral Benson's birthday. He never recovered fully from this setback.

Admiral Benson retired a disappointed officer. He had hoped to leave the service at the rank of full admiral, given his accomplishments within the Navy Department and at the Paris peace conference, but no action was taken to authorize such an honor. Despite this circumstance, a letter from his closest and oldest friend in Washington, Rear Admiral Charles J. Badger, must have brought him satisfaction. Neither he nor Benson, wrote Badger, had just cause for regret at the end of their active careers: "We have both done our best—it is not possible to do more." More important, "no man could or did take a more prominent part in the great events connected with the Navy of the past few years[,] and you carry with you into retirement all the honors which this and the other governments involved in the great war can bestow for duty well done."[33]

Another close associate, Captain Pratt, later praised the most important of Benson's qualities—his "sterling character." Pratt believed that Benson "possessed that quality to a marked degree, without which no man can be a great leader[,] for it is the first in the category of essential qualities a leader should possess. . . . The country may well be thankful it had such a capable man to direct its naval destinies through those crucial days."[34]

Benson's service to the nation had not come to an end. He was soon recalled to the government in a new role—as a member of the United States Shipping Board. The most important event in his life soon after he left the Navy Department, however, was a sensational investigation of the Navy Department's performance during the war, which came about at the instigation of Admiral Sims.

CHAPTER XIV

UNEXPECTED BROADSIDE: THE NAVAL INVESTIGATION OF 1920

Admiral Sims returned from Europe in a very agitated state, convinced that the Navy Department had seriously compromised the service during the war. On 13 August 1918, almost three months before the armistice, he had written to Pratt ominously: "When the history of this war comes to be written there will be a number of features that will not be very creditable to the United States Navy. If hearings are held on the conduct of the war, a number of rather disagreeable facts must inevitably be brought out." Later on, after Pratt had prepared a report on naval operations during the war, Sims complained bitterly. How could Pratt have written in such positive terms about the flawed performance of the Navy? Who had instigated his misrepresentations? Pratt replied that he had composed the report entirely on his own. In doing so, he was "faced with the necessity of looking at our preparations from the broader point of view, in taking into consideration all of the operations in which we were involved." This exchange ended a long personal association between Sims and Pratt. It clearly indicated how alienated Sims felt from the Navy Department and the Office of Naval Operations.[1]

When he undertook the writing of a book of memoirs about the naval war, Sims had to avoid criticizing the administration or the Navy Department. This requirement of all officers on active duty was specified in Article 1534 of the naval *Regulations*. Sims informed his collaborator, Burton J. Hendrick, that the work would "contain nothing at all of a political nature and no criticism of the Department." He wrote sourly to Admiral Fullam, explaining the constraints that had been imposed on him. In concluding, he wrote: "You may be sure, however, that at the proper time I will tell the whole truth as I understand it." Fullam replied: "Personally I hope for the good of our country, that Congress *will* investigate the conduct of the War. The pre-war neglect was criminal." In response Sims commented bluntly: "You know I entirely agree with you that the country has got to be informed as to the condition of the Navy in the immediate past and its condition now." The matter would have to rest for the moment, but those who had "camouflaged the subject cannot escape very long."[2]

An opportunity to precipitate a naval investigation developed in connection with a controversy over the award of decorations to naval personnel. In December 1919 the Navy Department published a list of 1,620 recipients of decorations. Admiral Sims quickly wrote a letter to Secretary Daniels complaining bitterly. The awards did not reflect the "relative merit of the services performed," a circumstance that would "necessarily result in serious discontent and a sense of injustice." To underline his position, Sims declined the Distinguished Service Medal that had been awarded to him. Admiral Fullam sensed the significance of this action. "Bully for you! . . . Sims, the Navy has been under the autocratic rule of ignorance, injustice, and even neglect for such long years. . . . I hope you will fight to the last—I *know* you will." Sims's letter to Daniels was soon made available to the press, and others who disliked Daniels and Benson soon rallied to Sims, including Admiral Fiske, who wrote: "I fancy this investigation will not be confined to medals. *It must not be.*"[3]

On 5 January 1920 the Senate Committee on Naval Affairs appointed a subcommittee to investigate the awards, and hearings began on 16 January, but during the interim Sims added to the controversy. On 7 January he wrote once again to Daniels, this time summarizing his overall indictment of the Navy Department, which stressed the failure of the department to honor his recommendations during the crisis of the submarine war in 1917. This letter also was soon leaked to the press: Albert W. Fox broke the story on 14 January in the *Washington Post*. Daniels summarized its content succinctly: "Sims virtually indicted the whole Navy Department."[4]

Appearing before the subcommittee, Sims read his charges into the public record, and the group decided to hold a second set of hearings. One of Sims's allegations caused a considerable sensation. He maintained that when he had been called to Washington in March 1917 prior to his departure for Great Britain, he had been told by Admiral Benson: "Don't let the British pull the wool over your eyes. It is none of our business pulling their chestnuts out of the fire. We would as soon fight the British as the Germans." Benson's explanation of this statement downplayed the anti-British aspects, stressing instead his desire to maintain neutrality. "I endeavored to impress upon [Sims] as emphatically as I could that he must not do or say anything which would embarrass the United States in its then position of neutrality." He had in mind prior indiscretions of Sims, especially a pro-British oration in 1910 at the Guildhall in London that had earned a presidential reprimand.[5]

A number of senior officers urged Daniels to relieve Sims as president of the Naval War College or even to court-martial him. Admiral Robert E. Coontz, Benson's successor as chief of naval operations, favored a court-martial: "I can assure you that there would not be the slightest doubt of his conviction." Daniels, perhaps mindful of his desire to run for the presidency, and perhaps because it appeared to him that the admiral seemed mostly interested in attacking the Office of Naval Operations, appeared reluctant to take any action against Sims. When he took up the question with President Wilson, Daniels said he feared that punishment might allow Sims to "pose as a martyr." Wilson agreed, and no action was taken against Sims.[6]

The first phase of the hearings on the naval awards continued until 10 February; for the moment Admiral Benson kept his own counsel. He expressed himself forthrightly, however, in a letter to Commander Walter B. Woodson. He had sought to "keep absolutely quiet . . . although, as you say, it has been very difficult to exercise forbearance." What were Sims's motives? "He has, all along, posed in an absolute false light, and he is continuing to do so, and is apparently attempting to work up a feeling throughout the country that he is a much abused individual, instead of what he really is." Noting that Sims had considerable standing among younger officers, he thought it important to consider Sims's early career. Sims had "never done any very great things. . . . He is naturally a fluent writer and loves to indulge in such pastimes but the burden of his song has always been criticism and faultfinding of the American people in general and the U.S. Navy and Naval profession in particular." Benson categorically rejected the charges that Sims had levelled before the congressional subcommittee. Sims, Benson believed, demonstrated a "most lamentable ignorance, not only of conditions in general, but of the Navy in particular."[7]

On 7 March the hearings on the naval awards came to an end without significantly affecting the final list of recipients. The Republican majority condemned the actions of the secretary of the navy, but the Democratic minority defended him. Sims apparently thought that many officers would follow his lead in declining a decoration, but he was disappointed in this expectation. Daniels conducted a review of the original list and made some minor adjustments, and the awards were bestowed on Armistice Day, 1920.[8]

Nevertheless, Sims had accomplished what he had set out to accomplish—the hearings on the naval awards led to a full investigation of his charges against the Navy Department. A second round of hearings was scheduled to begin on 9 March. Admiral Benson was recalled to active duty and given an opportunity to prepare his testimony carefully. Secretary Daniels also asked the bureau chiefs and other responsible officers to prepare reports on their wartime activities. In Newport, Sims sought assistance from his circle. Daniels seems to have concluded that he would escape unscathed; the real contest would be between naval factions. On 29 February he wrote: "The Sims letter [of 7 January] & Benson's reply will make it an Admiral's fight."[9]

The second phase of the hearings began on 9 March and continued until 28 May, a marathon that produced over two and a half million words. Sims's charges masked the issue that had led to the selection of Admiral Benson as the first CNO in 1915—the question of whether to establish a powerful naval general staff. Naval reformers such as Fiske, Fullam, and Sims wanted to minimize civilian control of the navy in the interest of efficiency. They developed a great dislike of Admiral Benson precisely because he supported civilian supremacy. To Benson's critics among the reformers, this behavior appeared craven, a surrender to incompetency, and was symbolized in their minds by Secretary Daniels. As Sims put it in a letter to Fullam: "Politicians have been able to surround themselves by naval officers who will do exactly what they want." Fullam, commenting on a proposal to make Benson a full admiral for life, was more specific: "The elevation of Admiral Benson to High Admiral, under all the circumstances, can only be regarded as a reward for personal and political service—nothing more or less." Benson had "never seen any Naval duty that entitled him to the rank of Farragut, Porter, and Dewey."[10]

The account that follows is not a full examination of the hearings; rather, it treats those aspects of the proceedings that help to illuminate the activities of Admiral Benson.

Sims and Daniels both sought to shape public opinion, mostly by attempting to influence journalistic coverage of the hearings. Sims was prepared to expend his own funds, if necessary, to carry the day. He paid for the printing of various materials to help reporters "get up their stories." He explained to his wife that the cost, perhaps $2,000, was justified: "We must win this fight." Fiske busied himself with a "newspaper offensive," hoping to obtain coverage of the case against the Navy Department in various metropolitan newspapers. Daniels tried to obtain favorable publicity for the Navy Department. Admiral Benson refrained from such activities. Remaining noncommittal in public, he preferred to withhold his comments until he testified before the subcommittee. His one initiative was a successful effort to obtain the next-to-the-last word; only Daniels was to testify after him.[11]

Admiral Sims offered direct testimony to the congressional subcommittee from 9 March to 18 March, elaborating on the charges contained in his letter to Daniels of 7 January. He insisted that the navy had not been prepared for the war. It lacked adequate material and personnel, and it failed to prepare sound war plans. For these reasons the navy performed well below acceptable levels during 1917: "Owing to [our lack of preparedness] and to the lack of proper organization of our Navy Department . . . we failed, for at least six months, to throw our full weight against the enemy; . . . during this period we pursued a policy of vacillation, or in simpler words, a hand to mouth policy, attempting to formulate our plans from day to day, based upon an incorrect appreciation of the situation." The consequences, Sims maintained, were horrendous. The six-month delay cost the Allies half a million lives, two and a half million tons of shipping, and expenditures totalling $15 billion.[12]

These charges caused great resentment among the officers whom the Navy Department called to testify. Admiral Benson thought them "an outrage to the honorable record of the United States Navy" that, if permitted to stand, would constitute an "everlasting disgrace." Admiral Mayo condemned Sims's view as a "wild statement, not at all susceptible of proof," and an "unwarranted attack upon the Navy Department and the Navy." Admiral Wilson insisted that the "American naval forces materially aided in shortening the war, saving untold life and property." Admiral Rodman observed that there were three kinds of lies—"lies, damned lies, and statistics"—and that Sims's comments belonged to the last category. Rear Admiral Joseph Strauss, commander of the force that built the North Sea barrage, said: "As to Sims's charges of losses my answer is NO." Both of Benson's assistants emphatically rejected the accusations. Pratt maintained that, if all the American antisubmarine craft had been dispatched to Europe immediately, the war would not have been shortened by a single day. McKean made perhaps the most angry statement: "The charge is monstrous and an insult to the Navy. Had it been invented by the inflamed, exaggerated diseased ego of a patient at St. Elizabeth's [an institution for the mentally ill in Washington, D.C.], no one would have been surprised. . . . Made by an officer of the Navy it is an insult to every officer and man now in the Navy." Badger deemed Sims's statement "utterly unfounded," and Fletcher agreed with Pratt, claiming that the "delays charged did not prolong the war for a single day."[13]

Senator Frederick Hale (R-Maine), a friend of Admiral Sims, while cross-examining him, brought up the statement reportedly made by Benson about the British pulling the wool over Sims's eyes. Sims responded that he "regarded this as a personal idiosyncrasy of the admiral: I had known the general opinion that he was intensely anti-British, but it did not affect me particularly." He claimed to have maintained the "best possible relations" with Benson and, furthermore, that the CNO alone had been responsible for the opportunity given him to serve during the war in Europe. Although there was nothing personal in his criticism, he concluded that the "spiritual foundation of every war is the will to victory, and if any man, no matter how honest, has an invincible prejudice against the people that we are fighting alongside of, it is very probable that it has an unconscious influence upon him." This explained why he had mentioned Benson's remarks.[14]

Before Admiral Benson took the stand he received a singular honor; Pope Benedict XV had named him a Knight of the Order of the Grand Cross of St. Gregory the Great, Military Class, and the recipient of the silver medal of that order. Secretary Daniels wondered whether Benson should accept this award, because the pope headed a state as well as the Roman Catholic Church, but a ruling of the attorney general cleared the way: the pope had acted in his capacity as a churchman rather than as a statesman. Others feared that anti-Catholic sentiment might cloud the issues raised during the naval investigation. Benson nevertheless decided to proceed. On 11 April he received the award from James Cardinal Gibbons in Baltimore. Bishop William T. Russel of Charleston, South Carolina, delivered some remarks on the biblical text "Render, therefore, to all men their due. Honor to whom honor is due." Then he said, apparently referring to Admiral Sims: "True patriotism comprises loyalty to one's country, obedience to its laws, respect for its authority and a readiness to sacrifice all for its cause. . . . The man who refuses to allow his country's interests to predominate, and who permits his personal opinions to obtain, is no less a traitor than the man who refuses to fight for his land."[15]

Some of Admiral Benson's adherents feared that his acceptance of the award would provoke an outburst of anti-Catholicism. One correspondent, a retired lieutenant commander, R. Mason Lisle, counseled postponement: "There are many Catholic Irishmen and many Irishmen are Sinn Feiners. . . . Delay the decoration ceremonies until the Senate is entirely through with its investigation." Some criticism of the admiral appeared; for example, James F. Dailey of Philadelphia wrote to Daniels and accused Benson of "attending 'retreats' at the Roman Catholic Cathedral" in Philadelphia during the war. "Americanism has never been taught from any cathedral throne, and the one in Philadelphia is no exception." Dailey was of the opinion that "Benson was then a Sinn Fein sympathizer if not an actual member of that organization of secret assassins. Every Sinn Fein is a Romanist sworn to aid the Vatican politicians, and Benson is a Romanist." Some objections surfaced in the Georgia legislature, but the papal award does not appear to have influenced the conduct of the congressional hearings.[16]

Admiral Benson began his testimony on 4 May 1920. His former aide, Commander Carter, had urged him to offer a prepared statement and to "insist upon reading it *without interruption* before answering questions. If you don't some one with a lawyer's trickery will try to break in just as he thinks you are about to make a point he doesn't want brought out." Benson did not follow this advice. He began by saying: "I have intentionally avoided preparing a studied statement. I have attempted to keep my mind as free as possible from any of the

On 11 April 1920 Admiral Benson was decorated in the name of Pope
Benedict XV as a Knight of the Order of the Grand Cross of St. Gregory by
James Cardinal Gibbons (*center*) in the presence of Secretary Josephus
Daniels (*left*) and many prominent persons. From *The Wilson Era: Years of
War and After*, by Josephus Daniels. Copyright 1946, The University of
North Carolina Press. Reprinted by permission.

influences that might have been produced by hindsight." He did not intend to shirk blame or to incriminate or defend anyone. He would assume responsibility for naval policy during his tenure as chief of naval operations. "As naval advisor to the Secretary of the Navy," he noted, "I was responsible for the naval operations of the Navy."[17]

Admiral Benson offered a judicious explanation for the behavior of the Navy Department before and during the war. He admitted some prewar errors, arguing that he "would have had the Navy prepared for war at all times," but, he argued, "This was not the attitude of the people of the United States and not the attitude of the Administration." He did not possess authority to prepare the navy for war without political direction as long as the official national policy was neutrality. "There were many things that I felt as a naval officer that we ought to do that [Secretary Daniels] felt as a politician we ought not to do."

To allegations that he had failed to respond promptly to the needs of the Allies after the American intervention, Benson maintained that his first duty was "to safeguard American interests regardless of any duty to humanity or anything else." For this reason he believed that "we should be first able to protect our coast and then do everything we could to help them on the other side." No doubt bearing in mind Sims's charges concerning the lack of a war plan, Benson argued: "This war was not altogether our war. The Allies had been in it for some years and they had, or should have had, very definite policies and plans upon which they were conducting war and we were going to join them." The requests French and British naval representatives made in Washington "were more than satisfied." Thereafter the United States prompted the Allies to much more ambitious war measures. Benson insisted that during the war the navy's performance had been excellent.[18]

Admiral Benson lived up to his old nickname "Judge" during the hearings, adopting a simple, straightforward presentation that commanded respect because it was less partisan than those of others. His defense of the navy's performance in the given circumstances rather than an unqualified endorsement may have been more acceptable to Sims and his circle than to Daniels. Fullam recognized in Benson's testimony sympathy for an increase in the authority of the CNO. To Fullam's surprise, Benson had "out-Fisked Fiske." Fullam overstated the case, but certainly Benson proved himself a strong proponent of measures to give the CNO powers commensurate with his responsibility. Sims admitted to Fullam: "Perhaps the best news of all is that Benson has come out so strongly for reorganization, as this is what the Republicans want and what the Democrats particularly do not want. This is, in reality, the most effective criticism of the handling of the Navy Department by the present incumbent [Daniels]."[19]

Sims and Fullam recognized that Admiral Benson was by no means an unqualified admirer of Secretary Daniels. Benson probably shared the sentiments of Commander Wilson Brown, once assigned to the Office of Naval Operations, who reminded his former chief of the difficulties Benson had encountered during the prewar years and during the early days of the American intervention. He hoped that Benson would not "assume the whole burden . . . when you testify . . . as you did while you were Chief of Naval Operations." He thought that "what the Navy accomplished was accomplished to a large extent in spite of the Secretary." Benson's testimony could be a "great step . . . towards the accomplishment of the dream of all true Naval officers—that is to say, the establishment of a properly organized Navy Department presided over in its technical and military features by the Chief of Naval Operations whose position cannot be assailed."[20]

During the hearings Benson, as he usually did, expressed himself with utter clarity in behalf of strengthened authority for future chiefs of naval operations. "The office of the Chief of Naval Operations should have the responsibility for the preparation of the Navy as a whole. He should be strictly responsible for that, but he should have the authority that enables him to discharge that; all, of course, under a civilian Secretary of the Navy." Specifically, the CNO should have "authority to coordinate all the technical activities of the Navy Department [the bureaus], and he should be held responsible for their efficient coordination and cooperation." Benson believed it was also necessary to keep the CNO "fully informed as to the policies of the Government—I mean the political policies of the Government; what international problems were pending, what the international policy of the administration is at the time, any changes that might involve the distribution of forces." By this device the navy's activity could be subordinated appropriately to the political purposes of the president, a means of countering Daniels's fear that a strengthened naval staff would "Prussianize" the navy.[21]

A number of years later Admiral Benson frankly expressed his view of Secretary Daniels, something he had kept to himself as chief of naval operations. It was not a flattering view. Writing in 1927 of the war years, he noted:

> It was unfortunate that at this period we had as Secretary of the Navy a man who, while he was honest, earnest and sincere in his efforts to do the best with the situation, due to a very meager experience and lack of knowledge of international affairs, could not appreciate the fact that we could be drawn into the European struggle, and in addition to that, was more or less suspicious of military and naval men, believing their principal effort was to do things that would redound to their military glory [rather] than to the best interests of the country. He was honestly and firmly of the opinion that we could not be drawn into the war, consequently when requests were made upon him for increased appropriations, more officers or material, he often could not see his way clear to give full and wholehearted co-

operation and sometimes even refused consent. He was at times suspicious of changes in organization and things of that sort.

It is a tribute to Benson's tact that apparently his civilian chief never realized that the admiral respected his humanity but not his leadership.[22]

The hearings included some discussion of the "wool-pulling" statement Benson had made to Sims in March 1917. Benson did not deny that he had said something of the sort. Although he could not remember his exact words, he characterized them as a "figure of speech to impress upon Sims the delicacy of the situation." He deemed caution necessary in view of Sims's well-known sympathy for Great Britain, but he regretted that such things had been made public outside of the navy. Such disclosures did not contribute to the desirable Anglo-American relationship that had been established during the war.[23]

A journalist writing in the *Washington Post* on 13 May 1920 maintained that British officers attached little importance to the remarks Sims attributed to Benson, but Admiral Benson was greatly concerned that his naval associates in Great Britain might take offense. To Admiral Browning, perhaps his closest friend among British officers, he wrote in apparent distress: "I would very much like to have a long talk with you, and explain to you many things that I cannot in a letter." He had in mind especially the "unfortunate Sims affair that has weighed very heavily on my mind, because of the great admiration I have always had for the English people as a nation. . . . To have an attempt made to create a wrong impression in regard to my real feelings has been very painful. . . . Even now, many things are said in which I am misquoted, and a wrong use is made of my expressions and views."[24]

When Admiral Sims issued a concluding statement that reiterated his charges and argued that the former CNO had in effect corroborated them, Admiral Benson decided to provide a written refutation to be included in the published report of the hearings. He revealed the depth of his feelings in a letter to Commander Wilson Brown: "The point that really gives me worry is the fact that such things can be in our Navy, and that people who do such grave injustice, and whose actions are so injurious to naval morale and discipline, go apparently unpunished."[25]

In his refutation, Benson informed Senator Hale that his testimony "not only did not confirm but denied and refuted Admiral Sims' most serious charges." Admiral Benson summarized his views: "As Chief of Naval Operations I had the authority and responsibility of controlling operations. It was Admiral Sims' duty, as my assistant in Europe, to furnish all possible information, to make recommendations, and to carry out orders that were issued to him. It was my duty to make decisions and issue orders." He was convinced that the Navy Department had met its obligations "with efficiency and success; that the policies we adopted and our plans in accordance therewith were thoroughly justified by events, that the Office of Naval Operations, as well as the Navy as a whole, performed well a difficult task; cooperating from beginning to end with the Allies and rendering them every assistance in our power, and contributing very materially to the general result." He believed that his testimony and that of his assistants, Pratt and McKean, did not support Sims but instead constituted the "strongest refutation of his most serious charges."[26]

The hearings then came to an end and soon passed from the consciousness of the nation, becoming simply part of the preliminaries to the presidential campaign of 1920. If Sims had hoped to catapult himself into the position of chief of naval operations or at least commander in chief of the Atlantic Fleet, his hopes were shattered. Warren G. Harding, at the time running as the Republican candidate for the presidency, refused even to consult with Sims. Captain Pratt later concluded that Sims had allowed himself to be used for partisan purposes: "I have always felt and do now that the real motive behind it was political, not military." Daniels had been the prime target, but Pratt was sufficiently objective to recognize that some of the responsibility for prewar failures lay with the uniformed service. "They were the technicians, but there was too much petty animosity, too many bickerings over unessential details for anything big to really get over. If I may say so, it was all small stuff, too much of the personal equation entered into it." When the subcommittee reported its conclusions in 1921, three Republicans supported Sims, but two minority reports absolved the Navy Department. Those who had forced the hearings to be conducted had to contend with the fact that the navy's wartime performance had been excellent. Sims's charges appeared to reflect his pique at not having been able to dominate decision making from London.[27]

Although Admiral Benson emerged generally vindicated at the conclusion of the naval investigation, he suffered later at the hands of scholars and publicists. Sims and his circle advanced their view in varied forums and convinced many of their validity. Sims's book *The Victory at Sea*, which won the Pulitzer Prize in 1921, served to publicize its author, although it did not take up the issues of the naval investigation. Sims's biographer, Elting E. Morison, added to Sims's image as a progressive officer who had been badly treated because of his innovative ideas and forceful personality. Benson remained silent, convinced that this course was in the best interest of the naval service. He composed no memoir, and no one prepared a biography. These circumstances partly explain the failure of many to recognize the accomplishments of the United States Navy during World War I and to grant to Admiral Benson an appropriate measure of credit for his contributions to the victory of 1918.[28]

As it happened, however, the naval investigation of 1920 was not the last event in the career of the wartime CNO. Shortly after Admiral

Benson left the Navy Department, President Wilson asked him to lead the organization charged with the task of strengthening the United States merchant marine. The distinguished former naval officer was to devote many years to the United States Shipping Board.

CHAPTER XV

THE UNITED STATES SHIPPING BOARD 1920–1928

On 16 February 1920, Admiral Benson informed Secretary Daniels that Edith Bolling Wilson, the president's wife, had conveyed to him the hope that he would accept appointment as the chairman of the United States Shipping Board. The outgoing chairman, John Barton Payne, had been appointed secretary of the interior. Benson had expressed his reluctance to attempt "another hard job," and he had already accepted an invitation to become professor of international relations at the University of Notre Dame. Given the president's ill health, however, he felt compelled to accept the appointment to the board. His selection was announced on 17 February, and it became effective on 13 March. Later, when reporters asked him why Wilson had selected him, Benson responded that the president had not given him his reasons, but that his designation might have stemmed from a "feeling that I handled naval operations during the war in a manner that would assist in merchant marine affairs."[1]

The Shipping Board, a promotional and regulatory body intended to support the American merchant marine, had come into existence by act of Congress on 7 September 1916. The board's first chairman, Edward N. Hurley, served throughout the war, and John Barton Payne was the board's general counsel. When the United States entered the war, President Wilson established the Emergency Fleet Corporation, which was authorized to acquire, construct, and operate merchant shipping. Benson had concurred in Hurley's strong advocacy of a great merchant fleet and in his assumption that Anglo-American commercial rivalry would materialize during the postwar period.[2]

In assuming direction of the Shipping Board, Benson took on a formidable task. The merchant marine had expanded considerably during the war. In 1914 it had carried only 9.7 percent of the nation's waterborne foreign commerce, valued at $368,359,756, but for the fiscal year ending 30 June 1920, the volume increased to 42.7 percent, worth $5,071,623,227. Benson hoped to preserve this growth, but he recognized that foreign trade competitors planned to recapture prewar markets. Furthermore, American wartime enthusiasm for the merchant marine cooled rapidly, given an oncoming recession and the politics of the presidential election in 1920. After the armistice the Emergency Fleet Corporation had curtailed its program of acquisitions, making the adjustment to peacetime. Neither Hurley nor Payne had managed to accomplish much toward reorganization of the postwar merchant marine.[3]

During his first meeting with the Shipping Board, Benson gave notice of his intentions. He put himself on record as a proponent of an all-American merchant marine, consisting of ships built by Americans, owned by Americans, and operated by "out-and-out American personnel," sailing under the American flag to all parts of the world.[4]

As the leader of the Shipping Board, Benson emphasized two fundamental purposes. The merchant marine should constitute both an auxiliary force in support of the regular United States Navy and a powerful instrument for the accumulation of national wealth. He believed that such a merchant marine would serve others as well as the United States, because it would decrease the dependency of all nations on any single great maritime power. The nation he had in mind was Great Britain. Foreign rivals, he noted early in his tenure at the Shipping Board, must not be allowed to intimidate American shipping companies in order to dominate world trade: "We know that if they can get it by frightening our steamship companies they would do so." This point of view reflected his continuing commitment to the sturdy nationalism that had determined his course as chief of naval operations.[5]

Benson gave early notice of his activist approach to trade through his attitude toward the disposition of German ships that had been seized during the war and operated under the American flag. The Shipping Board had attempted to sell the vessels to private owners, but a federal judge had enjoined this policy. Responding to the inquiries of reporters, Benson argued that the vessels clearly belonged to the government and that the board was studying the matter. They might be allotted to American companies, a step that would require their reconditioning. When reporters asked whether some arrangement concerning the ships might be negotiated with the Hamburg-American Line, Benson indicated that none would be transferred to German control, but that U.S. "plans contemplate[d] the employment of German docks and terminals." He believed that other countries would take over these facilities should American companies refuse to use them. No doubt Benson took this position because of information he had received about British and Scandinavian efforts to employ German installations.[6]

On occasion Admiral Benson's activities at the Shipping Board revived old charges that he was prejudiced against Great Britain. Certainly his earlier concerns about British trade domination frequently influenced him, but it is important to distinguish between nationalist sentiments and Anglophobia. It is difficult to imagine that anyone dealing with trade questions after World War I, and especially a convinced nationalist, would not on occasion express concern about British activities. In a world of nations, nationalism is defensible until it degenerates into chauvinism. Benson's joust with Sims over the "wool-pulling" incident naturally meant that any action of his that could be construed as a function of prejudice would draw attention. If such a standard—nationalism—is to be used to define an Anglophobe, then the same label would have to apply to many other statesmen of the era, including President Wilson and Colonel House. It would just as surely become necessary to label as Americanophobes such stalwart British nationalists as Prime Minister Lloyd George, Sir Arthur Balfour, Sir Eric Geddes, and Admiral Wemyss.

Benson's suspicions of British intentions came to the surface when Sir Auckland Geddes, a brother of Sir Eric, became the British ambassador to the United States. Minister of national service in Lloyd George's government from 1917 to 1919, and, later, president of the Board of Trade, Sir Auckland came to his post with a considerable commitment to British trading interests. This circumstance disturbed President Wilson, who hoped to prevent the appointment. To Frank L. Polk, counsellor of the State Department, he wrote: "It is evident to me that we are on the eve of a commercial war of the severest sort, and I am afraid that Great Britain will prove capable of as great commercial savagery as Germany has displayed for so many years in her competitive methods." He inquired whether Polk thought it either "too late or unwise to suggest to the British Government through our Ambassador [John W. Davis] that we would welcome the appointment of someone who represented the political policies of the British Empire rather than its commercial policies." Admiral Benson shared this view, which was not without basis. Speaking of Sir Auckland's mission to Washington, his wife, Lady Isabella Gamble Geddes, said in 1957: "You do know why my husband was selected for this post? It was because of his commercial trade background."[7]

Shortly after Sir Auckland Geddes assumed his duties in Washington, he and Admiral Benson entered into a controversy over oil. Benson pursued an effort to ensure adequate oil supplies for the American merchant fleet as earnestly as he had sought while CNO to safeguard oil for the navy. He expressed himself on this question regularly;

for example, on 29 April 1920, before the chamber of commerce in Atlantic City, New Jersey, he said: "The modern ship must use oil . . . if it is to compete for world trade. If we are forced to return to coal as fuel we might as well give up the fight." Unfortunately, America's competitors had "obtained to an almost complete extent the absolute control of the foreign oil supply." There was real danger in this circumstance: "If legislation is not soon passed which will enable us to obtain foreign sources of oil supply we will awaken to find that there is no place in the world outside of our own ports where an American ship can be sure of obtaining fuel." Given British maritime interests and control of the world's oil supply and reserves, the United States "must approach the question of more trade in a spirit of friendly rivalry." Sir Auckland Geddes took issue with Benson during a speech the ambassador delivered in New York City on 25 May 1920. Referring to reports that Great Britain had acquired an "oil monopoly" and proposed "to hold the world to ransom," he claimed that 70 percent of the world's output of oil came from American wells and another 16 percent from Mexico. Americans, he continued, sought oil in at least ten other nations and held 82 percent of the world's supply at the time.[8]

Geddes chose to disregard the core of Admiral Benson's argument, which emphasized oil reserves rather than current oil production. American officials estimated that the United States held only 12 percent of the recoverable oil in the world and Mexico but 7.5 percent. This minor skirmish suggests the degree of tension that developed between the United States and Great Britain shortly after World War I as each nation sought to strengthen its position in world markets.[9]

One of Admiral Benson's early accomplishments at the Shipping Board was to settle the vexing question of how to dispose of ships owned by the government, as well as how to operate them pending their sale. On 15–16 April 1920 he convened a conference of seventeen leading businessmen, Hurley and Payne among them, to discuss the estimated three billion dollars worth of property in the hands of the Shipping Board. An overwhelming majority supported private ownership of the merchant marine. As a result, a committee was formed to draw up a plan within thirty days to specify the method, price, and terms of sale to private purchasers. By August 1920 the terms of sale were established, and the government-owned fleet was placed on the market.[10]

By far the most important achievement of Benson's tenure as chairman of the Shipping Board was the passage of the Merchant Marine Act of 1920, an important attempt to eliminate the historic disadvantages of American shippers. Vessels sailing from the United States could easily find cargoes, but they were often unable to locate them for the return voyage. British traders did not face this problem because, unlike America, Great Britain had to import large amounts of raw materials.

Further disadvantages stemmed from high construction and labor costs in the United States as well as expensive maintenance and insurance. In remarks to Senator Wesley Jones (D-Wash.), the sponsor of the legislation often known as the Jones Act, Benson insisted that the means of ensuring Americans a competitive position in world trade was to provide a range of subsidies.[11]

The Jones Act did not pass Congress without opposition. Postmaster General Albert S. Burleson and Secretary of Agriculture David F. Houston questioned certain provisions during a discussion of the act in the cabinet. Critics feared a trade war. Benson's answer was that the bill would "meet and offset the countless discriminations by other nations against American shipping with which Shipping Board ships and privately owned vessels of the United States have had to contend." This argument prevailed; Congress passed the Jones Act only thirty minutes before adjournment, and President Wilson signed it on 5 June 1920. This action was an early step away from the principles of free trade competition, one of many that occurred during the 1920s, even before the Republican party gained ascendancy.[12]

In addition to enacting measures to protect American commerce, the Jones Act defined the postwar functions of the Shipping Board. The organization was charged to encourage a merchant marine "of the best equipped and most suitable types of vessels sufficient to carry the greater proportion of its commerce and serve as a naval or military auxiliary in time of war or national emergency" and to dispose of government-owned ships and shipping property. A multitude of problems came under its jurisdiction, including repair, maintenance, and operation of government-owned ships, docks, and other facilities until disposal, sale, or lease; maritime insurance and labor unrest; and technical matters such as diesel engines, electrical drives, fathometers, and salt detectors. Benson aptly summarized the intent of the board's missions: "The purpose of the Board is to establish a permanent American merchant marine ultimately resting on private enterprise and private capital." Why was it important to accomplish this task? Benson answered: "If it is the desire of the American people to maintain their present high standards of living and to retain even approximately their present position in finance and trade, our annual surplus must be sold in foreign markets; and in order to do this it is necessary to have a merchant marine owned and controlled by American citizens."[13]

Admiral Benson did not believe that the legislation of 1920 was sufficiently rigorous, but it aroused considerable criticism at the time and since. British interests argued that preferential treatment violated the freedom of the seas: during peacetime, they claimed, the phrase meant nothing "unless ships of all nationalities receive[d] equal treatment in every port." Lloyd's of London warned that activation of certain provisions in the Jones Act would force the company to withhold insurance from American shippers. For the same reason other nations, for example, Japan, threatened to divert tonnage from the United States. Benson argued that the American measures were justifiable if others used "unfair methods." Although he thought trade wars "deplorable," he argued that the United States could not "submit to insulting restrictions imposed by any foreign nation." His objective was "ship independence," and he believed that his nation was in a position to achieve this goal: "We've got the ships, we've got the money too." Critics of Benson adjudged these views "anti-foreign" or even "xenophobic," but Benson considered his preferred course to be not only in the national interest but also a contribution to equal opportunity for all nations on the high seas.[14]

Another dispute developed between the United States and Great Britain when an American company made an agreement with the Hamburg-American Line. On 19 June 1920 the American Ship and Commerce Corporation, whose president was W. Averell Harriman, concluded a two-pronged agreement with the German firm that provided reciprocal services between Atlantic-Gulf ports and Germany and also between Germany and ports elsewhere in the world. Benson responded to accusations that Germany and the United States had begun a trade war against Britain with a question: "Is the writer aware that Great Britain has chartered to Germany many of the former German vessels in order to compete with us for German trade?" Benson defended his position in a letter to his friend Admiral Browning, beginning with a familiar generalization: "My idea is that most of the troubles that begin between nations and finally produce wars, arise from commercial envies and jealousies." His position, he continued, was "one of conciliation, an effort to give the other fellow a fair show, and to do everything that I can to bring commercial interests in various countries to a realization that the ocean is a free field, and that everyone must have his just and fair proportion of the fruits of this field, depending entirely upon his own initiating energy and efficiency."[15]

Benson encountered some opposition to the Hamburg-American deal within his own organization, especially from the general counsel, Robert A. Dean, who thought it unduly favorable to German interests. He argued that it violated the intent of the Jones Act because it promoted German as well as American trade. When Harriman learned of these objections, he responded that no alien money was invested in his company and that it was entirely invulnerable to foreign control. The services in question were simply "feeder" aids of the type that all shipping companies required; he promised that Germany would never gain control of such services. Benson then maintained that the agreement was "nothing short of heaven-sent from the standpoint of the future of the American mercantile marine." It was important to make use of the vast volume of shipping that had become available as a consequence of the war. "If we hadn't accepted the [German] offer," he said, "the British would have, and Scandinavian shippers were nibbling at it too."[16]

Resignations from the Shipping Board, the president's slowness in filling vacancies, and the president's reluctance to put into effect the protective provisions of the Jones Act hampered Admiral Benson's activity. Wilson's tactics raised the question of whether he intended to reappoint Admiral Benson as chairman of the Shipping Board. Benson's advocates expressed concern and support. A writer in the *Charleston American* maintained: "There will be jubilation in Liverpool if Benson is not reappointed. There will be great rejoicing in the ranks of the pro-British in America. Will Benson have to pay the price of being an American in the Wilsonian era?" His former aide Commander Carter wrote from Boston: "How difficult indeed it is for an honest man with the good of his country at heart to accomplish anything constructive when the law is circumvented by those in highest authority and political expediency is permitted to take precedence over great national principles."[17]

President Wilson eventually selected new members of the Shipping Board and reappointed Admiral Benson to a six-year term, but he did not act until after the presidential election, which went against the Democratic party. The newly appointed members were given recess appointments and sworn in on 1 December 1920, but they were unable to act effectively until the Senate confirmed them and voted an appropriation to finance operations. The Sixty-sixth Congress, meeting in a lame duck session, took no action. It seemed unlikely that the new president, Warren G. Harding, would reappoint Benson and others, although the admiral enjoyed some support from prominent Republicans, according to a report in the *Washington Times*. Commander Carter gloomily anticipated the worst: "The general tendency seems to be to wield the knife. . . . While nothing would please me so much as to see you triumph when the time comes and see your own clean work stand out in such a pronounced manner that you will be an exception to the general rule, I think you should be prepared to be displaced."[18]

After his inauguration, President Harding asked Admiral Benson to carry out the functions of the Shipping Board until he made other arrangements. Benson agreed to remain in harness, informing the new chief executive: "Having now been assured of your desires, it is a pleasure to serve until such time as to suit your convenience." This outcome must have provided a certain satisfaction, given the doubts cast on Benson's performance during the waning moments of the Wilson administration.[19]

Meanwhile Admiral Benson found himself involved in a difficult situation that had been developing for some time, a general maritime strike. The wage agreement that had been negotiated in May 1919 expired one year later at a most difficult moment—a general depression

W. S. Benson, chairman, and members of the United States Shipping Board,
1 December 1920.

in the worldwide shipping industry had struck American companies
with particular force because of high operating costs. Benson was anxious to ensure a square deal for merchant seamen, but he was also
concerned about the plight of the shippers. Informing labor and management that it was absolutely essential to cut operating expenses to a
minimum, he proposed to reduce wages in government-owned ships by
25 percent and to eliminate overtime at sea.[20]

When representatives of labor rejected Benson's proposal and
threatened to call a strike, management responded with a compromise
that led to a crisis. The American Shipowners' Association proposed to
reduce wages by 15 rather than 25 percent. Benson insisted on lower
subsistence payments and elimination of overtime at sea. After the
workers rejected this position, Benson ordered the wage cut, and the
merchant seamen called a strike to begin on 1 May. To put teeth into
his stand, the admiral called on former members of the navy to operate
the ships and pledged the support of the Shipping Board to those merchant seamen who remained on the job. Benson and Secretary of Labor
James J. Davis worked together to arrange a settlement. At length, on
13 June, the workers accepted an agreement that included a wage cut
of 15 percent and the elimination of compensation for overtime.[21]

The settlement of the maritime strike was Admiral Benson's last
act as chairman of the Shipping Board. Appointing Albert D. Lasker
to this position, President Harding nevertheless asked the admiral to
remain for a year as a member of the board. Harding wanted to achieve

continuity by taking advantage of Benson's knowledge and experience. Although reluctant to continue, Benson agreed to stay on, informing the president that he had "sacrificed his natural inclination" to retire. At the end of Benson's tenure as chairman, members of the staff of the Shipping Board and representatives of shipping companies gave him a bust, the work of the noted sculptor Jo Davidson, which bore the inscription: "To Rear Admiral W. S. Benson, U.S.N. (Ret.), Chairman of the United States Shipping Board, presented by some of his loyal friends and admirers of America." On 14 June the new members of the Shipping Board were sworn in and held a conference with the president. Lasker characterized Harding as supportive of the reestablishment of a strong merchant marine, although he opposed operation of ships "at ruinous losses to accomplish that end." Benson then took a vacation— he had not taken one during his eighteen months as chairman of the Shipping Board—and on his return to Washington represented himself to Charles Belknap as in the best of health: "Physically I never felt better in my life."[22]

From the earliest moments, Admiral Benson expressed great doubt about the international conference on naval armaments that the Harding administration arranged to take place in Washington toward the end of 1921. Naval officers had played a minimal role in preliminary planning. How prepared was the Republican leadership to sacrifice naval power at the altar of political expediency? Benson wondered whether Harding and his secretary of state, Charles Evans Hughes, might make unwise concessions as compensation for the failure of the United States to enter the League of Nations. On 16 May 1921 Benson sent the president a memorandum that outlined his views forcefully. Harking back to his confrontation at the Paris peace conference with British naval leaders, particularly Admiral Wemyss and Walter Long, he interpreted British motives as a "deliberate intention . . . to use every possible influence" to block the American building program and to place "every possible obstacle" in the path of the American merchant marine. The same British government was still in power. It still hoped to "hamper . . . and if possible destroy our commercial development." This objective lay behind British "propaganda for disarmament and other features tending to keep the United States in a position subordinate to the British Empire." Benson called for every possible effort "to meet and defeat the efforts of British propagandists."[23]

In September 1921 Benson returned to these views in responding to a questionnaire the General Board sent to twenty-six high-ranking naval officers, asking for their views on a "basic plan" for the conference. In particular, the board sought opinions on two questions: "Under present world conditions what would be an equitable ratio of naval strength of Great Britain, United States, Japan, France, and Italy?" and "What is the minimum relative strength appropriate to the American

Navy if the Anglo-Japanese Alliance continues?" Members of the panel were also asked to comment on twenty-one proposals that were under consideration, one of which was a plan to prohibit both direct and indirect subsidies for merchant fleets. Admiral Benson was well prepared to respond to the General Board; these issues had been on his mind for many years.[24]

For the moment Benson ignored the board's two basic inquiries, choosing instead to identify certain principles that ought to guide the United States as it considered placing limitations on naval armaments. No plan for disarmament should "apply to any instruments of warfare which (because of their nature and size) could be secretly made and stored in peace time by nations acting in bad faith." He also expressed concern about activities that "can be evaded or can be concealed, though built into final position"—his response to the idea of prohibiting subsidies. With these observations, he concluded his remarks, noting that he would comment later on subjects he had not covered in his initial communication.[25]

A few days later Benson extended his comments on naval disarmament, preparing a document titled "Notes Relating to the International Conference on the Limitation of Armaments." Once again he noted the "determination of Great Britain to maintain a position of dominance in world affairs, and a determination to so manipulate the interests of the minor powers as to secure sufficient nations to outvote and block the United States in any efforts which might in any way interfere with British domination." He presumed that before the Washington Conference began, other powers would reach "secret understandings." What posture, then, should the United States assume toward the forthcoming negotiations? The nation, which had emerged from the war "practically unharmed financially," had called the conference "out of a feeling of sympathy" for suffering European nations. The United States should be prepared to accept proposals that would permit those countries to "reduce very materially their expenses for armaments and rehabilitate themselves." Obviously Benson did not think that the United States should accept proposals that endangered its naval position. Because other nations owed the United States large sums, the American negotiators were in a position to "dictate terms of naval disarmament."[26]

About a month later Benson completed his second letter for the General Board on the disarmament conference, in which he reiterated views that had been with him from the time of the Paris peace conference. He opposed any reduction in the naval building program, preferring expansion until the nation possessed a "complete naval establishment in the Pacific independent of that in the Atlantic, and ample to meet all reasonable demands there in time of war." If this goal could not be adopted at present, it should be established as a future objective.

Only by this policy could the United States ensure safety on both maritime fronts, "even if disaster befell the [Panama] Canal." This point of view breathed continuing distrust of Great Britain and Japan, especially in combination. Finally, Benson once again professed his faith in the good intentions of the United States and the nation's significance for others: "The nations of the world have confidence in our justice and contentment. They are not suspicious of us, for they know we have no desire for conquest." The United States Navy took on great importance in this context. Other nations believed that the United States Navy was "intended only for defense; also with possibilities of use in the protection of world wide international rights, generally, as in the great war."[27]

In these terms Benson staked out views that represented his experience as chief of naval operations during World War I and the Paris peace conference. Some observers thought that Admiral Benson was the logical choice as President Harding's adviser on naval questions during the conference because of his wartime experience and later service at the Shipping Board, but these were surely unrealistic expectations. Benson's outlook was at variance with the premises that underlay the negotiating position of the United States during the disarmament negotiations of 1921–22. The "basic plan" that the General Board submitted to Secretary of State Hughes was rejected and the task transferred to a "more reasonable group."[28]

Benson made one more attempt to influence the negotiations after learning of the proposal to establish a ratio of 5:5:3 between the navies of the United States, Great Britain, and Japan, writing the assistant secretary of the navy, Theodore Roosevelt, Jr., to complain about the "decidedly unbalanced situation" that would result from any such agreement. A solution might be found, Benson suggested, by allowing France sufficient strength to "offset Japan's naval strength." This expedient would deal effectively with a potential Anglo-Japanese combination. The interests of Britain and Japan overrode those of any other two nations: "In case of trouble they would naturally stand together. This would permit a combination against the United States."[29]

Nothing came of the objections that Admiral Benson and other exponents of a dominant navy and merchant marine posed to the arrangements that issued from the Washington conference despite the decision to terminate the Anglo-Japanese alliance, an apparent indication that the British preferred to cast their lot with the United States than with Japan. Benson, unsatisfied, viewed the Washington negotiations as merely a "sequel" to the heated exchanges that took place in 1919 between Daniels, Long, Wemyss, and himself. To Daniels he wrote in distress: "I shall always feel that the British, being unable to accomplish their desired end of remaining supreme on the sea in any other way, brought about this conference, the result of which leaves them decidedly superior on the sea."[30]

Admiral Benson's reservations about British naval intentions did not affect his close friendship with Vice Admiral Browning. When Browning paid a visit to the United States in 1923, he became Benson's house guest. Acknowledging the Bensons' hospitality, he wrote to Mrs. Benson: "It will always be a pleasure to look back upon this visit to your house and to feel that that friendship was cemented that I have felt from the first for the Admiral and afterwards for yourself." To Benson he wrote: "After the great privilege of seeing a home life which is really a beautiful instance of life long devotion and which you allowed me to witness for myself I am the more anxious that the sea shall not be allowed to completely separate us."[31]

Developments at the Shipping Board were as disturbing to Admiral Benson as the course of the Washington conference. President Harding showed no more inclination to enforce the Merchant Marine Act of 1920 than had his predecessor. The new chairman, Lasker, was inclined to recall the ships operated by the board from active service. Benson did not question Lasker's good intentions, but he thought that those who believed economies would result from reducing operations failed to "grasp the great principle involved that if, by doing so, we withdraw our ships from the trade routes already established we simply abandon them to our foreign competitors."[32]

The lassitude of the Harding administration probably lessened the pleasure that Admiral Benson derived from its continuing confidence in his ability, reflected in further service on the Shipping Board. When Benson's one-year appointment expired early in June 1922, President Harding named him to a full six-year term. For this reason Benson continued in government service until 1928, although most of his old naval colleagues, including Sims, left the public stage shortly after the war.

Admiral Benson had refused to offer an account of his service as chief of naval operations, but in 1923 he wrote a book about his views on the merchant marine titled *The Merchant Marine: "A Necessity in Time of War; A Source of Independence and Strength in Time of Peace,"* which included a systematic presentation of his views on naval and maritime affairs. He discussed the role of sea power in the rise of great nations, describing the early activity of Great Britain in developing a merchant marine. He then reviewed the growth of the American merchant marine and the nature of government assistance to shipping. Although he refused to comment on whether the executive was justified in failing to put the Merchant Marine Act of 1920 into effect, "ignoring a policy and direction so definitely ordered by Congress," he questioned the failure of both Wilson and Harding to order protective tariffs. His prime objective was to urge government aid for the American merchant marine so that it could compete successfully with the merchant marines of other nations.

In 1923 Admiral Benson took advantage of an invitation to review Winston Churchill's account of World War I, *The World Crisis*, to answer those who accused him of unreasoning anti-British sentiments. In a sympathetic review, he argued that Americans should learn from the British how to serve their national interest. "Self-interest naturally plays a large part in international relations; nor should it be otherwise. Officials of Governments are appointed to protect and enforce, consistently with honor and their obligations, the people's rights; it is not their privilege or function to spend either the lives or the wealth of the people in a spirit of chivalry, apart from the *interests* of the people they represent." Churchill had revealed "nothing discreditable to the English people" in arguing that it was in the national interest to aid France. He hoped that every American would read the book "not only to gain an insight of European diplomacy and international dealings, but in the hope that the American reader will imbibe some of that splendid love of country that so strongly dominates the author."[33]

Admiral Benson's service on the Shipping Board extended to a third presidential administration on 2 August 1923, when, on the death of President Harding, Calvin Coolidge became chief executive, but Benson's last years in government were generally frustrating. He devoted himself to certain issues in which he had a special interest, but his activism, especially his advocacy of strong governmental intervention in mercantile affairs, ran counter to the desires of the Coolidge administration.

Beginning in 1921 Benson strongly advocated conversion of merchant ships to diesel power. A test of reconversion, which equipped the *William Penn* (12,500 tons deadweight) with diesel engines, proved successful. The vessel left New York for the Far East on 3 September 1921 and returned 197 days later (19 March 1922), having traversed 28,500 miles without needing repairs by shore establishments. The diesel engines functioned without difficulty, maintaining speed and low fuel consumption. Encouraged by this outcome, Benson led a drive to convert other merchant ships to diesel power, a costly project. He proposed the use of the merchant marine construction fund to equip vessels owned by the Shipping Board. Congress eventually passed legislation that authorized this procedure for 375 selected ships. Unfortunately, the conversion proved financially unsuccessful. Many years later Captain Richard D. Gatewood recalled that the converted vessels were not fully utilized because few marine engineers were acquainted with them and few schools existed to provide necessary training. The country was not yet prepared for this policy; Gatewood thought that the situation "was a little like the present day potentialities of atomic energy." Only in later years did the merchant marine realize the economy inherent in diesel operation.[34]

Admiral Benson also encountered frustration in another farsighted campaign, an attempt to provide for construction of modern merchant ships. The policy of the Shipping Board was to sell ships in the hands of the government to private interests. This initiative encountered difficulties, partly because economic recession made it difficult to find buyers. The board then faced a choice between operating vessels or laying them up. These obsolete ships were unable to compete with the modern vessels of other nations. Therefore, Benson proposed to construct 230,000 tons of new shipping annually, along with two passenger liners at 30 thousand tons each with a speed of 20 knots to operate in the North Atlantic. Noting that American vessels carried less than 19 percent of American exports and that American shipping earned only 30 percent of the charges for transporting both imports and exports, Benson called for government action to place American interests "more nearly on a parity with foreign competitors." The United States, he continued, had constructed only 18 of the 1,300 ships built since the end of the war. "We have slid back to tenth place," he said. "Even Russia has passed us." Arguing that the combined strength of naval and merchant tonnage constituted the true measure of maritime power, he insisted that after the Washington Treaties the United States did not have "parity with Great Britain in naval strength as was originally intended, and that with respect to other nations the United States had dropped considerably below the ratio agreed to in principle at the Washington Arms Conference." Unless the ratio included auxiliary vessels, measures of comparative naval strength lacked reality.[35]

When he failed to gain support despite the encouragement of many people in shipping, Benson unveiled his distress in a letter to Josephus Daniels. He thought the Coolidge administration terribly remiss in permitting a situation to develop "so un-American and so contrary to the fundamental principles of our Government" as he understood them; "It has been almost impossible for me to remain on the Board. . . . I am staying on as a public duty, and at great personal sacrifice and discomfort."[36]

Interspersed with frustrations were gratifying moments. As Benson approached his seventieth birthday, having served his country for fifty years, an "Honorary Committee of One Hundred" composed of prominent men from all sections of the country sponsored a testimonial dinner to mark the occasion. When Bernard M. Baruch accepted membership on the committee, he described Benson as "a real tower of strength in war and in the period which followed." President Coolidge wrote to the sponsors: "It is very seldom that one person has an official connection with the Government for so long a time." On 19 September, at a special meeting, the Shipping Board passed a resolution that extended heartiest congratulations to Benson and expressed the hope that he would be "spared to us and to the country for many, many years."

That evening dignitaries of the cabinet, Supreme Court, army, navy, diplomatic corps, and the Catholic hierarchy were among those in attendance at a dinner in the grand ballroom of the Mayflower Hotel. Secretary of the Navy Curtis D. Wilbur conveyed the official congratulations of the Navy Department: "From John Paul Jones to Admiral Benson the same spirit of self-sacrifice has actuated the men of our Navy. Thank God that at the head of our Navy in the last war was a man who believed not only in man, but in God." Newton D. Baker extolled Benson for "flawless cooperation between the Army and Navy," crediting him with the successful operation of the convoy system and the construction of the North Sea barrage. Bishop C. Boyle of Pittsburgh said that Benson "would have been an ideal citizen of an imaginary commonwealth where every citizen was imbued with the ideal of unselfish service."

Benson especially appreciated the presence of many of the officers with whom he had been associated during the war. He wrote to Secretary Baker and Admiral Mayo to thank them for being present, and he received warm replies. Mayo wrote: "Not only did I consider it a pleasure to take part in the testimonial banquet in your honor, but I considered it a duty I owed you in appreciation of our long and close associations in the Service, and also because I felt that, owing to our close association during the World War, . . . I could show by my presence at this testimonial that I had appreciated the great value of your services to the Navy and to the country." He added: "And may I also at this time again assure you that I really did appreciate your consideration of me during the time that I was Commander-in-Chief." Baker's accolade must have been especially welcome: "The fact is, that we have treated our War leaders shabbily. England gave hers Earldoms and fortunes, we hardly know the names of ours! Your case is peculiarly impressive since you have never said a word or nodded a hint in your own behalf—so I simply must do it for you if history is to tell the truth!"[37]

The situation at the Shipping Board did not improve as time passed. In 1926 Benson experienced a particularly galling setback. A new chairman, T. V. O'Connor, acting with the support of several other new members of the Shipping Board who had been appointed to succeed "those who had voted against Administration policies," deposed the president of the Emergency Fleet Corporation, Captain Elmer E. Crowley, over the objections of Benson and another member. To Edward N. Hurley, Benson wrote: "I do not mind telling you that I do not think I have ever been so completely down and out in my life." He had entertained a high opinion of his fellow board members and hope for improvement in the merchant marine, but the vote against Crowley

William Shepherd Benson. From the program book of the "Testimonial Dinner" held 19 September 1925 in honor of Admiral Benson on his seventieth birthday.

"knocked the very last pin of hope from under" him: "I shall try not to let it discourage me to the extent of giving up the fight."[38]

Admiral Benson's term on the Shipping Board was scheduled to expire in June 1928, and it seemed unlikely that President Coolidge would reappoint him, given Benson's opposition to the administration's views. Although he remained unhappy with the situation on the Shipping Board, he did not relish the thought of being "dropped out as undesirable," hoping instead that he would enjoy the option of resigning after an offer of reappointment. This was not to be; he and a fellow member, Philip S. Teller, were replaced by appointees prepared to support the "Coolidge policy of placing the shipping business in private hands." Benson revealed his disappointment at this outcome in a sad letter to his son Howard: "You no doubt will be glad to know that circumstances have conspired to compel me to take a rest. Ere this reaches you, you will know that the President has refused to reappoint me. . . . The way it has been done hurts my pride."[39]

Benson, the proponent of subsidies and protective tariffs—energetic governmental activism—found himself generally in the minority during the affluent 1920s. His greatest success was the Merchant Marine Act of 1920, but the promise of that legislation was never realized. Captain Gatewood summarized the difficulties that the admiral encountered on the Shipping Board: "There were days when few appreciated the importance of the merchant marine. Out of the relatively few people who did, many wanted to make money quickly." Benson left the Shipping Board full of honor and respect, despite his inability to sway three presidents to his views on maritime questions. Just before Benson retired, his colleagues adopted a resolution that conveyed "their appreciation of the ability and zeal so conspicuously displayed by Admiral Benson as a Commissioner of this Board and to extend to him their most sincere congratulations on his long and distinguished career in the service of his Country, and to express to him the high esteem in which they personally hold their association with him." This testimonial came at the end of over half a century in the service of his country.[40]

CHAPTER XVI

LAST DAYS

William S. Benson became a private citizen at the age of seventy-three, retaining his permanent rank of rear admiral. Although disturbed at the manner of his departure from public service, he soon warmed to the joys of retirement. He wrote to his son Howard: "Each day increases my satisfaction in being free [from Washington routine] . . . and I feel quite sure time will increase that feeling." From Admiral Browning came a sad but loving encomium: "I find time hanging heavily on hand, with little to do except the garden, chickens, ducks, and beer. I am afraid you may be undergoing the same experience, but you have put in so much useful work for your country before retirement, and that will be lasting consolation."[1]

Unlike many of his World War I associates, Benson chose not to write his memoirs. Although he began the task, he soon abandoned it, concerned that his story might have a negative effect on his two sons, both naval officers. Admiral Benson discussed this possibility with them. Rear Admiral Samuel McGowan, former chief of the Bureau of Supplies and Accounts, was present during one such session. Concerned that Benson's sons might not recognize their father's importance, he praised the admiral highly and later wrote: "I am glad Wyse was there to hear what I had to say [about you]. It's *due* to your children that they know from outside and direct from truthful people who know, that their honored father is not only a *big* man but a *great man*! Anybody who thinks otherwise is either a fool or a knave—or both." McGowan added: "I know it, and it gives me genuine joy to proclaim it from the house-tops." Both Howard and Wyse had great respect for their father. They deplored the situation that developed just after the war and felt that the hearings injured their careers.

Although Benson did not record his personal comments, he was anxious to preserve a sound historical record for future generations. For this reason he proposed to Admiral Coontz, his successor as CNO, the establishment of a historical division to store information "for the benefit of American naval history." He suggested as a specific project the editing of war films to "bring before the people the real part the Navy played in the Great World War."[2] Others shared Benson's views. The Navy Department soon created a historical division headed by Dudley Knox.

Family life had always served as Admiral Benson's refuge, and his retirement allowed him to indulge this interest. The comfortable home he had been able to build at 2420 Tracy Street in northwest Washington provided shelter for much of his family. In residence was Mrs. Benson's mother, Mrs. Frances O. Wyse. Herman Krafft, Benson's son-in-law, and Benson's son Wyse were on duty at the Naval Academy, a billet that allowed them to bring their children frequently to the house of their grandparents. Howard's children came less often because he lived on the West Coast, but young "Howdy" occasionally came for an extended stay.

The Benson grandchildren loved both the admiral and Mrs. Benson, but Howdy recalls that "Grandfather . . . awed us. . . . I remember him as being very dignified and quite regal. Although he enjoyed his grandchildren, we were always children." Benson's mien bespoke a man used to command, but his kindly eyes revealed a gentle consideration. The youngsters would sit on his lap, and he would take out his pocket watch for them to listen to. Wyse's daughter Dorothy wrote: "He always seemed so kind." He nevertheless sought to inculcate in them, as he had in his own children, values that he treasured: honesty, reliability, integrity, loyalty, patriotism, respect for authority, acceptance of responsibility, and religious faith.[3]

Admiral Benson frequently took part in the activities of his grandchildren. When Frederic Krafft, May's son, undertook to build a boat, his grandfather offered assistance and then had to suspend his boat-building efforts because of a sore knee. Benson wrote Frederic to say that when he recovered he would resume the hunt for a propeller: "You have done a splendid job on your boat and I am anxious to help you out." He also encouraged the lad to continue his membership in the Boy Scouts: "You are the one to whom the boys look for example. God bless you my dear boy, will be the constant prayer of your affectionate Grandpa." On one occasion Frederic resisted his parents' desire that he attend a private school run by the Benedictine order. He succeeded in gaining the intercession of his grandfather, which proved decisive. Benson then told Frederic that his parents, in yielding to his wishes, had made a "very great concession"; the "burden of responsibility" now rested with him:

> I would suggest you show in every way you can to your Daddy that you appreciate his wanting to send you and his concession in yielding to your wishes in the case. . . . Now, my dear boy, please do not think I am preaching. It is only my affection for you and my desire to help you. Although I am seventy-six years old, I have not forgotten my boyhood days. Nor must you think I want to make you take too serious a view of life. On the contrary, I want you to hold your head high and with a clear conscience look everybody in the eye and be happy. Now is the time to lay the foundation of the great fundamentals of life.

Surely this advice reflected Benson's own experience and the stance he had maintained throughout his own life.[4]

Benson never forgot the estrangement from his mother that developed because of his conversion to Roman Catholicism. He loved her dearly and sought to eradicate the memory of the strain that had developed between them. In 1929 he took action, presenting to the Wesleyan Female College of Macon a beautiful copy of Raphael's *Madonna of the Chair*. Shirley Ann Bakewell, a great-great-niece of Admiral Benson's mother, unveiled the picture on 6 January 1929. On this occasion Benson wrote to the *Wesleyan Alumnae* in praise of his mother: "I consider it a great privilege to have been given the opportunity of making this offering which may be to the world and posterity a token of filial affection to the dearest and best of mothers—she who instilled into me the fine principles of right living that have carried me successfully through life." It was "also a token of the appreciation of the splendid institution, the Alma Mater of my mother, as well as of many other noble women of the Southland who have from the beginning exerted such an exalted and ennobling influence, not only upon the South, but upon the entire country."

This tribute to Benson's mother brightened the celebration of the fiftieth anniversary of the admiral and his bride. Good weather blessed the occasion, the garden was beautiful, and the celebrants included many loved ones: all three of the children, the grandchildren, and Mrs. Benson's brother Dr. William Wyse and his wife, Winfred.[5]

One shadow darkened the Bensons' otherwise happy domestic life. The failure of the nation to grant the admiral the rank of full admiral embittered Benson; he felt so humiliated that he suspended the exchange of visits with naval friends that was of great importance to the sociable Mrs. Benson. Sensitive to his wife's feelings, he explained the situation to his son Howard: "Mama does not seem at all inclined to take the car and make visits. She will not go anywhere unless I go with her . . . and I do not feel at all inclined to call under the circumstances, so we do very little calling."[6]

Fiftieth anniversary of Benson's wedding. Picture was taken on 6 August 1929 at 2420 Tracy Place in Washington, D.C. *Left to right:* Francis Wyse Benson, Mrs. W. S. Benson, Admiral Benson, Mrs. Mary ("May") Benson Krafft, and Howard H. J. Benson.

Happily, on 21 June 1930, Congress rectified this situation. On that date 302 retired officers of the army, navy, and Marine Corps were restored to their wartime ranks. Benson was one of ten naval officers who received full brevet rating. On this occasion Vice Admiral Browning wrote: "I am so very glad that your rank of full Admiral has been restored to you, though unaccompanied with the pay proper to the rank. It was an ill reward for all your great services to your country when Congress deprived you of it, & I cannot understand their attitude, for you were never a political admiral." Colonel House wrote in a similar vein: "I have always felt that your remarkable services in the Great War were never wholly appreciated."[7]

Benson did not completely abandon his past; during his retirement he sustained certain of his friendships and nursed certain of his antagonisms. He remained in contact with Josephus Daniels, although he had become quite irritated in 1921 when the former secretary of the navy had failed to give due notice to the Office of Naval Operations in a series of articles printed in the *Washington Evening Star*. To Charles

Belknap he noted that it was difficult to understand "how an honest man can take refuge behind the work of other people and attempt to reap the credit that is due them"; it was best to "let bygones be bygones" and instead to "look forward with buoyant hope to an awakening of the American people that will arouse the real, true, patriotic element to a sense of their individual as well as collective responsibilities." Benson felt much differently about Colonel House, who took advantage of several opportunities to honor his former colleague. In 1929 he arranged for Benson to become one of his wartime associates depicted in the stained-glass windows that graced the room at Yale University where the House papers were deposited for the use of scholars.[8]

Admiral Benson never became reconciled to Admiral Sims's pretensions about his position in London. When authorities in Lowell, Massachusetts, proposed to honor Sims as the commanding officer of the navy during the war, as one who held a position similar to that of General Pershing in the army, Benson wrote to a newspaper in Lowell noting that there was "absolutely no comparison whatever between the position held by General Pershing in the Army and that of Admiral Sims in the Navy." Sims, he continued, "lived in a hotel in London, and the U.S. Government gave him an allowance for his living expenses. He was provided with ample office room. . . . At no time was he afloat, except in making trips across the Channel or during the visits to the Grand Fleet or visiting some station for inspection purposes."[9]

The building program of the navy and the periodic conferences on limitations of naval armaments continued to hold Admiral Benson's interest. When the nation debated the question of whether to accept membership in the World Court, he took occasion to render a cautionary comment on the League of Nations and disarmament conferences as well as on the court. As always, he stressed that "national preservation and expediency are the prime factors that control [European statesmen] in all their international dealings." He declared support for the league and other such organizations, but only in appropriate circumstances, noting that the league of 1919 was "nothing more than an attempt to have the United States guarantee that those nations which had divided up the territory taken from Germany, Austria, and other countries, would hold their ill-gotten gains for all times." When naval disarmament discussions took place in 1927 and 1930, Benson strongly supported the views of Admiral Hilary Jones, a principal naval adviser on both occasions, who manifested Bensonian doubts about the good faith of the European negotiators.[10]

After the London Naval Conference of 1930 Admiral Benson communicated to his friend Admiral Browning a valedictory pronouncement on such international enterprises. He opposed them because the "conditions and interests of various nations are too varied and diverse to try to equalize such matters. There is always danger in the suspicions that arise that each is trying to get some advantage over the others. When such is the case it is apt to create unkind feelings rather than increase more kindly feelings." Benson was among the many participants in World War I whose support of unilateralism reflected disappointment at the peace settlement arrived at in 1919–20.[11]

As CNO Benson had established good relationships with the several bureau heads in the Navy Department, and during the postwar years he had reorganized the office; he remained interested in this area after he left operations. In retirement he deprecated the failure to sustain what he considered a sound conception of the office. His wartime colleagues recognized this commitment. His former assistant, Pratt, wrote: "When I first came to you, I had long been associated with Sims, but when I had been with you for some time, I knew that it was the most fortunate thing which could happen that you not Sims was the Chief of Naval Operations. The Service owes you a debt of gratitude which few ever will know but which I do know." McGowan expressed similar views: "As Chief of Naval Operations you literally held the Navy by one hand and its unpopular civilian head by the other and (by doing every hour of every day exactly what you considered right and all that was *right* and only what was *right*) you thereby saved the day and successfully handled a delicate situation in a manner more masterly than any other man on earth could have done! To *me* you were a veritable inspiration and a tower of strength always."

Benson hoped that Pratt would become CNO and augment the powers of that office. He wrote to him:

> When this new tour is ended I shall hope to be able to welcome you here in Washington to continue the building up of the organization you did so much to lay the foundation for. I do not believe the Service generally and the various bureaus, offices of the Navy Department in particular have yet grasped the full force of what was intended in the establishing of the Office of Operations. They do not fully appreciate that the chief of that office is the technical head of the Navy and that all chiefs of bureau[s] and offices are his aids and that their efforts must be coordinated by the Chief of Naval Operations. We started it all right but there has been a very perceptible weakening at times since.

As Benson had desired, Pratt had an opportunity to help develop Operations. He became chief of naval operations in September 1930.[12]

Admiral Benson may have given more attention to social and philanthropic interests during his last years than to public affairs. Among other things he devoted considerable time to the Army, Navy, and Marine Corps Country Club in Arlington, Virginia, after becoming its president in 1925. He believed one purpose of this organization was to foster sound associations among officers. Writing to graduates of the Naval Academy, he noted: "We trust that our club may be of service to you in creating opportunities for close contact, not only with officers of your service, but with those of the other services as well, and also with civilians interested in national defense." His labors bore fruit: the membership of the club greatly increased during his presidency, as did the quality and quantity of its facilities.[13]

Benson also interested himself in the condition of minority groups at home and abroad. He headed the Washington Committee for the American Christian Fund for Jewish Relief, which sought to raise funds in support of suffering Jews in Eastern Europe. He also helped to strengthen the Cardinal Gibbons Institute, a boarding and day school for young black people. To James M. Curley of Boston he wrote in explanation of his activities: "I was born and raised on a southern plantation. My father was a slave-holder, and I remember well the plantation life of my boyhood days. I had an opportunity to judge the loyalty and fine qualities of these people when properly appealed to and trained, and I am a great believer in the latent possibilities of the race."[14]

Although Admiral Benson was a devoted husband, he did not entertain advanced views concerning the status of women. He valued the contributions of women to national life and took advantage of opportunities to praise their participation in the war effort, but he believed that a woman's place was normally in the home. He did not object to those women who wished to enter politics or business, but he thought it false that a "woman must do man's work to be man's equal. It is a fallacy which all history disproves."[15]

Perhaps Admiral Benson's most ardent commitment was to the Roman Catholic Church. A devout convert, he was critical of nominal practitioners: "Since coming into the Church it has been my belief that one of the greatest handicaps to her work is the 'nominal' Catholic. We must force 'nominal' Catholics to have something besides inert faith; we must make him zealous and active in belief of God's Church." He practiced what he preached, involving himself in varied activities and organizations of the church, among them the Knights of Columbus, the National Council of Catholic Men, and the Catholic Veterans. Perhaps sensitive to false charges of religious bias, he maintained firmly that "Our [religious] tolerance must be as broad as that of our constitution which guarantees to us and those of the other communions complete freedom of conscience and of worship." Benson thus proved himself an exponent of religious freedom.[16]

During the presidential campaign of Governor Alfred E. Smith of New York, the Democratic party's candidate in the contest with the Republican Herbert Hoover in 1928, ugly religious prejudice seemed likely to develop because Smith was a Roman Catholic. An educational foundation known as the Calvert Association sought to campaign against religious intolerance. Benson was asked to participate in this endeavor, but he declined, taking the position that such action would stimulate undue attention to the religious issues: "By degrees similar actions on the part of others would soon justify our opponents in making religion the only issue." Later in the campaign he opposed a general meeting of federated Catholic societies because an attempt might be made to have the organizations endorse the candidacy of Governor Smith, another step that might backfire.[17]

This brief review of Admiral Benson's familial, professional, philanthropic, and religious activities demonstrates the truth of his assertion that time did not hang heavy on his hands. As he had throughout his public career, he retained a most active interest in the world around him and a strong commitment to its improvement.[18]

Admiral Benson died suddenly at his home at the age of seventy-six on 20 May 1932, the victim of a cerebral hemorrhage. It was fitting that the announcement of his death should issue from Admiral William V. Pratt, the incumbent chief of naval operations:

> It is with great regret and with the deepest sympathy that I have just learned of the death of Admiral Benson, whose assistant I was during the World War. In my association with him during those trying days of 1917 and 1918 two characteristics stood up to the front—his determination to carry through once he had made up his mind to a certain course of action which he thought right, and the second was his sterling integrity of character. Coupled with these traits of character, his judgment invariably was sound. He stood like a rock at a time when the navy needed such men, and his name will go down to posterity as one of the finest characters that has ever worn the navy cloth.

Telegrams and letters poured in from around the world, but these words from Admiral Pratt, one of the original "band of brothers" that coalesced around Admiral Sims before World War I, were the most heartfelt and fitting.[19]

The funeral services for Admiral Benson took place on 23 May 1932. A requiem mass was held at St. Matthew's Church in Washington, the Benson parish, with Archbishop Michael J. Curley of Baltimore presiding and Apostolic Delegate Monsignor Pietro Fumansoni-Biondi among the mourners. Josephus Daniels attended the mass. Admiral Benson was buried at Arlington National Cemetery. Captain Russell Train, the naval aide at the White House, represented President Hoover. Admiral Pratt led the list of honorary pallbearers. Archbishop Curley spoke eloquently of the admiral in a final tribute: "Admiral Benson had a real spiritualizing influence on all who knew him. He was a man among men. He was a great character who carried the American Navy in his heart and mind." Although he was "among the Navy's greatest leaders . . . he was at the same time a man of the deepest simplicity."[20]

Admiral Benson's career in the United States Navy unfolded during the years when the navy accomplished the transition from sail and wood to steam and steel, when it grew from a small force to a fleet of the first rank. He saw the evolution of ship-to-shore communication from carrier pigeon to radio transmission, as well as the emergence of the battleship as the measure of naval power. Like his close contemporaries Fiske, Sims, and Fullam, he lived through a period that necessitated marked changes in the organization of the fleet and required equally significant changes in ship construction and naval administration. Like them, he was a reformer, very much interested in technical advances, and a proponent of a strong naval staff to provide central direction for the operations of the fleet. Unlike Fiske, Sims, and Fullam, he demonstrated constant fidelity to the principle of civilian supremacy. A man of the highest character, he proved worthy of the greatest responsibilities.

Benson's most significant contributions came during his tour as the first chief of naval operations. He directed the navy during the intervention of 1917–18 with notable success, at the same time establishing the importance of his office. Taking a broad view of his duties, he earned the enmity of the principal naval officer in Europe during the war, Admiral Sims. After serving as the naval adviser to President Wilson at the Paris peace conference, he served three presidents as a member of the United States Shipping Board, far outdistancing his contemporaries in length of service to his country.

Admiral Benson's strong nationalist commitment was at once a source of strength and a basis for criticism. He proved fully capable of protecting the nation's interests, but his distrust of Great Britain at times may have passed beyond reasonable limits. A convinced follower of Admiral Alfred Thayer Mahan, he is best understood as a navalist and a nationalist in the model of his distinguished mentor.

Evaluations of the performance of the United States Navy during the First World War that are made in the future should elaborate on the existing story, especially by taking into account a complete and balanced version of Admiral Benson's contributions. His place is secure in the naval history of his beloved country, along with many others of his time—friends and foes—who nurtured the United States Navy.

NOTES

CHAPTER 1

1. Notes, 1 January 1929, in Admiral William Shepherd Benson Papers, Library of Congress, Manuscript Division, Washington, D.C. Hereafter cited as Benson Papers.
2. James B. Morrow, "Who Should Run Our Ships?" *Nation's Business*, October 1920, p. 15.
3. For this information see Benson's Notes, 1 January 1929, Benson Papers; Doc. 2157, 17 and 18 April 1872, in Correspondence re Midshipmen (1862–1911), Record Group 24, National Archives, Washington, D.C. The latter collection is cited hereafter as NA, RG 24. All information concerning Benson's experiences in gaining admission to the Naval Academy and his years there is drawn from RG 24 unless other sources are noted.
4. Speer is quoted in "Became Distinguished Admiral Despite Early Flunk in Math," *Evening Star* (Washington), 24 October 1922, Benson Scrapbook, Benson Papers. Most newspaper items cited in this work are in the Benson Scrapbooks. For Benson's appointment see Doc. 2157, Correspondence re Midshipmen, NA, RG 24.
5. Worden to Benson, 2 July 1873, U.S. Naval Academy Misc., vol. 37, NA, RG 24; J. E. Brown to Simon Cameron, 25 June 1873, doc. 2157, NA, RG 24.
6. Harrington's report, 31 December 1878, is in the Benson Papers, as is Schley's report, 21 April 1879.
7. Benson recounted the experience at Bar Harbor in his Notes, 1 January 1929, Benson Papers.
8. Robert Seager II, *Alfred Thayer Mahan: The Man and His Letters*, pp. 127–28, 630–31.
9. For the rescue of the Greely expedition see Benson's account in his Notes, 1 January 1929, Benson Papers. Commander Woodward's report, 30

November 1882, and Commander Wilde's report, 14 October 1884, are in Benson Papers.

10. For information about the United States Fish Commission see Dean C. Allard, Jr., *Spencer Fullerton Baird and the U.S. Fish Commission: A Study in the History of American Science.* For the fitness report see Lieutenant Commander Zera L. Tanner to Secretary of the Navy, 29 November 1887, Benson Papers.

11. George Dewey, *Autobiography of George Dewey, Admiral of the Navy,* p. 164; Wilde to Secretary of the Navy William C. Whitney, 3 October 1888, Benson Papers.

12. Commodore Howard H. J. Benson to author, 25 January 1972, Klachko Files.

13. Fitness Report, 26 November 1895, Naval Examining Board Records, case 6, vol. 121, Record Group 125, National Archives, Washington National Records Center, Suitland, Md. Hereafter cited as NA, RG 125, WNRC.

14. Commodore Benson to author, 26 December 1967, Klachko Files.

15. *Address of Honorable Theodore Roosevelt, Assistant Secretary of the Navy, Before the Naval War College, Newport R.I.* (2 June 1897) (Washington, D.C.: Government Printing Office, 1897); Benson's Notes, 1 January 1929, Benson Papers; Commodore Benson to author, 26 December 1967 and 29 January 1969, Klachko Files.

16. Bureau of Navigation to Benson, 12 May 1898, Benson Papers; Benson to Luce, 12 June 1898, Admiral Stephen B. Luce Papers, Library of Congress, Naval Historical Foundation, Manuscript Division, Washington, D.C. Hereafter cited as Luce Papers.

17. Captain Caspar Goodrich to Benson, 16 July 1898, Spanish Prisoners Papers (1898), U.S. Naval Museum, U.S. Naval Academy, Annapolis.

18. Benson to Luce, 1 August and 29 November 1898, Luce Papers. The title of the revision was *Text-Book of Seamanship: The Equipping and Handling of Vessels under Sail for the Use of the United States Naval Academy,* by Rear Admiral Stephen B. Luce, USN, revised by Lieutenant W. S. Benson, USN, with illustrations by Lieutenant S. Seabury, USN (1898).

CHAPTER 2

1. For Captain Tilley's report see his Fitness Report, 12 August 1905, NA, RG 125, WNRC.

2. Benson to Howard Benson, 29 June and 23 September 1905, and Commodore Benson to author, 25 January 1972, all in Klachko Files.

3. For Benson's service at Newport see Chief of Bureau of Navigation to Rear Admiral William Shepherd Benson, USN, "Transcript of Record Service," 29 July 1921, NA, RG 24. A copy is also in the Benson Papers. For information about the Naval War College during these years see Austin M. Knight and William D. Puleston, "History of the United States Naval War College," and U.S. Naval War College, "Outline History of the United States Naval War College, 1884 to Date." Both items are in the Naval War College Archives, Newport, R.I.

4. Benson to Sims, 12 November 1906, Admiral William Sowden Sims Papers, Library of Congress, Naval Historical Foundation, Manuscript Division, Washington, D.C. Hereafter cited as Sims Papers. Benson's recommendations to Assistant Secretary of the Navy Truman H. Newberry, 3 September 1906, Benson Papers.

5. For educational policies see Benson to a future Academy commandant, Captain Wat T. Cluverius, 18 June 1919, in Subject Files, 1911–1927, UB-Admiral Benson's Personal Correspondence, Record Group 45, Naval Records Collection of the Office of Naval Records and Library, National Archives, Washington, D.C. Hereafter cited as Subject Files, NA, RG 45.

6. For information on this incident see "Wants to Have the Fleet Quit New London for Good," *Telegram* (New London, Conn.), 5 July 1908; Captain Charles Badger to Benson, 15 July 1908, Benson Papers. For Badger's commendation, see Fitness Reports, NA, RG 125, WNRC.

7. Benson to Sims, 14 March 1908, Sims Papers.

8. Sims to Benson, 26 June 1908, Benson Papers.

9. Benson to Sims, 6 August 1908, Sims Papers.

10. Benson to Howard Benson, 16 November 1919, Klachko Files; Benson to von Lengerke Meyer, 13 July 1909, NA, RG 125, WNRC.

11. USS *Albany* Logbook, 23–25 April 1909, NA, RG 24.

12. Naval Examining Board Records, 24 July–31 December 1909, NA, RG 125, WNRC.

13. Chief of Bureau of Navigation to Benson, "Transcript of Record Service," 29 July 1921, NA, RG 24. For the interlude at the Naval War College see Benson's testimony, 5 May 1920, in U.S. Congress, Senate, *Naval Investigation: Hearings before the Subcommittee of the Committee on Naval Affairs, United States Senate*, 66th Cong., 2d sess., 1920, 2:1833. Hereafter cited as U.S. Senate, *Hearings*, 1920.

14. Rear Admiral Griffin to author, 24 January 1969; Rear Admiral Griffin to Commodore Benson, 11 January 1968, both in Klachko Files; "The Ranking Admiral of the Navy," *Washington Star*, 4 February 1917, which describes Benson's attitude toward his crew. Performance records are reported in "The Giant *Utah* Shatters Speed Records of Navy: In Dash at Twenty-Two Knots Proves Herself Fastest of Battleships," *New York Herald*, 12 September 1911; Franklin D. Roosevelt to Benson, 31 July 1913, NA, RG 125, WNRC.

15. Fitness Report, 30 September 1912–3 January 1913, NA, RG 125, WNRC; Badger to Benson, 16 June 1913, Benson Papers.

16. Henry T. Mayo, Aid for Personnel, to Benson, 29 May 1913, Benson Papers; Bradley A. Fiske, *From Midshipman to Rear Admiral*, p. 585; Secretary of the Navy Josephus Daniels to Benson, 11 July 1913, Benson Papers; Benson to William H. Hayes, 11 February 1915, Benson Papers.

17. Benson to Daniels, 3 March and 1 June 1914, and Daniels to Benson, 11 April and 6 June 1914, all in Benson Papers. In the 6 June communication, Daniels wrote: "I never doubted that you in this matter, as in all matters, would do what was best."

18. For information on these subjects see Fiske, *From Midshipman to Rear Admiral*, pp. 530–32, 541; Ronald Spector, *Admiral of the New Empire: The Life and Career of George Dewey*, p. 193; Rear Admiral Bradley A. Fiske Diary, 15, 20, 22, and 27 June 1914 and 8 and 24 July 1914. Vol. 1 of the diary (6 January 1913–24 September 1914) is in the U.S. Naval Academy Museum, Annapolis; vol. 2 and vol. 3 (26 September 1914–18 September 1918) are in the Library of Congress, Naval Historical Foundation, Manuscript Division, Washington, D.C. Hereafter cited as Fiske Diary.

19. For indications of the developing relationship between Benson and Daniels, see Daniels to Benson, 2, 6, and 13 January 1914, and Benson to Daniels, 5 and 15 January 1914, all in Benson Papers. On the Marines

see undated handwritten memorandum by Russel C. Gross, Post 562, American Legion, Overbrook, Pa., Benson Papers. For Mexican affairs see Daniels to Benson, 29 April 1914, NA, RG 125, WNRC. For the invitation to the ceremonies at the Philadelphia Navy Yard see Benson to Daniels, 30 June 1914, Benson Papers.

CHAPTER 3

1. For the actions of the General Board see file no. 420-1, General Board Papers, Operational Archives, Naval Historical Center, Washington Navy Yard, Washington, D.C. Hereafter cited as General Board Papers.
2. For the activities of Congressman Gardner see William Reynolds Braisted, *The United States Navy in the Pacific, 1909–1922*, pp. 175–76. For Fiske's response, see entry for 20 October 1914, Fiske Diary.
3. Entry for 20 October 1914, Fiske Diary. Jonathan Daniels, son of the secretary of the navy, noted Roosevelt's differences with the Wilson administration over naval matters in *The End of Innocence* (p. 148). For Mahan's view see Mahan to Carter H. Fitzhugh, 23 September 1914, Area Files, 1911–1927, Record Group 45, Naval Records Collection of the Office of Naval Records and Library, National Archives, Washington, D.C. Hereafter cited as Area Files, NA, RG 45.
4. For Fiske's criticisms see his *From Midshipman to Rear Admiral*, p. 558. Daniels's comment is in U.S. Navy Department, *Annual Reports of the Navy Department for Fiscal Year 1914*, p. 53. Hereafter cited as U.S. Navy Department, *Annual Reports (year)*.
5. Meyer is quoted in Josephus Daniels, *The Wilson Era: Years of Peace, 1910–1917*, p. 119. Daniels's reaction to the reform proposal is in entry for 4 January 1915, Fiske Diary. He elaborated his criticism in *Years of Peace* (p. 243). Only two chief executives before Wilson took up the cause of naval reform: Ulysses S. Grant was strongly in favor, whereas Theodore Roosevelt manifested mild interest (Robert Greenhalgh Albion, *Makers of Naval Policy, 1798–1947*, ed. Rowena Reed, p. 217). For a detailed account of the legislative struggle that led to the establishment of a chief of naval operations, see Paolo E. Coletta, *Admiral Bradley A. Fiske and the American Navy*, pp. 149–62.
6. The Appropriations Act is printed in *U.S. Statutes at Large*, 1913–1915, 38:929. The incorrigible Fiske unsuccessfully suggested that the new chief of naval operations be made an ex officio member of the General Board to enable "all possible and desirable cooperation between the department and the General Board" (entry for 6 March 1915, Fiske Diary). For a summary of the legislative process see David F. Trask, "William Shepherd Benson: 11 May 1915–25 September 1919," in *The Chiefs of Naval Operations*, ed. Robert William Love, Jr., pp. 4–5.
7. For disputes between Daniels and Fiske see entries for 26 November 1913, 19 January, 19 March, and 21 and 29 May 1914, Fiske Diary. Fiske listed possible candidates from the reform faction in *From Midshipman to Rear Admiral* (p. 585). Fiske reported Fletcher's assessment of Benson in his entry for 28 April 1915, Fiske Diary (italics in original). On Sims, see Elting E. Morison, *Admiral Sims and the Modern American Navy*, pp. 317–18. Daniels's comment on Winslow is in *Years of Peace*, p. 244.
8. This account is contained in Rear Admiral Francis W. Benson to author, 21 July 1967.
9. For the public announcement of Benson's appointment see "Captain Ben-

son Is Appointed Chief of Naval Operations," *Philadelphia Inquirer*, 29 April 1915.

10. Fiske, *From Midshipman to Rear Admiral*, p. 585 (italics in original).
11. Fullam to Benson, 29 April 1915, Benson Papers (italics in original). For Daniels's activities see Trask, "William Shepherd Benson," p. 4.
12. Sebree to Benson, 9 May 1915, Benson Papers (italics in original).
13. "New Navy Boss a Hard Worker: Rear Admiral Benson Takes Firm Hold as Chief of Naval Operations, Experienced by Long and Varied Service," *Public Ledger* (Philadelphia), 16 May 1915.
14. Speech before the Naval Academy Graduates Association, 1 June 1916, Josephus Daniels Papers, Library of Congress, Manuscript Division, Washington, D.C. Hereafter cited as Daniels Papers. Benson testimony during the naval investigation hearings, 4–5 May 1920, is in U.S. Senate, *Hearings*, 1920, 2:1820, 1869.
15. Interview, author with Commodore Howard H. J. Benson, 29 September 1965 and 3 January 1968, Klachko Files.
16. "Fiske Says Navy Is Unprepared to Guard Coast," *New York Times*, 15 June 1915; Sims to Fiske, 10 June 1915, Sims Papers.
17. "Prepare for War to Assure Peace, Advice of Admiral Benson," *North American*, 6 June 1915.
18. For a negative assessment of Benson see Morison, *Admiral Sims*, p. 396. For Pratt's statement see his "Autobiography," p. 218, in Admiral William Veazie Pratt Papers, Operational Archives, Naval Historical Center, Washington Navy Yard, Washington, D.C. Hereafter cited as Pratt, "Autobiography." Some Pratt materials are in the U.S. Naval War College, Naval Historical Collection, Mahan Library, Newport, R.I. Hereafter cited as Pratt Papers. For Train's statement: interview, author with Admiral Train, 26 March 1968, Klachko Files. For that of Ingersoll: interview, author with Admiral Ingersoll, 5 January 1968. Admiral Benson once described his relations with Daniels favorably: "All that has been required of me has been to present the need and desirability of changes and improvements in order to receive the Secretary's sympathetic attention. He does not blindly yield to suggestions but gives them the most earnest and thoughtful consideration" (speech before the Naval Academy Graduates Association, 1 June 1916, Daniels Papers).
19. Jones to Fiske, 5 January 1921, Admiral Hilary P. Jones Papers, Library of Congress, Naval Historical Foundation, Manuscript Division, Washington, D.C. Hereafter cited as Jones Papers. Admiral Arleigh A. Burke, a forthright CNO of recent vintage (17 August 1955–1 August 1961), maintained that protest resignations usually have little effect on policy. Their main utility is to allow an officer to remove himself from a personally unbearable situation. Burke to author, 30 July 1982; Dean C. Allard, Jr., to author, 29 July 1982, Klachko Files.
20. Pratt to Howard Benson, 14 August 1952, Klachko Files. See Pratt's "Autobiography," p. 209.
21. 5 March 1915, file no. 446, General Board Papers.
22. Daniels, *Years of Peace*, pp. 505–6.
23. Ibid., pp. 506–7. For the Benson-Dewey effort on behalf of Badger see Daniels to Dewey, 7 July 1915, Admiral George Dewey Papers, Library of Congress, Naval Historical Foundation, Manuscript Division, Washington, D.C. See also "Proceedings of the General Board, 1915," 8:215, General Board Papers.
24. For this episode see Commodore Benson to author, 14 September 1973,

Klachko Files; Benson to Fullam, 28 March and 27 June 1916, Benson Papers; Mrs. May Krafft to author, 18 September 1973, Klachko Files; Fullam to Benson, 13 May and 24 August 1916, Benson Papers. Italics in original.

25. For information about the bureaus see Charles Oscar Paullin, "A Half-Century of Naval Administration in America, 1861–1911," *U.S. Naval Institute Proceedings*, September 1913, p. 1259. For the advisory organ, including Daniels's comment, see "Advisory Council Created in June 1915," and for Benson's observation see Benson to Secretary of the Advisory Commission, 4 August 1915, both in Daniels Papers.

26. Sims to Assistant for Operations (Chase), 7 July 1915, Sims Papers.

27. For the exchange between Sims and Benson see Sims to Benson, 21 July 1915 and 10 April 1916, and Benson to Sims, 23 July 1915, all in Sims Papers.

28. Benson statement on 16 March 1916, in U.S. Congress, House, Committee on Naval Affairs, *Hearings . . . on Estimates Submitted by the Secretary of the Navy*, 1916, 64th Cong., 1st sess., 1:3105.

29. Ibid., 3:3104.

30. These family recollections are in interview, author with Ingersoll, 5 January 1968, and in Commodore Benson to author, 10 December 1967, Klachko Files.

31. For Daniels's comments see Fitness Reports, 11 May–22 November 1915 and 23 November 1915–31 March 1916, NA, RG 125, WNRC.

CHAPTER 4

1. Benson expressed himself publicly on the question of preparedness shortly after becoming CNO: "Prepare for War to Assure Peace, Advice of Admiral Benson," *North American*, 6 June 1915.

2. For Fiske's proposal and the refusal of Daniels to act on it see file no. 425, 13 March 1915, General Board Papers; Fiske, *From Midshipman to Rear Admiral*, pp. 579–82. For the order to put the Fiske-Benson proposal into effect see Secretary of the Navy to the General Board, 28 May 1915, file no. 425, General Board Papers. Braisted compares Benson favorably to Fiske in *The United States Navy in the Pacific* (p. 183).

3. Memorandum for the Secretary, 30 September 1915, Benson Papers.

4. File no. 422, 3 August 1915, General Board Papers; U.S. Navy Department, *Annual Reports, 1915*, p. 10. U.S. Navy Department, *Annual Reports, 1916*, p. 87.

5. For the presentation to the General Board and adoption of the proposal see Benson to General Board, 24 May 1915, and Dewey to Secretary of the Navy, 5 June 1915, file no. 420; "Proceedings of the General Board," 1915, 7:153–54, all in General Board Papers. For Daniels's opposition see Admiral Benson's Notes, 28 December 1919, Benson Papers; Interview, author with Commodore Benson, 29 September 1965; Speech before the Naval Academy Graduates Association, 1 June 1916, Daniels Papers. Benson's evaluation is in Admiral Benson's Notes, 28 December 1929, Benson Papers.

6. For correspondence on these matters see Rear Admiral Victor Blue to Sims, 7 September 1915; Benson to Sims, 8 September 1915; and Sims

to Benson, 10 September 1915, Sims Papers; Morison, *Admiral Sims*, p. 318. Fletcher retained the command of the Atlantic Fleet until Rear Admiral Henry T. Mayo succeeded him in June 1916. On 16 April 1916, Navy Department General Order no. 209 renamed Plunkett's organization the Office of Gunnery Exercise and Engineering Performance.

7. Benson's speech before the Naval Academy Graduates Association, 1 June 1916, Daniels Papers; Chief of Naval Operations to Bureau of Supplies and Accounts, 22 June 1915, General Board Papers.

8. Daniels, *Years of Peace*, pp. 490 ff.

9. Benson's speech before the Naval Academy Graduates Association, 1 June 1916, Daniels Papers; "Statement by the Chief of Naval Operations," U.S. Navy Department, *Annual Reports, 1916*, p. 89.

10. Yates Stirling, *Sea Duty: The Memoirs of a Fighting Admiral*, pp. 151, 154–56. Stirling became Grant's assistant. For Benson's role see press notice, 28 May 1915, Daniels Papers; Benson to Grant, 7 July 1915, Area Files, NA, RG 45; Benson to Daniels, 30 September 1915, Benson Papers; Testimony of Captain Harris Laning, 24 March 1920, in U.S. Senate, *Hearings*, 1920, 1:389–90.

11. For these developments see Archibald D. Turnbull and Clifford L. Lord, *History of United States Naval Aviation*, pp. 8–9, 21, 28, 52; Mark L. Bristol to Navy Department via Chief of Naval Operations, "The Organization of Our Air Fleet," 8 June 1915, Daniels Papers; Testimony of Josiah McKean, 29 April 1920, U.S. Senate, *Hearings*, 1920, 1:1725. For criticisms of Benson's actions see Turnbull and Lord, *History of United States Naval Aviation*, pp. 51–52, 54–55, 82. For Bristol's command of the *North Carolina* see Chief of Naval Operations to Chief of the Bureau of Navigation, 25 February 1916, Benson Papers.

12. Turnbull and Lord, *History of United States Naval Aviation*, p. 69.

13. Ibid., p. 82; U.S. Senate, *Hearings*, 1920, 2:1862.

14. Benson's activity in relation to Haiti is apparent in Robert Lansing to President Wilson, 7 August 1915, Woodrow Wilson Papers, Library of Congress, Manuscript Division, Washington, D.C. Hereafter cited as Wilson Papers. See also Benson to the naval commander at Port au Prince, USS *Washington*, 9 August 1915, and Lansing to President Wilson, 10 August 1915, Wilson Papers; Benson to Boaz Long, 23 September 1915, with attachments titled "Draft of the Order for Issue by the Secretary of the Navy" and "Memorandum Relative to the Establishment of a Haitian Constabulary," Subject Files, UB-Admiral Benson's Personal Correspondence, NA, RG 45. For the purchase of the Danish West Indies see file no. 427, General Board Papers.

15. Daniels's attitude toward Wilson is reflected in a statement he made many years afterward to the president's biographer. As secretary of the navy he had done all that he could, "consistent with loyalty to the 'Old Man,' to keep America out of war." Daniels to Ray Stannard Baker, 29 November 1935, Ray Stannard Baker Papers, Library of Congress, Manuscript Division, Washington, D.C. For House's view see House to Wilson, 14 July 1915, Edward M. House Papers, Yale University Archives, Historical Manuscripts, Yale University, New Haven. Hereafter cited as House Papers or House Diary. For the president's request for a naval program see Wilson to Daniels, 21 July 1915, Wilson Papers. An authoritative evaluation of this step toward preparedness is in Braisted, *The United States Navy in the Pacific*, pp. 188 ff.

16. The program of 30 July 1915 is contained in file no. 4202, General Board Papers.
17. Benson memorandum for the Secretary, 19 August 1915, Wilson Papers.
18. Memorandum for the Secretary, "Four Battleships," 22 September 1915, and memorandum for the Secretary, 25 September 1915, both in Benson Papers.
19. For information concerning the preparation of the five-year program see memorandum by the Division of Operations, "Ships Built, Building, and a Program for Five Years together with Cost," 6 October 1915, file no. 420-2; Minutes of the General Board, 6, 7, 8, 9, 11, and 12 October 1915, in "Proceedings of the General Board," 1915, 7:293 ff., all in General Board Papers. Details of the proposal to the Department of the Treasury are in *New York Times*, 20 October 1915.
20. For the president's speech see Ray Stannard Baker and William E. Dodd, eds., *The Public Papers of Woodrow Wilson*, 3:384–92.
21. For Wilson's speech of 3 February 1916 see Baker and Dodd, eds., *Public Papers of Woodrow Wilson*, 4:414. For his statement at the cabinet meeting see Josephus Daniels, *The Wilson Era: Years of War and After, 1917–1923*, p. 41. For Wilson's motives in supporting naval expansion see David F. Trask, "Woodrow Wilson and International Statecraft: A Modern Assessment," *Naval War College Review* 36 (March–April 1983): 63–64.
22. For Benson's testimony see U.S. Congress, House, Committee on Naval Affairs, *Hearings . . . on Estimates Submitted by the Secretary of the Navy*, 1916, 64th Cong., 1st sess., 3:3194 ff. His comment on his office is reported in the *New York Times*, 18 and 19 May 1916.
23. For Fiske's testimony see U.S. Congress, House, Committee on Naval Affairs, *Hearings . . . on Estimates Submitted by the Secretary of the Navy*, 64th Cong., 1st sess., 3:3194 ff. Benson's comments are in his speech to the Naval Academy Graduates Association, 1 June 1916, Daniels Papers. For the insurgents' views see entry for 2 June 1916, Fiske Diary; Fullam to Sims, 17 June 1916, Sims Papers.
24. For information about the action of the House of Representatives see a file titled "Appropriations," Navy Department, 18 May 1916, Daniels Papers.
25. For House's reaction to a conversation with the French ambassador, Jules Jusserand, about the implications of the Russo-Japanese understanding see House to Wilson, 1 June 1916, House Papers. For Mexican developments see Benson memorandum for the Secretary of the Navy, 27 June 1916, Daniels Papers.
26. For Kitchin's statement see U.S. Congress, *Congressional Record*, 1916, 12698, col. 53 (italics in original). The total authorized construction included ten first-class battleships, six battle cruisers, ten scout cruisers, fifty torpedo boat destroyers, nine fleet submarines, fifty coastal submarines, one submarine with a Neff propulsion system, three fuel ships, one repair ship, one transport ship, one hospital ship, two destroyer tenders, one fleet submarine tender, two ammunition ships, and two gunboats.
27. For Benson's proposals see Benson to Daniels, 26 June 1916, Benson Papers. For the provision relating to the CNO see *U.S. Statutes at Large*, 1915–1917, 39:558.
28. For the Daniels telegram see Daniels to Benson, 29 August 1916, Benson

Papers. For the reaction of the reformers see Sims to Hutch I. Cone, 29 August 1916, Sims Papers.

CHAPTER 5

1. Captain Pratt did not take up full-time responsibilities until 10 May 1917. The leading work on Pratt is Gerald E. Wheeler, *Admiral William Veazie Pratt, U.S. Navy: A Sailor's Life*, but see also Craig L. Symonds, "William Veazie Pratt: 17 September 1930–30 June 1933," in Love, *The Chiefs of Naval Operations*, pp. 69–86. Benson's interest in encouraging enlistments is mentioned in his postwar testimony on 4 May 1920 in U.S. Senate, *Hearings*, 1920, 2:1187 ff. For the retention of Admiral Badger see Benson to Fletcher, 30 August 1916, and Fletcher to Benson, 1 September 1916, Area Files, NA, RG 45. For the comment to Fullam see Benson to Fullam, 28 October 1916, Benson Papers. For his communication to Gleaves see Benson to Gleaves, 14 November 1916, Area Files, NA, RG 45.
2. For the training cruise see Commodore Benson to author, 20 February 1969, Klachko Files. See also Benson to Sims, 3 October 1916, Sims Papers.
3. For success in developing an electric drive see Benson to Mayo, 18 November 1916, Benson Papers. For the meeting of the General Board see file no. 420-2, 16 October 1916, General Board Papers.
4. Speech on "The Relations of Inland Waterways to Naval Efficiency," 6 December 1916, Benson Papers.
5. Chief of Naval Operations to All Fleets, Reserve Forces, All Bureaus, Naval Districts, and All Department Offices; Subject: "Mobilization Plan, 11 December 1916," Area Files, D-Navy Department, NA, RG 45.
6. For Wilson's last attempt to arrange American mediation see Trask, "Woodrow Wilson and International Statecraft," pp. 62–64.
7. For the German decision to resume unrestricted submarine warfare see David F. Trask, *Captains and Cabinets: Anglo-American Naval Relations, 1917–1918*, pp. 30–34.
8. Daniels to Wilson, 2 February 1917, Wilson Papers.
9. Benson memorandum titled "Regarding Belligerents in Neutral Jurisdiction," 2 February 1917, Daniels Papers.
10. Benson memorandum titled "Situation: The United States Being at Peace, and Germany Having Declared Zones as Per Present Information. Required: An Examination of the Question of Convoy by Vessels of the United States Navy," 2 February 1917, Daniels Papers.
11. For the meeting of 5 February 1917 see Benson to Daniels, 7 March 1921, Benson Papers. For Benson's views on arming merchant vessels see Benson memorandum to Daniels, "On Arming Merchant Vessels," 14 February 1917, Daniels Papers (italics in original).
12. For information about the discovery of the German overture to Mexico made by the German foreign minister, Arthur Zimmermann, see Barbara Tuchman, *The Zimmermann Telegram*. British intelligence intercepted this message in January 1917, but it was not forwarded to the United States until five weeks later. For Wilson's speech on arming merchant vessels see Baker and Dodd, eds., *Public Papers of Woodrow Wilson*, 4:432. For the arming of vessels on executive authority see a memorandum prepared in Benson's planning section, "Arming Merchant Vessels," 5 March 1917, and Daniels to Wilson, 9 March 1917, both in Daniels Papers; entries for

8 March and 11 March 1917, Daniels Diary in Daniels Papers. Hereafter cited as Daniels Diary. I prefer to cite the original rather than the published version, *The Cabinet Diaries of Josephus Daniels, 1913–1921*, ed. E. David Cronon (Lincoln: University of Nebraska Press, 1963).

13. For the Caribbean concentration see entry for 11 March 1917, Daniels Diary. For the decision to concentrate the fleet in the Chesapeake Bay see Braisted, *The United States Navy in the Pacific*, p. 292; "Proceedings of the General Board," 6 March 1917, General Board Papers. For Admiral Mayo's position see Pratt to Sims, 27 May 1917, Sims Papers. For measures in home waters see Benson to Commandants of Naval Districts 1–8 and 15, "Defense in Home Waters," 19 March 1917, Subject Files, NA, RG 45.

14. For the decision to go to war see Trask, *Captains and Cabinets*, pp. 49–51. For Wilson's decision to communicate with Congress see *New York Times*, 22 March 1917; Ray Stannard Baker, *Woodrow Wilson: Life and Letters*, 6:504.

15. These events are traced in Trask, *Captains and Cabinets* (pp. 52–55). For Page's suggestion see Page to Lansing, 23 March 1917, Walter Hines Page Papers, Houghton Library, Harvard University, Cambridge. Hereafter cited as Page Papers or Page Diary. For the president's instruction see Wilson to Daniels, 24 March 1917, Daniels Papers.

16. For the consideration of Captain Wilson see entry for 25 March 1917, Daniels Diary. Various people claimed credit for choosing Sims to go to London. Daniels did so in Daniels to Sims, 15 December 1917, Daniels Papers. Roosevelt did so in a speech delivered at the Brooklyn Academy of Music, 1 February 1920, Franklin D. Roosevelt Papers, Franklin D. Roosevelt Library, Hyde Park, N.Y. Hereafter cited as F. D. Roosevelt Papers. Sims informed his wife that Benson not only had approved of his selection but had made the choice. In so doing he had antagonized officers of greater seniority who wanted the assignment. Sims to Mrs. Sims, 10 December 1917, Sims Papers. Years later Benson's son Francis Wyse Benson wrote: "I know from my father that he personally selected Sims to go to London as a naval liaison officer" (Rear Admiral Francis W. Benson to author, 3 November 1965). In *Admiral Sims* (p. 340), Elting E. Morison, Sims's son-in-law and biographer, gives the credit for the selection to Roosevelt and Benson. For Sims's description of his orders see William Sowden Sims, *The Victory at Sea*, ed. David F. Trask, p. 3. His secret departure for Europe is described in U.S. Senate, *Hearings*, 1920, 1:268.

17. For the testimony before the congressional committee see Trask, *Captains and Cabinets*, p. 55.

18. Trask discusses this question in *Captains and Cabinets* (pp. 362–65). See also two articles by Dean C. Allard, Jr., "Admiral William S. Sims and United States Naval Policy in World War I," *American Neptune*, April 1975, pp. 97–110, and "Anglo-American Naval Differences during World War I," *Military Affairs*, April 1980, pp. 75–81.

19. Memorandum, February 1917, Daniels Papers.

20. Admiral William S. Benson, "Estimate of the Situation," 13 March 1917, Subject Files, NA, RG 45 (italics in original).

CHAPTER 6

1. For the ignorance rife among members of the British government concerning the emergency see Lord Beaverbrook, *Men and Power, 1917–*

1918, p. xxxv. See also Sir Charles E. Madden to Admiral Sir John R. Jellicoe, 8 March 1917, Admiral Sir John R. Jellicoe Papers, British Museum, London. Hereafter cited as Jellicoe Papers. For Sims's state of mind see Sims, *Victory at Sea*, p. 6.

2. British reluctance to show eagerness for American participation in the war is revealed in Foreign Office to Colville Barclay, 21 March 1917, file 137, book 1436, Papers of the Admiralty, Public Record Office, London. Hereafter cited as Adm. (file/book). For the British plan see memorandum for Naval Attaché, Washington, D.C., 24 March 1917, and for the role of Roosevelt see Decypher, Barclay, no. 791, 25 March 1917, both in Adm. 137/1436. For the president's reaction see Wilson to Daniels, 24 March 1917, Daniels Papers.

3. French Naval Attaché to Secretary of the Admiralty, 4 April 1917; Admiralty to de Lostende, 6 April 1917; and Browning to Secretary of the Admiralty, 13 April 1917, all in Adm. 137/1436.

4. Browning to Secretary of the Admiralty, 13 April 1917, Adm. 137/1436.

5. For information about the naval conference see Benson memorandum for the Secretary of the Navy, 26 February 1921; Badger memorandum, 25 February 1921; Mayo memorandum, 26 February 1921; Roosevelt to Daniels, 25 February 1921, all in Daniels Papers.

6. For the Anglo-American relationship see Browning to Secretary of the Admiralty, 13 April 1917, Adm. 137/1436; Benson testimony, 4 May 1920, U.S. Senate, *Hearings*, 1920, 2:1817 ff. For de Grasset's views see Trask, *Captains and Cabinets*, p. 64. Browning's observations on de Grasset are in Browning to Secretary of the Admiralty, 13 April 1917, Adm. 137/1436. Later in the war de Grasset encountered Admiral Mayo in London and said: "You did much more for us than I had believed possible" (Mayo memorandum for Secretary of the Navy, 26 February 1921, Daniels Papers).

7. General Board memorandum, 5 April 1917, Daniels Papers.

8. For Benson's statement see his testimony in U.S. Senate, *Hearings*, 1920, 2:1824.

9. For Sims's arrival in England see Sims to Daniels, 19 April 1917, Subject Files, TD-Admiral Sims's Personal File, NA, RG 45. For his first impressions see Sims, *Victory at Sea*, pp. 7, 47.

10. Copies of Sims to Navy Department, 14 April 1917, are in many locations, including Benson, Daniels, and Sims Papers.

11. Sims to Secretary of the Navy, 19 April 1917, Area Files, NA, RG 45.

12. For the destroyer's orders see Daniels to Taussig, 18 April 1917, Area Files, NA, RG 45. For Sims's desires see Sims to Mrs. Sims, 27 April 1917, Sims Papers.

13. For Sims's orders see Daniels to Naval Attaché, London, 28 April 1917, Sims Papers. For Taussig's instructions see Sims to Taussig, 29 April 1917, Sims Papers. On 2 June 1917 Benson sent a memorandum to Sims titled "Organization of U.S. Forces Operating in European Waters," in which Sims was designated "Commander, United States Naval Forces in European Waters." Area Files, NA, RG 45.

14. Page to Wilson, 4 May 1917, Page Papers.

15. Entry for 23 April 1917, Daniels Diary.

16. For the instructions of the Balfour Mission see War Cabinet Minutes (W.C. 116), 10 April 1917, Cabinet file 23, book 2, Records of the War Cabinet, Public Record Office, London. Hereafter cited as Cab. (file/book). Sims gave notice of what to expect from Admiral de Chair—a shopping list of

needed materials—in Sims to Navy Department, 23 April 1917, Benson Papers.

17. Balfour is quoted in Trask, *Captains and Cabinets*, p. 74. For the British view see memorandum for the War Cabinet, "Cooperation with the United States," 4 April 1917, Records of the Foreign Office, Public Record Office, London, Foreign Office file 800, book 208, p. 67936. Hereafter cited as F.O. (file/book).

18. For information about naval support allocated to France see memorandum titled "Conference between Chief of Naval Operations and Vice Admiral Chocheprat, French Navy," 27 April 1917, Daniels Papers. Benson signed this document. For Sims's view see his *Victory at Sea* (p. 349).

19. Among authorities who treat Benson as an Anglophobe are Jeffrey J. Safford, *Wilsonian Maritime Diplomacy, 1913–1921*, and Wheeler, *William Veazie Pratt*.

20. For this interpretation see Trask, "William Shepherd Benson," p. 11.

21. Entry for 13 May 1917, House Diary; House to Wilson, 8 July 1917, House Papers. For a discussion of possible means of compensating the United States for suspending its efforts to build a balanced battle fleet during the emergency see Trask, *Captains and Cabinets*, pp. 102–25. In the end President Wilson did not pursue the matter.

22. For a summary of the introduction of the convoy system see Trask, *Captains and Cabinets*, pp. 71–73.

23. For the Benson-Pratt view see Pratt to Sims, 6 May 1917, Area Files, NA, RG 45.

24. For Pratt's comment see his "Autobiography," p. 216. For directions for Sims see OPNAV to Sims, 1 July 1917, Sims Papers. For the injunction to Sims see Daniels, *Years of War and After*, p. 95.

25. For the development of the naval transport system see Lewis P. Clephane, *History of the Naval Overseas Transportation Service in World War I*. For the activity of the Shipping Board see Edward N. Hurley, *The Bridge to France*. For the working arrangement that was established between the chief of naval operations and the army's chief of staff see Newton D. Baker to P. R. Duffy, 25 August 1932, Benson Papers; Thomas G. Frothingham, *The Naval History of the World War*, 3:162.

26. Josephus Daniels, "The Navy Transports Set Records to Carry Out Gigantic Task," *Evening Star* (Washington), 13 May 1921. The United States had not notified either Germany or neutral Switzerland that a state of war existed with Germany. On 8 May the chief of the naval staff of Germany, seeking to avoid accusations of having started the war with the United States, ordered: "American warships must not be attacked at present, and the utmost caution must be observed towards them, as it is not known what their orders are." Supplement no. 63 to "Declaration of War . . . " (B. 15781. O/1.), Subject Files, NA, RG 45. This order remained in effect until 1 August 1917. See Sims, *Victory at Sea*, p. 317.

27. Robert Debs Heinl, Jr., *Soldiers of the Sea: The United States Marine Corps, 1775–1962*, p. 195. Colonel Heinl interviewed General Thomas Holcomb, who, as a captain, had served as General Barnett's aide from 1914 to 1920. Heinl had been under the impression that Benson was anti-Marine, but Holcomb said that "Benson had been capable and fair and, from the Marine Corps viewpoint, a fine CNO." Colonel Heinl to author, 5 March 1968. See also Major General John Archer Lejeune, *The Reminiscences of a Marine*, pp. 222–23.

28. For the Navy Department's concern about the disintegration of the battle

fleet see Daniels to Lansing, 3 July 1917, U.S. Department of State, *Papers Relating to the Foreign Relations of the United States, 1917: The World War*, Supplement 2, 1:116–17. Hereafter cited as *Foreign Relations, 1917*. For Sims's view see Sims to Wilson, 11 July 1917, *Foreign Relations, 1917*, Supplement 2, 1:124–26. The position of Admiral Benson and the final results are in Pratt to Sims, 2 and 22 July 1917, Sims Papers. See also Braisted, *The United States Navy in the Pacific*, pp. 293–300; Trask, *Captains and Cabinets*, p. 96.
29. Trask, *Captains and Cabinets*, p. 139.

CHAPTER 7

1. For an example of the CNO's views on British operations against the submarine see Benson to Browning, 9 July 1917, Benson Papers. For Jellicoe to Browning, 7 July 1917, see A. Temple Patterson, ed., *The Jellicoe Papers: Selections from the Private and Official Correspondence of Admiral of the Fleet Earl Jellicoe*, vol. 2, *1916–1935*, pp. 181–82. Hereafter cited as *Jellicoe Papers*.
2. Pratt to Sims, 27 May 1917, Sims Papers.
3. Pratt to Sims, 2 July 1917, Sims Papers.
4. Chase's policy statement is in Subject Files, OP-Plans and Policies, NA, RG 45.
5. Wilson to Daniels, 2 July 1917, and Wilson to Sims, 4 July 1917, both in Daniels Papers.
6. Sims to Wilson, 11 July 1917, Daniels Papers. Italics in original. A draft of this letter in the Wilson Papers is more critical than the final version. Sims apparently wrote his response on 7 July, but he probably did not send it until 11 July. It arrived in Washington on 12 July 1917. Trask, *Captains and Cabinets*, p. 97.
7. "Notes on Interview between President Wilson and Sir William Wiseman," 13 July 1917, F.O. 800/209. For Pratt's opinion see Pratt, "Autobiography," p. 222.
8. Gaunt to Admiralty, 5 July 1917, Adm. 137/1437. For the exchange between Benson and Browning see Benson to Browning, 9 July 1917, Benson Papers, and Browning to Benson, 26 July 1917, Daniels Papers.
9. "British Naval Policy," 1 July 1917 (initialled by Jellicoe), Cabinet Paper G.T. 1272, Cab. 24/18.
10. Pringle to Sims, 13 September 1917, Sims Papers; entry for 24 July 1917, Daniels Diary.
11. Emmet to Sims, Subject Files, TD-Admiral Sims's Personal File, NA, RG 45.
12. For Roosevelt's involvement see Frank Freidel, *Franklin D. Roosevelt: The Apprenticeship* (vol. 1), p. 309. Wilson to Daniels, with Churchill report enclosed, 2 August 1917, Daniels Papers.
13. Pratt to Sims, 22 July 1917, and Belknap to Sims, 26 July 1917, both in Sims Papers; Earle to Sims, 28 August 1917, Subject Files, TT-British and US Navies, Cooperation Between, NA, RG 45.
14. For Wilson's speech see Daniels, *Years of War and After*, p. 44, and David Lawrence, *The True Story of Woodrow Wilson*, pp. 221–22.
15. For the origin of the Mayo Mission see entry for 24 July 1917, Daniels Diary. For Daniels's conversation with Phillips see entry in William Phillips Journals, 28 July 1917, Houghton Library, Harvard University, Cambridge. Hereafter cited as Phillips Journals. Italics in original. For infor-

mation about arrangements see Benson to Sims, 15 August 1917, Area
Files, D-Navy Department, NA, RG 45. Franklin D. Roosevelt wanted to
undertake the mission, but Secretary Daniels vetoed the idea (Trask, *Captains and Cabinets*, pp. 147–48).

16. Entry for 16 August 1917, Daniels Diary.
17. For Mayo's preparations see his report, 11 October 1917, Area Files, D-Navy Department, NA, RG 45. For the observations of the First Lord of the Admiralty see Geddes to Prime Minister [Lloyd George], 29 August 1917, in David Lloyd George Papers, Beaverbrook Library, London, F/17/6/8. Hereafter cited with F and identification numbers. Geddes enclosed a document titled "Admiral Mayo's Notes on the Purpose of His Visit."
18. For an early report on the conference see Mayo to Benson, 6 September 1917, Subject Files, QI-International Naval Conference, NA, RG 45. For a description of the conference see Trask, *Captains and Cabinets*, pp. 149–53.
19. Jellicoe to Benson, 22 September 1917, Subject Files, UB-Admiral Benson's Personal Correspondence, NA, RG 45; Sims to Benson, 1 September 1917, Benson Papers. For indications of Sims's reaction to Mayo's presence see Sims to Pratt, 7 and 11 September 1917, Sims Papers.
20. For the misunderstanding about communications see Gaunt to Jellicoe, 11 September 1917, Adm. 137/1437; Sims to Benson, 28 October 1917, Benson Papers; Page to Wilson, 25 September 1917, Page Papers; Sims to Admiralty, 11 October 1917, and Barclay to Balfour, 8 October 1917, both in Adm. 137/1437. For the procedure established to improve Anglo-American naval communications see Office Memorandum no. 216, M.O. 13494/17, 15 October 1917, and "Procedure for Informing United States Naval Authorities of Naval Staff Matters," 17 October 1917, both in Adm. 137/1437.
21. "General Report, . . . " 11 October 1917, Area Files, D-Navy Department, NA, RG 45. Daniels recorded Mayo's optimism in entry for 13 October 1917, Daniels Diary.
22. Benson to Jellicoe, 17 October 1917, *Jellicoe Papers*, 2:221. Benson's four-page typed letter is in Jellicoe Papers. A copy in NA, RG 45, is incorrectly identified as being from Jellicoe to Benson. For Wilson's reaction see entry for 19 October 1917, Daniels Diary.
23. Spring Rice to Balfour, 21 September 1917, F.O. 899/13. For Benson's decision see Pratt to Sims, 16 September 1917, and for Sims's reaction see Sims to Benson, 28 October 1917, both in Sims Papers. The judicious Wheeler's comment on this statement is: "Sims's response to Benson's letter is one of the most unique in his collection of correspondence" (Wheeler, *William Veazie Pratt*, p. 117).
24. For McKean's statement see U.S. Senate, *Hearings*, 1920, 1:1691–92.

CHAPTER 8

1. For the origins of the conference proposal see David F. Trask, *The United States in the Supreme War Council: American War Aims and Inter-Allied Strategy, 1917–1918*, pp. 15–16.
2. Ibid., pp. 16–17.
3. For the views of Jellicoe see Page to Wilson, 25 September 1917, Page Papers, and the entry for 2 March 1918, Page Diary. For Sims's recommendation see Sims to Pratt, 15 October 1917, Pratt Papers. For Daniels's statement to Benson see entry for 28 October 1917, Daniels Diary.
4. Pratt, "Autobiography," p. 211. For Pratt's letters see Pratt to Benson,

undated but c. 28 October 1917, Benson Papers; Pratt to Sims, 28 October 1917, Sims Papers.

5. Entry for 3 November 1917, House Diary.

6. Bliss to Mrs. Bliss, 6 and 7 November 1917, General Tasker Howard Bliss Papers, Library of Congress, Manuscript Division, Washington, D.C. For additional information about the voyage and the activities of the House Mission see Frederick Palmer, *Bliss, Peacemaker: The Life and Letters of General Tasker Howard Bliss,* pp. 186–97.

7. When the House Mission arrived in Plymouth, messages of relief and good will came from President Wilson, Secretary Daniels, and Captain Pratt. See cables from Daniels and Pratt, 8 November 1917, Benson Papers. For the announcement of the arrival of the mission in Europe see Department of State communiqué, 7 November 1917, Records of the U.S. Department of State, Decimal File 763.72/76198b, Record Group 59, National Archives, Washington, D.C. Hereafter cited as Decimal File (number/page), NA, RG 59. Sims's two letters to his wife, both dated 9 November 1917, are in Sims Papers. For his letter to the acting CNO see Sims to Pratt, 9 November 1917, Pratt Papers.

8. Auchincloss Diary, 14 November 1917, Gordon Auchincloss Diary and Papers, Yale University Archives, Historical Manuscripts, Yale University, New Haven. Hereafter cited as Auchincloss Diary or Auchincloss Papers.

9. For Benson's remarks of 8 November 1917 see "Statement of Admiral Benson, Chief of Naval Operations, November 1917," and for further information see "Record of the Activities of Admiral Benson while Serving as a Member of the American Mission Headed by Colonel House," undated (14 pages), both in Benson Papers. Unless otherwise indicated all information about Admiral Benson's activities as a member of the House Mission is drawn from the latter document and two others: information compiled by Lieutenant Commander Carter, "Chronological Record of Admiral Benson's Activities as Navy Representative on American Mission to Europe," undated, and a memorandum that Admiral Benson dictated on 6 July 1926, both in Benson Papers.

10. For Northcliffe's remarks see entry for 29 October 1917, Daniels Diary. For Pollen's comments see Pollen to Murray, 10 November 1917. Lord Elibank gave a copy of this letter to the author when she interviewed him in London in 1957 (18 April, 6 May, and 27 June). The letter is reproduced in full in Mary Klachko, "Anglo-American Naval Competition, 1918–1922," a copy of which is in Naval Historical Center, Washington Navy Yard, Washington, D.C.

11. Sims to Bayly, 10 and 12 November 1917, and Sims to Mrs. Sims, 1 and 15 November 1917, all in Sims Papers. To the American commanding the destroyers at Queenstown, Commander Joel R. Poinsett Pringle, Sims wrote of the value he attached to Benson's visit, of Benson's fairness, and of Benson's devotion to the cause of the Allies: "He is in entire agreement with me and with the Admiralty as to what should be done. It is very fortunate that he has come over here to look into matters himself" (Sims to Pringle, 12 November 1917, Sims Papers).

12. For information concerning the decision to send the four American battleships to Europe see Benson to Daniels, 9 November 1917, Benson Papers; entry for 10 November 1917, Daniels Diary; and Secretary of the Navy to Benson, rec. 13 November 1917, and OPNAV to Benson, 17 November 1917, both in Benson Papers.

13. "Record of the Activities of Admiral Benson while Serving as a Member of the American Mission Headed by Colonel House," undated, Benson Papers.
14. A description of Benson's suggested method of keeping mine anchors in place is in Mrs. Benson to James T. White & Co., Publishers, 11 January 1934, and Mrs. Benson to F. E. Compton & Company, 11 April 1934, copies in Klachko Files. For Jellicoe's views on attacks against German bases see his paper on the subject, June 1917, printed in *Jellicoe Papers*, 2:171–74, 178. Benson refused to reveal details of the plan to Daniels in 1921, when the former secretary of the navy was writing a book about his wartime service (Benson to Daniels, 30 August 1921, Benson Papers).
15. Jellicoe to Beatty, 9 November 1917, *Jellicoe Papers*, 2:225–26. Italics in original. The secret information that Jellicoe referred to in this passage was the signal intelligence derived from intercepts of German wireless messages. A group located in Room Forty of the Admiralty had succeeded in deciphering the intercepts. See Arthur J. Marder, *From the Dreadnought to Scapa Flow*, 4:264–68.
16. Benson to Daniels, 14 November 1917, Subject Files, VV-Visits, NA, RG 45. For British expectations of help with destroyers from the United States see "New Destroyers," *Journal of the Royal United Service Institution* 62 (1917): 155.
17. Sims's letter to his wife, 15 November 1917; and letters in a similar vein to Bayly, 20 November 1917; Pringle, 10 December 1917; Rear Admiral Albert P. Niblack, 10 December 1917; and Rear Admiral Hugh Rodman, the officer commanding the division of American battleships with the Grand Fleet, 12 December 1917, are in Sims Papers.
18. For British views on the employment of the Grand Fleet see "The Influence of the Submarine upon Naval Policy and Operations," memorandum for the War Cabinet by the First Sea Lord, 18 November 1917, Cab. 24/33, X.G. 7735. See also First Sea Lord, memorandum for the War Cabinet, 18 November 1917, "The Influence of the Submarine upon Naval Policy and Operations," Subject Files, NA, RG 45. A handwritten notation appears on the latter document: "Permission to print refused by the Admiralty, Oct. 1930." Presumably the U.S. Department of State requested permission to include this document in a volume of the *Foreign Relations* series, but the Admiralty refused to cooperate.
19. Benson to Daniels, 19 November 1917, Daniels Papers. In another message Benson directed the two officers to report directly to Sims. Benson to OPNAV, 22 November 1917, Subject Files, VV-Visits, NA, RG 45.
20. The Churchill proposal is in Churchill to Wilson, 22 October 1917, Daniels Papers. On 21 October 1917 Sims informed Mrs. Sims that "Cone, Babby [Babcock], and I had him [Churchill] to dinner to go over his first rough draft of his letter to W.W. We will see the final draft before it goes. I believe it will do a lot of good" (Sims Papers). For evidence of the close relations between Sims and Churchill see the latter's letter to Sims, 13 November 1917, Sims Papers. For Pratt's position see Pratt memorandum for the Secretary of the Navy, handwritten, undated, and for Daniels's suggestion that Benson and Churchill confer see Daniels to Benson, 12 November 1917, and Daniels to Churchill, 12 November 1917, all in Daniels Papers.
21. Benson to OPNAV, 11 November 1917; Benson to OPNAV (for Secretary of the Navy), 16 November 1917, both in Benson Papers. The statement about subordination to the American ambassador annoyed Sims, who

wrote to Pratt angrily: "Where did you people in Washington get the idea that the naval attaché was subordinate to the ambassador?" (Sims to Pratt, 21 November 1917, Sims Papers).

22. Benson's proposal is in Benson to Daniels, undated, Daniels Papers. Refusal to name Sims an honorary member of the Admiralty is in entry for 26 November 1917, Daniels Diary. Italics in original. For both the president's and Admiral Benson's views see entry for 31 January 1918, Daniels Diary; Wilson to Daniels, 31 January 1918, Daniels Papers.

23. For information about the luncheon at 10 Downing Street see "Procès-verbal of a Conference of the British War Cabinet and Heads of Government Departments with Certain Members of the Mission from the United States of America, held at 10 Downing Street, S.W., on Tuesday, November 20, 1917, at 11:30 a.m.," Bainbridge Colby Papers, Library of Congress, Manuscript Division, Washington, D.C. Hereafter cited as Colby Papers. See also David Lloyd George, *War Memoirs of David Lloyd George*, 5:3002–17, and "Secret Document Reveals Britain's Darkest Hour: Lloyd George's Moving Appeal to America—the United States Gives Pledges and Redeems Them," *Current History* 22, no. 4 (July 1925).

24. "Procès-verbal of a Conference," 20 November 1917, Colby Papers.

25. For the exchange between Daniels and Wilson see Daniels to Wilson, 21 November 1917, Wilson Papers; Wilson to Daniels, 22 November 1917, Daniels Papers. The British view of the proposed inter-Allied naval council was decided on 15 November 1917. See "Minutes of a Meeting of the War Cabinet, held at 10 Downing Street, S.W., on Thursday, November 15, 1917, at 11:30 a.m.," Cab. 23/4, X.G. 7729. The discussion of 20 November 1917 is reported in Sims to Pratt, 21 November 1917, Sims Papers.

26. For the views regarding Benson see entry for 19 November 1917, House Diary; "New Destroyers," *Journal of the Royal United Service Institution* 62 (1917): 155; entry for 21 November 1917, House Diary. At Calais, Benson was pleasantly surprised by the assignment of his son Howard, then with the United States Patrol Squadron based in France, to his staff for the stay in Paris. Benson's other aides were Lieutenant Commander Carter and Naval Constructor Lewis B. McBride.

27. For the meeting with Sharp see Francis Warrington Dawson, ed., *The War Memoirs of William Graves Sharp: American Ambassador to France, 1914–1919*, pp. 178–79. For the meetings with de Bon, Leygues, and Wemyss and consideration of Italian matters see Daniels to Benson, 6 November 1917, Benson Papers; Sims to Mrs. Sims, 30 November 1917, Sims Papers; Benson to Train, 26 November 1917; Train to Benson, 27 November 1917; Benson to Train, 29 November 1917, all in Benson Papers.

28. For the views of the naval leaders see "Record of the Activities of Admiral Benson while Serving as a Member of the American Mission Headed by Colonel House," and for the submission of the proposal to Washington and the president's response see Daniels to Benson, 26 November 1917, both in Benson Papers.

29. For these developments see Trask, *Captains and Cabinets*, pp. 179–80. See, for Geddes's view and other matters, the Minutes of the First Session, Allied Naval Council, 29–30 November 1917, Subject Files, QC-Records of the Allied Naval Council, NA, RG 45.

30. For an account of the session see entry for 29 November 1917, House Diary.

31. Sims to Mrs. Sims, 19 July 1918, Sims Papers.
32. Confidential "Doctrine," 1 December 1917, Area Files, D-Navy Department, NA, RG 45.
33. For Benson's message to Sims see Benson to Sims, 8 December 1917, Sims Papers. Sims delayed his reply until 18 January 1918: "I am sorry that I did not know that you had something more to tell me before I left the *Mount Vernon*. . . . I naturally supposed that as we had been together for three or four days that you had told me everything that you want" (Sims to Benson, 18 January 1918, Benson Papers).
34. Cravath to House, 6 December 1917, and Report of General Bliss, 14 December 1917, both in House Papers.
35. "A Brief Memorandum Covering What I Believe to Have Been Accomplished in Naval Matters during the Visit of the Mission to Europe, and Certain Recommendations for Future Action," written on board the USS *Mount Vernon*, 14 December 1917, by Benson (House Papers). See also "Report of the Special Representative of the United States Government (House)," *Foreign Relations, 1917*, Supplement 2, 1:385 ff.
36. Entry for 17 December 1917, Phillips Journals. In appreciation of Benson's services, Colonel House presented him a photograph inscribed: "To W. S. Benson, my friend and comrade in a great adventure, December 1917, EM House." Sims also presented a photograph to Benson inscribed: "To Admiral W. S. Benson, U.S.N., in grateful remembrance of his patience, square dealing, and unfailing support in carrying out my responsible duties in European Waters during the Great War. London, Nov., 1917. Wm. S. Sims." Both photographs from the Family Album are still in possession of Howard H. J. Benson, Jr., Admiral Benson's grandson.

CHAPTER 9

1. For Daniels's report see entry for 17 December 1917, Daniels Diary. Benson's observations are in the "Report of the Special Representative of the United States Government (House)," *Foreign Relations, 1917*, Supplement 2, 1:385. See Allard, "Anglo-American Naval Differences during World War I," p. 15.
2. Benson to Rear Admiral Walter McLean (Navy Yard, Norfolk, Va.), 1 February 1918; McLean to Benson, 4 February 1918; and Benson to W. A. Gracey, 19 April 1918, all in Benson Papers.
3. Pratt, "Autobiography," p. 204. Pratt to Sims, undated, in answer to Sims to Pratt, 12 March 1918, Subject Files, TD-Admiral Sims's Personal File, NA, RG 45.
4. Daniels to Sims and Benson to Sims, 22 December 1917, are in Subject Files, TD-Admiral Sims's Personal File, NA, RG 45. For Sims's reply see Sims to Daniels, 23 December 1917, Sims Papers. Congressman Oliver is quoted in *Washington Post*, 4 January 1918.
5. Entry for 9 January 1918, House Diary; entry for 28 January 1918, Daniels Diary.
6. Caperton to Benson, 11 January 1918; Knight to Benson, 1 February 1918, both in Benson Papers. For the views of Sims's subordinate see McBride to Sims, 9 January 1918, Sims Papers.
7. Entry for 26 January 1918, Daniels Diary; Babcock to Sims, 5 February 1918, Sims Papers.
8. Belknap to Sims, 2 March 1918, Sims Papers; Laning to Sims, 26 August 1918, Subject Files, TD-Admiral Sims's Personal File, NA, RG 45.

9. For the differing British and American views of the planning section see Sims to Secretary of the Navy (Operations); Subject: Planning Section on Force Commander's Staff, 21 January 1918, Subject Files, TD-Admiral Sims's Personal File, NA, RG 45. To this document was attached memorandum no. 2 of the planning section; Subject: Duties of Planning Section, 2 January 1918. It also appears in U.S. Office of Naval Records and Library, monograph no. 7: *The American Naval Planning Section, London* (1923), pp. 10–11. Twining's decision is in another memorandum attached to his report of 21 January 1918, titled "Memorandum Regarding Planning Section of Admiral Sims's Staff," 3 January 1918, Subject Files, TD File, NA, RG 45. Sims's judgment is in Sims to Benson, 7 March 1918, Sims Papers.

10. Benson to SIMSADUS, 2 February 1918, Subject Files, OP-Plans and Policies, NA, RG 45.

11. Special Board to Chief of Naval Operations, 1 February 1918, quoted in Captain Pratt's testimony on 19 April 1919 in U.S. Congress, House Committee on Naval Affairs, *Hearings on Naval Estimates for 1919*, 65th Cong., 3d sess., 1:1243–50.

12. Pershing's views on troop shipments are in his *My Experiences in the World War*, 1:250. For the Naval Overseas Transportation Service (NOTS), see Clephane, *History of the Naval Overseas Transportation Service*, pp. 8–9.

13. For Sims's views see Sims to Pratt, 14 August 1917. See also Sims to Bayly, 14 August 1918. His recommendation concerning reinforcement at Queenstown is in Sims to OPNAV, 8 January 1918. Pershing's statement is quoted in OPNAV to Sims, 8 January 1918. For Benson's views on the need to develop forces on the French coast see Benson to Sims, 8 December 1917. All of these communications are in the Sims Papers.

14. Benson to Sims, 3 January 1918, Area Files, European Area, NA, RG 45. For Sims's actions see Force Commander to Wilson, 12 January 1918, in the same location.

15. For Baker's role see Frederick Palmer, *Newton D. Baker: America at War*, 1:252.

16. For these episodes see Sims to Benson, 15 February 1918, Benson Papers; Sims to Benson, 16 April 1918; Sims to Pratt, 4, 16, and 29 April 1918; Pratt to Sims, 30 April 1918 (italics in original); Benson to Sims, 8 May 1918; Sims to Mrs. Sims, 10 May 1918; Sims to Pratt, 12 May 1918; Sims to Benson, 1 June 1918, all in Sims Papers. Elting E. Morison notes that when Sims became disturbed in May, "Benson, as he did so often during the war, came to Sims' support and assured him that no change was contemplated" (*Admiral Sims*, p. 385).

17. For information concerning the reaction to the appearance of German submarines in American waters see Daniels to Sims, 13 May 1918, Daniels Papers; Sims to Benson, 16 May 1918, Daniels Diary; Sims to Bayly, 1 June 1918, Sims Papers.

18. For information about the appearance of the U-boats in American waters see U.S. Office of Naval Records and Library, monograph no. 1: *German Submarine Activities on the Atlantic Coast of the United States and Canada* (1920); Benson to Howard Benson, 18 June 1918, Klachko Files.

19. "Reminiscences of Rear Admiral Harold Cecil Train," p. 62. Also author's interview with Train, 26 March 1968.

20. Taylor to Sims, 22 December 1917; Sims to Bristol, 24 January 1918, both in Sims Papers.

21. See "The North Sea Barrage," in U.S. Office of Naval Records and Library, *American Naval Planning Section, London*, p. 9. See also, in the same publication, "Further Characteristics of Northern Barrage," pp. 12–13.

22. For these developments see Daniels to Lansing, undated, with Benson's memorandum titled "Use of Japanese Shipping," 14 February 1918, attached, Daniels Papers; Benson to House, 28 February 1918, with Benson's memorandum titled "Memo for Colonel House" attached, House Papers.

23. Benson to Sims, 19 March 1918, Area Files, North Pacific, NA, RG 45.

24. For Pratt's leave see Pratt to Sims, 15 August 1918, Pratt Papers. For information about Benson's visit to Saranac Lake see Carter to Pratt, 2 September 1918, Benson Papers. For Daniels's observation see Patric R. Duffy, "A Great and Honorable Man," *Columbia*, April 1933, p. 13. Benson was a believer in prayer. Father Duffy reports that Benson once said to Secretary Daniels as they were leaving the Navy Department after a long workday: "Mr. Secretary, I want you to know that I pray for you every night—that your health may be preserved and that you will be guided in the great work entrusted to you."

25. For the characterization of Benson see "Persons in the Background," *Current Opinion*, 30 July 1918, pp. 86–87. See also "Our Ranking Admiral," *Boston Transcript*, 10 August 1918.

CHAPTER 10

1. Balfour to Wiseman, 5 March 1918, Arthur James Balfour Papers, British Museum, London. Hereafter cited as Balfour Papers. For a detailed analysis of the de Bunsen Mission see Klachko, "Anglo-American Naval Competition, 1918–1922," pp. 26–32. The mission first came to light in George Henry Payne's work *England: Her Treatment of America*. Balfour's description of the de Bunsen Mission is in Balfour to his Majesty's Representatives in South America, 4 April 1918, in "Correspondence of the British Mission to South America, 1918" (presented to Parliament by Command of His Majesty, May 1919). For Howard's dispatch and its suppression see Roy Howard to United States Press Office in Buenos Aires, 20 May 1918, in a memorandum sent by Lansing to President Wilson on 27 May 1918, Decimal File 033.4120/16½, NA, RG 59; Lansing to President Wilson, 27 May 1918, Decimal File 033.4120/16½, NA, RG 59.

2. For Benson's reaction see his letter to George Henry Payne, 13 September 1930, Benson Papers. The secretary of the navy expressed his view in Daniels to Lansing, undated but c. 17 July 1918, Decimal File 033.4120/18, NA, RG 59. A copy is also in Daniels Papers.

3. For the complaint about the activities of British agents in New York see Office of Naval Intelligence to Frank L. Polk, 8 June and 13 July 1918, Frank L. Polk Confidential Diaries and Papers, Yale University Archives, Historical Manuscripts, Yale University, New Haven. Hereafter cited as Polk Papers. For Willert's letter to Dawson, 21 July 1918, see *The History of the Times*, pt. 1, *1912–1920*, p. 440.

4. For the British reasons for seeking to arrange the postwar acquisition of American merchant ships see Admiralty memorandum [by the First Lord of the Admiralty] to the War Cabinet, "Naval Effort: Great Britain and the United States of America," July 1918, in Captain T. E. Crease Papers, Naval Library, Ministry of Defense, London. Rear Admiral Halsey to Sims, 17 May 1918, Subject Files, UP-Reports and Recommendations of the General Board, NA, RG 45. For the American attitude toward this

proposal see Freidel, *Franklin D. Roosevelt*, 1:353. For Sims's comments to his wife see his letter, 10 May 1918, Sims Papers. The exchanges between the Navy Department and Sims are covered in Sims to OP-NAV, 23 July 1918, Sims Papers; Daniels to Sims, 24 July 1918, Subject Files, Admiralty Navy Staff Duties, NA, RG 45; Sims to Daniels, 26 July 1918, Subject Files, TD-Admiral Sims's Personal File, NA, RG 45.

5. Benson to Sims, 16 August 1918, Subject Files, TD-Admiral Sims's Personal File, NA, RG 45; Force Commander (Sims) to Navy Department (Benson), Subject: Repair Facilities for United States Vessels in European Waters, Compensation to Great Britain, 15 August 1918; and Benson to Sims, 30 September 1918, both in Sims Papers.

6. For Geddes's activities see Minutes of the Board of Admiralty, 1 August 1918, Adm. 167/53; Statement to visiting congressmen, 2 August 1918, Geddes Papers, Adm. 116/1809; Sims's remarks to visiting editors, 6 September 1918, Pratt Papers; Minutes of Meeting of the Foreign Office, Lord Reading Presiding, 16 August 1918, p. 257, Balfour Papers. For Roosevelt's suggestion at the instigation of Geddes see "Report on Visit of Inspection in England, Scotland, Ireland, France, and Italy by Assistant Secretary of the Navy to the Secretary of the Navy of October 21, 1918," F. D. Roosevelt Papers. For Daniels's declination see Daniels to Geddes, 20 August 1918, Daniels Papers.

7. The invitation to Geddes is in Daniels to First Lord of the Admiralty, undated, F/18/2/13, Lloyd George Papers. For Sims's comments see Sims to Pratt, 30 August 1918, Pratt Papers. A copy is in Sims Papers.

8. Geddes is quoted in Daniels, *Years of War and After*, pp. 329–30. He based his comments on a memorandum titled "Proposition of German Submarine Fleet at Various Periods from Commencement of War," undated, in Daniels Papers. The Geddes Mission is discussed in Klachko, "Anglo-American Naval Competition, 1918–1922," pp. 34–36. Trask provides a detailed account based on Admiralty records (not available to scholars at the time of Klachko's research) in *Captains and Cabinets*, pp. 283–312.

9. Geddes's first interview is reported in the *Evening Star* (Washington), 9 October 1918. The second is in the *New York Times*, 10 October 1918.

10. For Wilson's irritation see entry for 13 October 1918, House Diary. For Lloyd George to Geddes, 12 October 1918, see F.O. 371/3493.

11. Geddes to Lloyd George, 13 October 1918, F/18/2/23.

12. For Geddes's guidance see First Lord, memorandum, 19 September 1918, Adm. 137/1622. For daily memoranda describing the meetings between the representatives of the Geddes Mission and the Navy Department see Subject Files, TT-British and U.S. Navies, NA, RG 45. See also Geddes Papers, Adm. 116/1809.

13. Benson to Pratt, 21 October 1918, Pratt Papers. See also Office of Naval Intelligence, U.S. Navy Department, "United States Activity in Connection with the Armistice of 1918 and the Peace Conference of 1918" (mimeographed), March 1944, Operational Archives, Naval Historical Center, Washington Navy Yard, Washington, D.C. Benson's request to the London planning section, 16 October 1918, is in the Benson Papers.

14. For Wiseman's reports see "Notes on Interview with the President at the White House, Wednesday, October 16, 1918," F.O. 800/214,

italics in original; "The Attitude of the United States and of President Wilson toward the Peace Conference," F.O. 800/214, italics in original.

15. Memorandum no. 59, "Armistice Terms," 24 October 1918, published in U.S. Office of Naval Records and Library, *American Naval Planning Section, London*, pp. 416–44; a copy is also in Benson Papers. For the action of General Bliss see Trask, *The United States in the Supreme War Council*, pp. 154–55.
16. Entry for 28 October 1918, House Diary.
17. Navy Department to Sims for Benson and House, 28 October 1918, Wilson Papers.
18. Sims's return to London is reported in Sims to Mrs. Sims, 4 November 1918, Sims Papers. For the exchange on freedom of the seas see Charles Seymour, *The Intimate Papers of Colonel House*, 4:165–66.
19. Benson to House, 30 October 1918, Subject Files, VA-Armistice, NA, RG 45.
20. Pratt to Daniels, undated, Pratt Papers. A copy in the Daniels Papers bears a cryptic pencilled comment by Franklin D. Roosevelt: "The sending of a sort of left-hand approval would help Benson's position a lot." For the secretary's message see Daniels to Benson, 29 October 1918, Subject Files, VA-Armistice, NA, RG 45.
21. For these two messages see Wilson to House, 29 October 1918, Wilson Papers; Official paraphrase of Wilson to House, 30 October 1918, House Papers.
22. Lloyd George's message is reported in House to Lansing, 30 October 1918 (second cable this date), House Papers. Lord Reading's observation is reported in Lady Wester Wemyss, *Life and Letters of Lord Wester Wemyss . . . Admiral of the Fleet*, p. 387.
23. Geddes's views are reported in Benson to House, 2 November 1918, House Papers. Benson's endorsement of the president's instructions is in Benson to Daniels, 10 November 1918, Daniels Papers. Pratt registered his view in "Memo for C.N.O. (secret)," handwritten and undated, Benson Papers. Sims to Mrs. Sims, 4 November 1918, Sims Papers.
24. For Lloyd George's proposal see Seymour, *Intimate Papers of Colonel House*, 4:131–32. For Benson's reservations see Minutes of the Sixth Meeting, Allied Naval Council, 1 November 1918, Fifth Session, Subject Files, QC-Records of the Allied Naval Council, NA, RG 45. For Foch's statement see Marshal Ferdinand Foch, *The Memoirs of Marshal Foch*, pp. 542–43.
25. Wilson's view is in his cable to House, 31 October 1918, House Papers. For the discussion on 3 November 1918 see entry for 3 November 1918, House Diary.
26. For the debate in the Allied Naval Council see Minutes of the Sixth Meeting, Allied Naval Council, 4 November 1918, Subject Files, QC-Records of the Allied Naval Council, NA, RG 45. The interned ships were six battle cruisers, ten battleships, eight light cruisers, two mine layers, and fifty destroyers. For the outcome in the Supreme War Council see Trask, *Captains and Cabinets*, pp. 347–48.
27. Trask, *The United States in the Supreme War Council*, pp. 170–71.
28. For the memorandum see Benson Papers or U.S. Office of Naval Records and Library, *American Naval Planning Section, London*, pp. 457–60. For an analysis of this memorandum see Trask, *Captains and Cabinets*, pp. 350–52.
29. Benson to Daniels, 10 November 1918, Daniels Papers.

CHAPTER 11

1. Sims to Mrs. Sims, 24 November 1918, Sims Papers; Benson to Daniels, 11 November 1918, and Daniels to Benson, 14 November 1918, both in Daniels Papers; Caperton to Benson, 12 November 1918, Benson Papers.
2. Commander in Chief, Grand Fleet, to Admiralty, 12 November 1918, no. 3065/H.F. 0013, Adm. 116/1825.
3. The terms of the armistice are given in full in Harry R. Rudin, *Armistice, 1918*, pp. 430–32. Information about the Paris meeting on 11 November 1918 and the Allied Naval Armistice Commission is in Benson to Daniels, "Report of Progress in Execution of the Armistice with Germany," 7 January 1919, Benson Papers. For Admiral de Grasset's attitude see Stephen Roskill, *Naval Policy between the Wars*, vol. 1, *The Period of Anglo-American Antagonism, 1919–1929*, p. 77. For the emergency meeting on 13 November 1918 see Allied Naval Council, "Report of the Emergency Meeting Held in London on Wednesday, 13th November 1918," Benson Papers. Another copy is in Adm. 116/1825.
4. For the Benson-Sims exchange see Benson to Daniels, "Report of Progress in Execution of Armistice with Germany," 7 January 1918, and for Sims's support for the British procedure see Sims to Benson, 20 December 1918, both in Benson Papers.
5. For Sims's description of the surrender see Sims to Cone, 23 November 1918, and Sims to Bayly, 25 November 1918, both in Sims Papers.
6. Twining to Benson, 23 November 1918; Benson to Sims, 17 December 1918; and Sims to Benson, 20 December 1918, all in Benson Papers. Roskill commented on Benson's letter to Sims as follows: it suggested that the "Chief of Naval Operations viewed with suspicion his colleague's well-known sympathy with the British point of view" (*Naval Policy between the Wars*, 1:77–78).
7. Chief of Naval Operations to Naval Attaché, Rome, Italy, "Italian Occupation of Istria and Dalmatian Coast," in response to Attaché Report, 25 November 1918, Benson Papers.
8. Benson to Daniels, 26 November 1918, Daniels Papers.
9. Benson to Daniels, 30 November 1918, Daniels Papers. For Daniels's response see Daniels to Benson, 30 November 1918, Daniels Diary. In January 1919, despite Benson's strenuous objections, President Wilson reached an agreement with Lloyd George concerning the interned submarines that resulted in the transfer of five to the United States for experimental purposes. For Benson's objection see Benson to Wilson, undated but c. 25 January 1919, and for the CNO's views on restoration of naval vessels to the Central Powers see Naval Advisory Staff memorandum, 17 December 1918, both in Wilson Papers.
10. For an indication that Benson's reasoning was accurate and that some officials advocated absorbing German ships into the Royal Navy see Lord Fisher's memorandum to the Secretary of the War Cabinet, 21 October 1918, and his explanatory remarks. Admiral of the Fleet Lord Fisher, *Memories and Records*, 2:233; N. E. Prothero, Board of Agriculture and Fisheries, to Prime Minister, 30 November 1918, F/15/8/46.
11. Benson to Daniels, 20 November 1918, Benson Papers.
12. For Mrs. Benson's reaction see entry for 3 December 1918, Daniels Diary. For Sims's reaction see Bayly to Sims, 5 December 1918, Fullam to Sims, 26 December 1918 (italics in original), and Sims to Fullam, 15 January 1919, all in Sims Papers.

13. President Wilson's speech is reported in *New York Times*, 3 December 1918.
14. U.S. Congress, House, Committee on Naval Affairs, *Hearings ... on Estimates Submitted by the Secretary of the Navy, 1918–1919*, 65th Cong., 2d and 3d sess., 1:821.
15. Lord Commissioners of His Majesty's Treasury to Lord Commissioners of the Admiralty, Treasury Chambers, 20 December 1918, Circulated to the Admiralty Civil Staff on 3 January 1919, Adm. 5433/18.
16. For information about the Inquiry see Lawrence E. Gelfand, *The Inquiry: American Preparations for Peace, 1917–1919*.
17. For the establishment and work of the communications center see Benson to Sims, 2 December 1918, and "Statement of Admiral Benson in Connection with His Mission as American Representative on the Inter-Allied Naval Council," dictated 7 October 1919, Benson Papers; also in Daniels Papers.
18. Unless otherwise indicated, reference to Benson's conferences with given individuals are based on the "War Diary of Admiral Benson, Admiral Benson's Personal File, October 1918–June 1919," in Subject Files, UB-Admiral Benson's Personal File, NA, RG 45.
19. Pershing to Benson, 25 January 1919, Benson Papers; Daniels to Wilson, 25 January 1919, Daniels Papers; Fitness Report on Admiral Bullard, 25 January 1919, Sims Papers; Mission no. 243 (report on Italian officer), 25 January 1919, Benson Papers; Benson to Robison, 25 January 1919, Subject Files, QN-Allied Naval Armistice Commission, NA, RG 45.
20. Benson to Mary Krafft, 28 December 1918, Klachko Files. Mrs. Krafft made available a copy of this letter.
21. For Churchill's speech at Dundee see "The War, Its Naval Side: Surrender of the German Fleet," *Journal of the Royal United Service Institution* 62 (1919): 129. For Sir Eric Geddes's public statement see "Delicate Anglo-American Relations," 10 December 1918, Subject Files, F-Freedom of the Seas, NA, RG 45. His secret statement is in his "Memorandum on Terms of Peace, November 15, 1918," Adm. 116/1852. Geddes remained a dedicated opponent of freedom of the seas. On 18 January 1919 he sent to Lloyd George a copy of a message dated 17 January 1919 from Benson to Daniels calling on the United States to stop Allied propaganda in American newspapers. Something must be done, Benson stated, to "stop Allied propaganda in the United States." Benson concluded with an endorsement of the naval construction scheme then before Congress: "Without appearing antagonistic it is necessary to insist on United States Shipbuilding programme to insure biggest Fleet. By no other means can Great Britain be forced to accept our terms at the Peace Conference." Geddes explained to Lloyd George that this message had fallen into British hands because a "friend" in the Navy Department was so "indignant" that he had handed over a copy. Geddes to Lloyd George, 18 January 1919, F/18/3/3. Geddes, incidentally, had just surrendered his position as First Lord of the Admiralty to Walter Long.
22. The plan for a league navy drafted on 11 November 1918, signed by Rear Admirals Coontz and McKean, Captains Pratt, Waldo Evans, and Yarnell, and Professor George G. Wilson, is in Benson Papers. The replacement plan, "Report of Planning Section Regarding the Establishment of a League Navy," 4 January [1919], is also in Benson Papers.
23. Lodge is quoted in *Congressional Record*, 65th Cong., 1st sess. (1918), 57:27. For President Woodrow Wilson's remarks see his speech at San

Diego, Calif., in Baker and Dodd, eds., *Public Papers of Woodrow Wilson*, 6:294.

24. Gilbert F. Close (confidential secretary to President Wilson) from Wilson to Benson for Daniels, 27 January 1919, Wilson Papers. See also entry for 28 January 1919 in Daniels Diary.

25. Benson to Wilson, undated but probably 25 January 1919, Wilson Papers; Wilson to Benson, 27 January 1919, Benson Papers.

CHAPTER 12

1. Memorandum of Proceedings, Admirals of the Allied and Associated Powers, 28, 29, and 30 January, and 13 February 1919, Benson Papers.

2. Benson memorandum for the President, 8 February 1919, Benson Papers.

3. The British draft terms are reported in Naval Advisory Staff, Paris, memorandum no. 18, 20 February 1919, Benson Papers. Benson's suspicions are in Benson to Wilson, 7 February 1919, House Papers. The Fuller-Leygues–de Bon discussions are in a memorandum written by Captain Fuller on 15 February 1919; it has an enclosure of seven pages titled "Programme of New Construction," F/192/1/3.

4. These developments are reported in Naval Advisory Staff, Paris, memorandum no. 18, 20 February 1919, and memorandum no. 20, 26 February 1919, Benson Papers.

5. Benson to Daniels, 22 February 1919, Daniels Papers.

6. The Wilson-Daniels exchange is in Wilson to Daniels, 1 March 1919, and Daniels to Wilson, 4 March 1919, both in Daniels Papers. Daniels's views on discussing the naval terms with Benson are in entry for 6 March 1919, Daniels Diary.

7. For information about the conference see House to Wilson, 7 March 1919, House Papers; entry for 6 March 1919, House Diary. The agreement is discussed in David Lloyd George, *Memoirs of the Peace Conference*, 1:187. Notice to Benson is mentioned in entry for 7 March 1919, Auchincloss Diary. The information sent to Wemyss is in Hankey to Wemyss, 7 March 1919, Auchincloss Papers.

8. Benson to Wilson, 14 March 1919, with memorandum no. 24, "Disposition of German and Austrian Vessels of War," 13 March 1919, Wilson Papers. In another letter of the same date, Benson objected to any interference with the control of German cables and advanced a general principle: President Wilson should not "participate in measures restricting the future sovereignty of Germany within her own borders as established by the Treaty of Peace" (Benson to Wilson, 14 March 1919, Wilson Papers). The Naval Advisory Staff, Paris, issued two memoranda on the problem of Allied control of German cables, memorandum no. 18, 20 February 1919, and memorandum no. 20, 26 February 1919, both in Benson Papers.

9. Benson to Wilson, "Naval Terms," 16 March 1919, Wilson Papers.

10. Minutes of the Council of Ten, 17 March 1919, in U.S. Department of State, *Papers Relating to the Foreign Relations of the United States, 1919: The Paris Peace Conference*, 4:355–403; Benson to Wilson, 18 March 1919, Wilson Papers.

11. Entry for 25 March 1919, Daniels Diary.

12. Memorandum by Admiral Benson, 16 May 1921, Benson Papers. This memorandum was first published in Payne, *England: Her Treatment of America* (pp. 214–21). Seeking to protect Benson from criticism, Payne wrote: "Probably, when this book is published [1931], Benson will be

accused of being anti-British and like Sumner, Seward, and most of the Presidents of the United States and the Secretaries of State, will be charged with prejudice. In this particular case Benson cannot be accused, as were Cleveland and others, of catering to the voters, as he has never run for public office and now, being retired at seventy-five years of age, is not likely to acquire the habit" (pp. 212–13). The secretary of the navy's account is in Daniels to Dudley W. Knox, 29 January 1937, Subject Files, UB-Admiral Benson's Personal File, NA, RG 45.

13. Entry for 27 March 1919, House Diary.
14. This account is based on several sources and authorities, including Daniels, *Years of War and After*, p. 368; Daniels to Wilson, 30 March 1919, Daniels Papers; Josephus Daniels, "March of Events: Britain Demanded at Paris to Woodrow Wilson Curtail the U.S. Navy," *New York Journal American*, 23 January 1927; Daniels to Knox, 29 January 1937, Subject Files, UB-Admiral Benson's Personal File, NA, RG 45.
15. The exchanges in this meeting are reported in Daniels, "March of Events."
16. Benson memorandum, 16 May 1921, Benson Papers. Some question the reliability of this memorandum because it was written more than two years after the conference. Long's memorandum of this gathering confirms Benson's report. The First Lord of the Admiralty, naturally, emphasized different details, but he conveyed the same impressions. Long to Prime Minister, 29 March 1919, F/192/1/4.
17. Daniels, *Years of War and After*, pp. 368, 371; Daniels to Wilson, 30 March 1919, Daniels Papers.
18. Long to Prime Minister, 29 March 1919, F/192/1/4.
19. Daniels, "March of Events."
20. See ibid.; Secretary of the Navy, memorandum for the President, 7 April 1919, Wilson Papers.
21. Entries for 1 and 3 April 1919, Daniels Diary. E. David Cronon believes that Benson's effort to keep Daniels out of the negotiations represented "disloyalty" to the secretary, who had complete trust in the CNO. (*Cabinet Diaries of Josephus Daniels*, p. 384). I suggest that Benson's commitment to naval parity was so strong that he felt he had no alternative but to do what was possible to exclude Daniels from future discussions.
22. Wemyss to Long, 3 April 1919, Admiral Sir Rosslyn Wester Wemyss Letters and Memoirs, Library of the University of California, Irvine. For Benson's advice to Daniels about meetings with the British leaders see entry for 7 April 1919, Daniels Diary.
23. For the Daniels-Long conference see entry for 7 April 1919, Daniels Diary; Memorandum for the President from the Secretary of the Navy, 7 April 1919, Wilson Papers; Long to Lloyd George, 7 April 1919, F/33/2/31; Daniels, *Years of War and After*, p. 382.
24. Naval Advisory Staff, memorandum no. 25, "United States Naval Policy," 8 April 1919, Benson Papers. One authority has noted: "The American naval professionals worked sincerely and stubbornly for a navy second to none; their attitude might have been less intense had the anglophile Admiral Sims been selected instead of Benson to head the expert staff" (Albion, *Makers of Naval Policy, 1798–1947*, p. 227).
25. For recent expressions of the view that Benson must be treated primarily as a nationalist see Allard, "Anglo-American Naval Differences during World War I," p. 75; Trask, "William Shepherd Benson," pp. 19–20.
26. Grayson's role is described in the entry for 6 April 1919, Diary of Admiral Cary T. Grayson. The diary is in the possession of Cary T. Grayson, Jr.,

who made excerpts from it available to me. For Admiral Benson's arrangements to bring the *George Washington* to France see Mission no. 396 and Mission no. 397 for OPNAV, both 8 April 1919, and Benson to Sims, 8 April 1919, all in Benson Papers. Benson to Sims, 8 April 1919, ordered Sims to prepare four destroyers to escort the *George Washington*.

27. Cecil to House, 8 April 1919, House Papers. This document is also in the Papers of Lord Algernon Robert Cecil, Viscount Cecil of Chelwood, British Museum, London. Hereafter cited as Cecil Papers or Cecil Diaries.

28. House to Cecil, 9 April 1919, House Papers; entry for 9 April 1919, House Diary. Also in Cecil Papers.

29. This account is based on entries for 10 April 1919 in the Cecil, Auchincloss, and House Diaries.

30. "Memorandum of Conversation between Colonel House and Lord Robert Cecil," 10 April 1919, House Papers. Cecil originally had named Benson as one of the high-ranking American naval officers. House, not wanting Benson by himself to be the object of criticism, asked Cecil to take out mention of the American admiral, noting that Wemyss and Long had also made some private comments that added to the difficulty of the situation. Cecil agreed. Entry for 10 April 1919, House Diary.

31. David F. Trask, "The American Navy in a World at War, 1914–1919," in *In Peace and War: Interpretations of American Naval History, 1775–1978*, ed. Kenneth J. Hagan, pp. 217–18.

32. Daniels, *Years of War and After*, p. 370; Pratt to Benson, 5 July 1927, Benson Papers.

CHAPTER 13

1. Benson to Pratt, 9 November 1918, Subject Files, UP-Reports and Recommendations of General Board, NA, RG 45; Benson to Daniels, 10 November 1918, Daniels Papers. When Pratt visited Paris briefly in December 1918 to confer with Benson, Rear Admiral Robert E. Coontz took his place. For Pratt's views on Benson's role see his "Autobiography," p. 204. An unsigned memorandum dated 29 November 1918 offered an argument against Benson's presence in Europe. The author of this memorandum feared that Benson might become subordinate in Paris to various figures, thereby damaging the status of the office of the CNO that he had built up since 1915. Area Files, D-Navy Department, NA, RG 45.

2. Benson to Daniels, 20 December 1918, Subject Files, VA-Armistice, NA, RG 45; Benson to Daniels, 23 January 1919, Daniels Papers.

3. For Benson's reaction to the Rodman incident see Pratt, "Autobiography," pp. 220–21. Pratt's annoyance is noted in Wheeler, *William Veazie Pratt*, p. 115. For Pratt's transfer see Daniels to Benson, 4 January 1919, Daniels Papers; Pratt to Benson, 25 January 1919, Benson Papers. Pratt soon took command of the *New York*.

4. Benson's protest is in Benson to Mayo, 25 November 1918, and the Commander in Chief replied in Mayo to Benson, 27 November 1918, both in Benson Papers. Benson's response is Benson to Mayo, 20 December 1918, Subject Files, VA-Armistice, NA, RG 45.

5. Sims to Pratt, 4 November 1918, Pratt Papers; Benson to Secretary Daniels, 18 December 1918, Sims Papers. For Sims's activities in Newport, especially his work on his memoir, see David F. Trask, "Introduction" to Sims, *Victory at Sea*, pp. xx–xxvii.

6. Benson to Pratt, 21 October 1918, Pratt Papers.

7. The secretary's request that Benson study the building program is in Daniels to Benson, 24 October 1918; Pratt's observation is in Pratt to Benson, 25 October 1918; the secretary once again sought the CNO's opinion on the building program in Daniels to Benson, 26 October 1918; for Benson's criticism of the armored cruisers see Benson to Daniels, Mission 185, 5 January 1919, all in Benson Papers. Benson later modified his views on armored cruisers, although for reasons of expediency, urging in May 1919 that the department begin construction of six battle cruisers, even if it became necessary to build fast battleships later, "the point being that our first three-year building program is already appropriated for and is well under way, and no one could object to our carrying it through to completion" (Benson to Daniels, 6 May 1919, Benson Papers).

8. These recommendations are in Benson to Daniels, 19 December 1918, Daniels Papers.

9. For a careful study of the fleet reorganization see Braisted, *The United States Navy in the Pacific*, pp. 441–76. For Daniels's response see Daniels to Benson, 4 January 1919, Daniels Papers. For the public announcement see entry for 25 July 1919, Daniels Diary. Fullam's views are in Fullam to Benson, 19 June 1919, Benson Papers. The infuriated Fullam wrote that he considered Rodman's appointment a personal slight, a "direct and undeserved reflection" if not a "persecution for reasons best known to the Department."

10. For the inspection issue see Benson to McKean, 26 January 1919, General Correspondence, 1916–1926, in General Records of the Department of the Navy (Confidential Records of the Secretary of the Navy, 1917–1919, and General Correspondence, 1916–1926), Record Group 80, National Archives, Washington, D.C. Hereafter cited as Confidential Records, NA, RG 80. For the shipping control question see Benson to McKean, 5 March 1919, Confidential Records, NA, RG 80.

11. Suda Lorena Bane and Ralph Haswell Lutz, eds., *The Blockade of Germany after the Armistice, 1918–1919*, pp. 573–75.

12. For information about the Marconi negotiations see Linwood S. Howeth, *History of Communications: Electronics in the United States*, p. 353. Benson's views are in Benson to Daniels, 2 and 5 May 1919, both in Daniels Papers; Benson to McKean, 6 May 1919, Benson Papers.

13. Benson to Daniels, 6 May 1919, Benson Papers.

14. Daniels to Wilson, 11 April 1919, Wilson Papers; Daniels to Benson, undated, Daniels Papers.

15. For an account of these matters see Lloyd George, *War Memoirs*, 3:545.

16. Benson to Wilson, 28 April 1919, Wilson Papers.

17. Benson to Wilson, 5 May 1919, Benson Papers; Wilson to Benson, 6 May 1919, Wilson Papers. For background on Benson's letter see Naval Advisory Staff, memorandum no. 27, 6 May 1919, Benson Papers.

18. Benson to Daniels, 6 May 1919, Daniels Papers.

19. For Benson's reference to the de Bunsen Mission see Benson to Daniels, 5 May 1919, Daniels Papers. President Wilson's message to Congress on its opening is in Baker and Dodd, eds., *Public Papers of Woodrow Wilson*, 5:489. Daniels's speech is reported in the *Washington Post*, 30 May 1919.

20. Benson to Wilson, 29 May 1919, and Wilson to Benson, 31 May 1919, both in Benson Papers; Benson to House, 2 June 1919, and House to Benson, 6 June 1919, both in House Papers.

21. Benson to Wilson, 8 June 1919, with enclosed undated memorandum, "To Their Excellencies, the President of the United States and the Envoys

Extraordinary of the Allied and Associated Nations to the Conference of Peace"; for additional information see Benson to Pietro Cardinal Gasparri, Vatican Secretary of State, 9 April 1919, both in Benson Papers; John de Salis to Sir Ian Malcolm, 4 June 1919, Balfour Papers. The Balfour Collection contains many documents pertaining to this question.

22. For the award of the Distinguished Service Medal see Roosevelt to Benson, 19 April 1919. For the award of the Grand Cross of the Legion of Honor see Director of Naval Intelligence to Chief of the Bureau of Navigation, 23 July 1919, Subject Files, UB-Admiral Benson's Personal Correspondence, NA, RG 45. For the letter of the peace commissioners see Lansing, House, Bliss, and White to Benson, 9 June 1919, and for Beatty's telegram see Beatty to Benson, 10 June 1919, both in Benson Papers.

23. Benson's statement is in *New York Herald*, 21 June 1919.

24. For the scuttling see paraphrase of Admiral Wemyss's report, 21 June 1919, F/192/1/1. For the British comment see Roskill, *Naval Policy between the Wars*, 1:93–94. For House's view see entry for 23 June 1919, House Diary. For the signature of the peace treaty see McNamee to Benson, 9 July 1919, Benson Papers.

25. See *Revised Organization Orders of the Office of Naval Operations*, 1 August 1919.

26. Inter-Division Order no. 10, 1 August 1919, Confidential Records, NA, RG 80.

27. For information on the Naval Overseas Transportation Service see Clephane, *History of the Naval Overseas Transportation Service*, pp. xvii–xix, 1–4, 6, 61–63. The report of the Plans Committee is Planning Committee to Chief of Naval Operations, 19 June 1919, Area Files, D-Navy Department, NA, RG 45. The special joint board included Admiral Benson as senior member; the other Navy Department member was Commander George S. Bryan. The remaining members were, for the Army, Brigadier General Frank T. Hines; for the Shipping Board, Karl Krogstad and A. Merritt Taylor; for the Department of Commerce, Charles A. McQueen and Dan Eldridge.

28. For expansion of the naval air service see Reginald Wright Arthur, *Contact: Careers of U.S. Naval Aviators Assigned Numbers 1 to 2,000*, p. 584. Additional information is in Turnbull and Lord, *History of United States Naval Aviation*, p. 600.

29. Craven's report, 23 May 1919, is in Daniels Papers. For the General Board's views see Senior Member Present to Secretary of the Navy, 23 June 1919, file no. 449, General Board Papers.

30. For the appropriations process see Statement of Captain G. W. Steele, 27 November 1918, U.S. Congress, House, *Hearings on Naval Estimates for 1919*, 1:133; U.S. Congress, House, Committee on Naval Affairs, *Hearings . . . on Estimates Submitted by the Secretary of the Navy*, 1920, 66th Cong., 2d sess., 1:1530. For the differing views of Benson and Daniels see CNO to Secretary of the Navy, 21 July 1919, Confidential Records, NA, RG 80; Secretary of the Navy to General Board, 24 July 1919, file no. 449, General Board Papers. In 1974 Admiral Hyman G. Rickover testified before a congressional subcommittee that Benson had manifested extreme shortsightedness in dealing with the development of naval aviation. He reported that in 1919 Benson had said: "I cannot conceive of any use that the fleet will ever have for aircraft. The Navy doesn't need airplanes. Aviation is just a lot of noise." U.S. Congress, House, Committee

on Appropriations, *Hearings before a Subcommittee: Department of Defense Appropriations for 1974*, pt. 3, 93d Cong., 1st sess., 1974, 3:135. Inquiry by the witness's staff concerning the source of this information led to Burke Davis, *The Billy Mitchell Affair*, p. 58. Davis identified Benson in text and index as "Admiral Charles Benson." He appears to have combined statements made by two persons. These statements are quoted in the book by Isaac Don Levine titled *Mitchell, Pioneer of Air Power*, p. 183. According to Levine, Harold Coffin made the first statement in 1919 but did not testify to that effect until 1924. See U.S. Congress, House, *Hearings by the Select Committee of Inquiry into Operations of the United States Air Services*, 1925, 68th Cong., 1st sess., 1:1238. Benson supposedly made his statement in 1917. Levine indicates that Benedict Crowell uttered the last two sentences attributed to Benson as "he recalled afterwards." Benson provided as much support to the air arm in 1919 as was possible. If he is to be criticized, it should be for his failure to press aviation questions more forcefully prior to the American intervention in World War I.

31. For Benson's directive to the director of plans that led to the Oliver report see Benson to Director of Plans, 30 July 1919, and for the Oliver report see Director of Plans Division to Chief of Naval Operations, 11 August 1919, both in Confidential Records, NA, RG 80. During this period Benson sought the views of the acting Chief of French naval aviation on this question. He learned that France expected to adopt a unified air service but that the French Navy opposed this step. The requirements of the sea service differed greatly from those of the land service. Rear Admiral Knapp, who obtained this information, summarized other important considerations: "Coordination of forces by Commander-in-Chief requires entire control at all times including training, experimental, and actual services. Minister of Navy should be responsible for expenditures from appropriation for Naval aviation; air minister not in position to allot funds to best advantage of navy." Knapp to Benson, 10 August 1919, Confidential Records, NA, RG 80.

32. For the announcement of Benson's retirement see Roosevelt to Benson, 15 September 1919; for Daniels's statement see Daniels to Benson, 24 September 1919; and for the statement of the Secretary of War see Baker to Benson, 26 September 1919, all in Benson Papers. On 11 September 1919 Benson received the Army Distinguished Service Medal from Secretary Baker.

33. Badger to Benson, 30 December 1919, Benson Papers.

34. Pratt, "Autobiography," pp. 217–18.

CHAPTER 14

1. Sims to Pratt, 13 August 1918, Pratt Papers; Chief of Naval Operations to Secretary of the Navy, Subject: "General Character of the Operations of Our Naval Forces during Present War" (drafted by Captain Pratt), 15 November 1918, Benson Papers; Sims to Pratt, 28 January 1919, and Pratt to Sims, 10 March 1919, both in Sims Papers. See also Wheeler, *William Veazie Pratt*, pp. 147–48.

2. For Sims's letter to Hendrick, 29 August 1919, see Trask, "Introduction" to Sims, *Victory at Sea*, p. xxii. See also Sims to Hendrick, 6 September 1919, Sims Papers. For the Sims-Fullam correspondence see Sims to Ful-

lam, 1 October 1919, Fullam to Sims, 4 October 1919, and Sims to Fullam, 3 November 1919, all in Sims Papers.

3. Sims to Daniels, 17 December 1919; Fullam to Sims, 24 December 1919; and Fiske to Sims, 6 January 1920, all in Sims Papers. Italics in original.

4. Entry for 14 January 1920, Daniels Diary.

5. For a discussion of the Benson-Sims conversation in March 1917 see chapter 5. This incident is summarized in Trask, *Captains and Cabinets*, p. 55. For Benson's explanation see an undated memorandum, c. 1920, in box 42, Benson Papers. For mention of this matter during the naval investigation see U.S. Senate, *Hearings*, 1920, 1:268–71; 2:1881–85. One newspaper commented editorially: "Because war with Germany was certain when Admiral Sims left this country, because no official in his senses would speak of war with Great Britain, we must set the words down as a bit of flippancy, as an example of our pungent American humor. If there was any serious intent in the warning, it was seriously phrased without impropriety." The editorialist thought the intent quite apparent: "You are going abroad to plan cooperation with the British. Do your duty by the Allies, but give a thought to American [interests] too" (*New York Evening Post*, 12 January 1920). For his part Sims explained his motives to Admiral Bayly: "As for the admonition 'Don't let the British pull the wool over your eyes, and so forth' it is my personal opinion that that will serve to clear the air. This certainly does not express, and did not express the sentiment of the American people, who were solidly behind the war, and it is well that those responsible for such an attitude should be brought to book" (Sims to Bayly, 27 January 1920, Sims Papers).

6. For Coontz's views see Daniels, *Years of War and After*, p. 503. Daniels's attitude is expressed in entry for 22 January 1920, Daniels Diary. For Daniels's discussion with President Wilson see his *Years of War and After*, p. 505.

7. Benson to Woodson, 25 February 1920, Benson Papers.

8. For Sims's views see Morison, *Admiral Sims*, pp. 439, 435. Daniels was somewhat compromised when it was observed that he had awarded a Distinguished Service Medal to his brother-in-law, David Worth Bagley. For a discussion of the awards controversy see Paolo E. Coletta, "Josephus Daniels," in *American Secretaries of the Navy*, ed. Paolo E. Coletta, 2:564–65.

9. For Benson's recall to active duty see Daniels to Benson, 21 January 1920, and for Daniels's call for reports from concerned officers see memorandum for Chief of Naval Operations (Coontz), 22 January 1920, both in Benson Papers. For Sims's request for assistance from his officers see Sims to Twining, 13 February 1920, Sims Papers. For Daniels's view see entry for 29 February 1919, Daniels Diary.

10. For a sound, succinct account of the hearings see Coletta, "Josephus Daniels," pp. 566–72. For Sims's views see Tracy Barrett Kittredge, *Naval Lessons of the Great War*, p. 65. This book is strongly pro-Sims. Kittredge was a member of Sims's staff in London. Sims's statement on those naval officers who did not oppose politicians is in Sims to Fullam, 8 November 1919; see also Fullam to Page, 18 January 1920, both in Sims Papers. Enclosed with this letter was a memorandum containing Fullam's attack on Benson.

11. Sims's explanation to his wife concerning printing costs is in Sims to Mrs. Sims, 10 March 1920; for Fiske's activities see Fiske to Sims, 15 and 25

April 1920, all in Sims Papers. Daniels commented on his activities in entries for 19 and 20 January and 3 February 1920, Daniels Diary. Benson's arrangements concerning the schedule for testimony are in memorandum for the Secretary of the Navy, 17 March 1920, Daniels Papers.

12. Coletta, "Josephus Daniels," pp. 566–67.

13. For these expressions see U.S. Senate, *Hearings*, 1920, 2:2181–89.

14. In his initial statement Sims did not identify Benson as the source. Daniels denied that he had been the author or that the views expressed were those of the Navy Department. Daniels to Page, 18 January 1920, Daniels Papers; entry for 18 January 1920, Daniels Diary; Freidel, *Franklin D. Roosevelt*, 2:40. For the Hale-Sims exchange see U.S. Senate, *Hearings*, 1920, 1:267–69.

15. For a report of the investiture see *Baltimore American*, 12 April 1920.

16. Lisle to Benson, 13 February 1920, Benson Papers; Dailey to Daniels, 12 May 1920, Daniels Papers; "Georgia Opponents Oppose Honor Benson," *Catholic Standard and Times*, 28 August 1920. It is possible that some Americans believed that Benson was an Irishman born to the Roman Catholic faith, although he was of English origin and a convert.

17. For the advice to prepare a formal statement see Carter to Benson, 3 February 1920, Benson Papers. Italics in original. For Benson's testimony, 4–8 May 1919, see U.S. Senate, *Hearings*, 1920, 2:1817–979.

18. For Benson's testimony see U.S. Senate, *Hearings*, 1920, 2:1817–19.

19. Fullam to Sims, 7 May 1920, and Sims to Fullam, 7 May 1920, both in Sims Papers.

20. Brown to Benson, 10 April 1920, Benson Papers.

21. Quoted in Trask, "Willaim Shepherd Benson," pp. 9–10.

22. Benson's memorandum, 16 March 1927, Benson Papers. Quoted in Trask, "William Shepherd Benson," p. 6.

23. For the "wool-pulling" incident see U.S. Senate, *Hearings*, 1920, 2:1881–85.

24. Benson to Browning, 24 August 1920, in Records of the United States Shipping Board, Benson Correspondence File, Record Group 32, National Archives, Washington, D.C. Hereafter cited as Benson Correspondence File, NA, RG 32.

25. Benson to Brown, 2 June 1920, Benson Papers.

26. Benson to Hale, 28 May 1920, Benson Papers.

27. Sims's ambitions are revealed in Sims to Yarnell, 8 November 1920; Sims to Fiske, 17 March 1921; and Sims to Twining, 25 March 1921, all in Sims Papers. Harding wrote to Sims: "Unquestionably, you could not come here at this time without incurring some degree of publicity. I could not consistently urge your visit at this time" (Harding to Sims, 3 September 1920, Sims Papers). For Pratt's judgment see his "Autobiography," pp. 208–9.

28. Some scholars in recent years have questioned the accuracy of the pro-Sims interpretation, for example, Allard, "Anglo-American Naval Differences during World War I," and Trask, "William Shepherd Benson."

CHAPTER 15

1. Daniels writes of Mrs. Wilson's proposal on 16 February 1920, Daniels Diary. About Benson's professorship at Notre Dame see *Religious Bulletin of Notre Dame University*, 23 May 1932. For information about Benson's

decision to accept the position see Benson to Vice Admiral Hilary P. Jones, 24 February 1920; Benson to House, 25 February 1920; and Benson to Casper Yost, 12 October 1926, all in Benson Papers. For Benson's comments on his appointment see *Chicago Daily Journal*, 21 February 1920. Benson on this occasion had gone to Chicago to address a Washington Day dinner at which 2,000 men were initiated into the Knights of Columbus, 800 of them former servicemen. Benson was a popular speaker before Roman Catholic audiences. On occasion he made use of such forums to speak in behalf of a strong merchant marine.

2. For a history of the Shipping Board that covers Benson's period of service see Darrell Hevenor Smith and Paul V. Bettors, *The United States Shipping Board: Its History, Activities, and Organization*. For the similarity of Benson's views with those of Hurley and Payne see Safford, *Wilsonian Maritime Diplomacy*, pp. 176, 183, 188, 193, 201–2, 204, 224–25, 256–61.

3. The statistics are drawn from William Shepherd Benson, *The Merchant Marine: "A Necessity in Time of War; A Source of Independence and Strength in Time of Peace,"* p. 167. The situation as Benson took charge is indicated in John Barton Payne's statement: "We have nothing but ships. We have no organization." Verbatim Minutes, United States Shipping Board, 11 March 1920, Records of the United States Shipping Board, Benson Reading File, Record Group 32, National Archives, Washington, D.C. Hereafter cited as Benson Reading File, NA, RG 32.

4. Benson's views are reported in *New York Commercial*, 16 March 1920; *Journal of Commerce*, 27 March 1920; *New York Times*, 12 and 13 April 1920.

5. For a succinct statement of Benson's overall views on the merchant marine see his *The Merchant Marine*, pp. vii–viii. For his statement on foreign rivalry see *Journal of Commerce*, 27 March 1920.

6. For this information see *New York American*, 27 March 1920; *Journal of Commerce*, 27 March 1920.

7. For the president's views see Wilson to Polk, 4 March 1920, Polk Papers. Lady Isabella's statement was made during the author's interview with her in London on 5 June 1957.

8. "Scarcity of Fuel Bared by Benson," *World's Business*, 30 April 1920. Geddes's remarks are analyzed in A. C. M., "Petroleum Emergency Memorandum," Department of State, Office of the Foreign Trade Adviser, 28 May 1920, Polk Papers.

9. See "Petroleum Emergency Memorandum," cited in note 8.

10. For the conference and its result see *Evening Star* (Washington), 26 April 1920. The specific arrangements were a price for steel vessels of $120 to $185 per deadweight ton, less depreciation. Sales required 10 percent down and 5 percent additional every six months to the end of the second year. The balance was due in installments every six months for ten years (*Fifth Annual Report of the United States Shipping Board, 1921*, p. 64). These arrangements prevented buyers from borrowing "large sums from banks to make the initial payments and then defer payments if freight rates or international trade was disturbed by unforeseen factors" (Benson to Wesley Jones, 19 April 1920, quoted in Safford, *Wilsonian Maritime Diplomacy*, pp. 227–28).

11. Benson to Wesley Jones, 19 April 1920, cited in Safford, *Wilsonian Maritime Diplomacy*, pp. 227–28.

12. For opposition to the bill see entry for 1 June 1920, Daniels Diary. Benson's view is expressed in Benson to W. T. Christenson, 21 July 1920, Benson Reading File, NA, RG 32.

13. Benson's view is in *Fourth Annual Report of the United States Shipping Board, 1920*, p. 9.

14. Safford provides a summary of objections made to the Jones Act in *Wilsonian Maritime Diplomacy*, pp. 232–39. For the British comments on the violation of freedom of the seas in time of peace see Archibald Hurd, "The World's Shipping: The Balance of Power," *Fortnightly Review*, 1 October 1920, p. 590. The warning from Lloyd's is noted in "The Merchant Marine," *Washington Post*, 5 July 1920. Benson's views on Japan are quoted in "Denies Pacific Rate War," *Washington Post*, 23 August 1920. For "ship independence" see "Ship Independence Is Aim of America," *Pittsburgh Dispatch*, 19 September 1920. Benson's answer to Lloyd's threat was to encourage development of American companies that could offer marine insurance.

15. For the American-German agreement see "U.S. German Ship Deal 100 Percent American, Admiral Benson Says," *Washington Herald*, 9 September 1920. For this letter to Browning see Benson to Browning, Benson Reading File, NA, RG 32.

16. "U.S. German Ship Deal 100 Percent American, Admiral Benson Says."

17. Opposition from the Department of State as well as from those cabinet members who had earlier attempted to block passage of the Jones Act along with John Barton Payne influenced the president. *Charleston American*, 13 October 1920; Carter to Benson, 25 October 1920, Benson Papers.

18. For the recess appointments see *Evening Star* (Washington), 1 December 1920. The group included Frederick L. Thompson (D-Ala.) for a five-year term, Joseph N. Teal (D-Oreg.) for a four-year term, Chester H. Rowell (R-Calif.) for a two-year term, and Guy D. Goff (R-Mo.) for a one-year term. Benson received a six-year term, and the only other holdover, John A. Donald, received a three-year term. For Carter's views see Carter to Benson, 24 January 1921, Benson Papers. For the report of Republican support for Benson see *Washington Times*, 2 March 1921.

19. Harding to Benson, 11 March 1921, and Benson to Harding, 11 March 1921, both in Benson Reading File, NA, RG 32.

20. *Evening Star* (Washington), 18 January 1921.

21. For information about the maritime strike see *Baltimore Sun*, 3 May 1921; *Evening Star* (Washington), 3 May 1921; *Philadelphia Inquirer*, 4 May 1921; *Washington Post*, 9 May and 14 June 1921; *Philadelphia Record*, 15 May 1921.

22. For Benson's letter of acceptance see Benson to Harding, 22 June 1921. For the initial activities of the new Shipping Board see *Evening Star* (Washington), 18 June 1921. For presentation of the bust see *Daily Marine Record*, 7 June 1921. The bust is now on exhibition at the United States Naval Academy. For Benson's comment on his health see Benson to Belknap, 22 August 1921, Benson Reading File, NA, RG 32.

23. Benson to Harding, 16 May 1921, Benson Papers. The government did not release this memorandum until 25 August 1953, but it was printed in full in Payne's *England: Her Treatment of America*, pp. 214–21.

24. General Board Questionnaire, 22 August 1921, Benson Reading File, NA, RG 32.

25. Benson to General Board, 17 September 1921, file no. 438, General Board Papers.

26. "Notes Relating to the International Conference on the Limitation of Armaments," 26 September 1921, Subject Files, UB-Admiral Benson's Personal File, NA, RG 45.
27. Benson to General Board, 24 October 1921, file no. 438, General Board Papers.
28. For mention of Benson as a logical adviser at the disarmament conference see *Daily Marine Record*, 3 November 1921. For the rejection of the General Board's plan see Theodore Roosevelt, Jr., to Mrs. Theodore Roosevelt, 26 October 1921, Theodore Roosevelt, Jr., Papers, Library of Congress, Manuscript Division, Washington, D.C. The author examined these papers at the home of Mrs. Theodore Roosevelt, Jr., at Oyster Bay, New York, before they were deposited at the Library of Congress. For additional information on the background of the Washington Conference see Klachko, "Anglo-American Naval Competition, 1918–1922," pp. 220–93.
29. Benson to Roosevelt, Jr., 19 December 1921, Benson Papers.
30. Benson to Daniels, 16 March 1922, Benson Reading File, NA, RG 32.
31. Browning to Mrs. Benson, 21 November 1923, and Browning to Benson, 24 November 1923, both in Benson Papers.
32. Benson to Senator Duncan U. Fletcher (D-Fla.), Chairman, Senate Commerce Committee, 25 August 1921, Benson Reading File, NA, RG 32.
33. "A Review by Rear Admiral W. S. Benson, U.S.N., of Winston S. Churchill's *The World Crisis*" (1923), Benson Papers. Italics in original.
34. For the test of the *William Penn* see Benson, *The Merchant Marine*, p. 162. For Benson's efforts to encourage diesel conversion see "Proceedings of a Conference Called by Commissioner W. S. Benson of the United States Shipping Board to Consider the Question of the Installation of Diesel Engines in Ships of the American Merchant Marine," 16 November 1922, and "Diesel Advisory Committee," U.S. Shipping Board Press Release, 16 June 1924, both in Benson Correspondence File, NA, RG 32; Benson to Browning, 6 June 1927 and 27 May 1928, Benson Reading File, NA, RG 32. Gatewood's views were expressed during author's interview with him on 21 April 1973. Benson made Gatewood manager of the Maintenance and Repair Division, Emergency Fleet Corporation, U.S. Shipping Board, in September 1920.
35. Benson's rationale for this program appears in "Sea Power and Its Relation to National Prosperity," undated but c. 1925, Benson Papers.
36. For indications of support for Benson's position among shipping people see *New York Herald Tribune*, 28 September 1925, and *New York Times*, 28 September 1925. For his letter to his former chief see Benson to Daniels, 7 October 1925, Benson Papers.
37. Baruch to Benson, 23 June 1925; Coolidge to Sponsors, 18 September 1925; and the Shipping Board's congratulations, 19 September 1925, all in Benson Papers. The testimonial dinner is reported in the *Washington Post*, 20 September 1925. Mayo to Benson, 24 September 1925, and Baker to Benson, 25 September 1925, both in Benson Papers.
38. For the removal of Captain Crowley see *New York Times*, 9 July 1926; Benson memorandum, 12 July 1926, Benson Papers. For his letter to Hurley see Benson to Hurley, 9 July 1926, Benson Papers.
39. Benson's views on reappointment are expressed in Benson to his son Howard Benson, 9 February 1928 and 22 April 1928, and his reaction to the president's decision is in Benson to Howard Benson, 17 May 1928, all in Klachko Files. This letter was misdated as 17 May 1929.

40. Interview, author with Captain Gatewood, 21 April 1973; Resolution of the Shipping Board, 15 March 1928, Benson Papers.

CHAPTER 16

1. Benson to Howard Benson, 27 June 1928, Klachko Files; Browning to Benson, 10 June 1928, Benson Papers.
2. Benson's brief work on a memoir is described in Benson to Howard Benson, 4 January 1929, Klachko Files. Benson's concern about the careers of his sons and their later experiences was revealed in the author's interviews with Commodore Howard H. J. Benson, 29 September 1965, and Rear Admiral Francis Wyse Benson, 3 January 1968. McGowan to Benson, 8 December 1929, AC 13,028, italics in original, and Benson to Coontz, 27 October 1932, both in Benson Papers.
3. Howdy's view is in Howard H. J. Benson, Jr., to his father, Commodore Howard H. J. Benson; for Dorothy's view see Dorothy Lucille Benson Smith to Howard H. J. Benson, 29 May 1969, both in Klachko Files.
4. Copies of Benson's letters to Frederic Krafft, 30 August 1931 and 29 September 1931, are in Klachko Files.
5. *Wesleyan Alumnae*, February 1929. An amusing story about the reproduction soon was circulated. When a guide explained to a visitor that Admiral Benson had recently donated the picture, the visitor regarded the lovely Madonna and the two children on her lap and said: "Mrs. Benson certainly had a nice face. And were those the two Benson boys?" (*Telegraph and Messenger* [Macon], 13 January 1929). The wedding anniversary produced the only photograph of Admiral Benson, Mrs. Benson, and all three children.
6. Benson to Howard Benson, 21 October 1928, Klachko Files. The original is misdated 1929.
7. Act of Congress approved 21 June 1930 (Public no. 406, 71st Cong.). Benson's commission for this advancement is dated 15 October 1930. Benson Papers. Other naval officers restored to their wartime ranks were William B. Caperton, Robert E. Coontz, Albert Gleaves, Hilary P. Jones, Henry T. Mayo, Hugh Rodman, William S. Sims, Joseph Strauss, and Henry B. Wilson. For congratulatory letters see Browning to Benson, 21 June 1931, and House to Benson, 11 August 1931, both in Benson Papers.
8. For his comment on Daniels see Benson to Belknap, 10 May 1921, Benson Reading File, NA, RG 32. For the Benson window portrait see House to Benson, 5 and 16 November 1929, both in House Papers. Others so honored were President Wilson, Premier Clemenceau, Prime Minister Lloyd George, Premier Orlando, Balfour, Grey, and General Bliss. The glass portraits are in the House Collection.
9. Letter to Editor, *Courier Citizen* (Lowell), 6 April 1922, Benson Papers.
10. For Benson's views on the World Court see Benson to S. C. Watkins, 18 July 1924, Benson Papers. For his views on the abortive naval negotiations of 1927 see Benson to E. C. Plummer, 30 July 1927, Benson Reading File, NA, RG 32. Also see a document titled "Our Interest in Sea Power and Its Equitable Limitation," undated, Jones Papers. Information about the relations between Jones and Benson is in F. W. Benson to Howard Benson, 6 September 1963, Klachko Files.
11. Benson to Browning, 14 July 1930, Benson Papers.
12. Pratt to Benson, 24 July 1928, and McGowan to Benson, 8 February 1930, italics in original, both in Benson Papers. Benson to Pratt, 28 March

1929, Pratt Papers. The Office of Naval Operations remained much as Benson had left it until 1942.

13. Circular letter to Naval Academy graduates, undated, and Benson to Browning, 14 July 1930, both in Benson Papers.

14. For an example of Benson's efforts in behalf of the American Christian Fund for Jewish Relief see Benson to William Howard Taft, 29 November 1926, Papers of William Howard Taft, Library of Congress, Manuscript Division, Washington, D.C. For his views on blacks see Benson to Curley, 14 July 1928, Benson Papers.

15. For Benson's views on women see *Washington Herald*, 5 June 1925.

16. For Benson's views on nominal Catholics see "Facts and Comments," *Catholic Mirror*, June 1921. For his views on tolerance see *Daily American Tribune*, 26 May 1925.

17. For Benson's views on the efforts of the Calvert Association see Benson to Michael Williams, 14 September 1928, and for his attitude toward the meeting of the federated societies see Father Albert Biever, S. J., to Benson, 9 October 1928, both in Benson Papers.

18. The admiral noted that he was quite busy after leaving the government in Benson to Howard Benson, 13 December 1928, Klachko Files.

19. Admiral Pratt's comments are in *New York Times*, 21 May 1932. Admiral Benson's wife, Mary Augusta Wyse Benson, died in May 1953 at the age of ninety-eight. His son Wyse died in 1968, and his son Howard in 1975. His daughter Mary Augusta "May" Krafft celebrated her 105th birthday on 2 May 1986.

20. *Baltimore Catholic Review*, 27 May 1932. Pratt wrote: Benson "was an ardent Catholic, and on his death the [C]hurch paid him as high a tribute as it is possible for a layman to receive" (Pratt, "Autobiography," p. 218).

BIBLIOGRAPHY

This biography is based on extensive research in archival collections, privately held records, and published sources and authorities. I had the distinct pleasure of using copies of some documents still in the possession of private individuals; in the notes, these are cited as being located in the Klachko Files.

The bibliography includes in the main those materials cited in the notes.

PRIVATE PAPERS AND MANUSCRIPTS IN THE UNITED STATES

U.S. Naval Academy Museum, U.S. Naval Academy, Annapolis. Bradley A. Fiske Diary (Vol. 1, 6 January 1913–24 September 1914) and Spanish Prisoners Papers (1898).

Houghton Library, Harvard University, Cambridge. Walter Hines Page Diaries and Papers and William Phillips Journals.

Franklin D. Roosevelt Library, Hyde Park, N.Y. Franklin D. Roosevelt Papers.

Library of the University of California, Irvine. Admiral Sir Rosslyn Wester Wemyss Letters and Memoirs.

Yale University Archives, Historical Manuscripts, Yale University, New Haven. Gordon Auchincloss Diary and Papers, John W. Davis Diaries and Papers (see also under Special Collection, Columbia University), Edward M. House Diary and Papers, Frank L. Polk Confidential Diaries and Papers, and Sir William Wiseman Papers.

Naval Historical Collections, Mahan Library, Naval War College, Newport, R.I. Admiral William Veazie Pratt Papers.

Special Collection, Columbia University, New York. John W. Davis (microfilm).

Princeton University Library, Princeton, N.J. Ray Stannard Baker Papers, Charles L. Swem Papers, and Woodrow Wilson Papers.

Washington, D.C. Cary T. Grayson Diaries (in possession of Cary T. Grayson, Jr.). Not open for study. Excerpts made available to author.

Library of Congress, Manuscript Division, Washington, D.C. Ray Stannard

Baker Papers, William Shepherd Benson Papers, Tasker Howard Bliss Papers, Bainbridge Colby Papers, Josephus Daniels Diaries and Papers (including Gilbert F. Close Diaries), Robert Lansing Diaries and Papers, William Gibbs McAdoo Papers, Theodore Roosevelt, Jr., Papers, William H. Taft Papers, Joseph P. Tumulty Papers, and Woodrow Wilson Papers.

Library of Congress, Naval Historical Foundation, Manuscript Division, Washington, D.C. George Dewey Papers, Bradley Fiske Diaries (Vol. 2, 26 September 1914–5 March 1917, and Vol. 3, 4 March 1917–18 September 1918), William Freeland Fullam Papers, Hilary P. Jones Papers, Stephen B. Luce Papers, Samuel McGowan Papers, and William Sowden Sims Papers.

National Archives and Records Administration, Washington, D.C.

Record Group 23: U.S. Coast and Geodetic Survey (logbooks).

Record Group 24: Records of the Bureau of Navigation and the Bureau of Naval Personnel (logbooks), Correspondence re Midshipmen (1862–1911), and U.S. Naval Academy Misc.

Record Group 32: Records of the United States Shipping Board (Benson Reading File and Benson Correspondence File).

Record Group 45: Naval Records Collection of the Office of Naval Records and Library (Subject Files, 1911–1927, and Area Files, 1911–1927).

Record Group 59: Central Files of the U.S. Department of State.

Record Group 80: General Records of the Department of the Navy (Confidential Records of the Secretary of the Navy, 1917–1919, and General Correspondence, 1916–1926).

Record Group 125: Records of the Office of the Judge Advocate General (Navy), including Fitness Reports and Naval Examining Board Records, Washington National Records Center, Suitland, Md.

Operational Archives, Naval Historical Center, Washington Navy Yard, Washington, D.C.

Central Subject Files of Correspondence and Studies.

General Board Papers.

"Proceedings of the General Board" (Vol. 7, 1915).

Special Series Relating to the Limitation of Naval Armament (1921–1968).

"United States Activity in Connection with the Armistice of 1918 and the Peace Conference of 1918" (1944). Mimeographed.

William Veazie Pratt Papers (including "Autobiography").

Joint Army and Navy Board Papers.

PRIVATE PAPERS AND MANUSCRIPTS IN GREAT BRITAIN

Beaverbrook Library, London. Private Papers of David Lloyd George (Earl of Dwyfor).

British Museum, London. Arthur James Balfour Papers (including the Ambassador to France Lord Derby Diaries and Papers), Lord Cecil's (Lord Algernon Robert Cecil, Viscount Cecil of Chelwood) Diaries and Papers, and Admiral Sir John R. Jellicoe Papers.

Foreign Office, Public Record Office, London. Memoranda and correspondence from Sir Cecil Spring Rice, Lord Reading, Sir William Wiseman, and other British representatives in the United States.

Naval Library, Ministry of Defense, London. Captain T. E. Crease Papers.

Private Collections, London. Lord Elibank (Lt. Col. Arthur Murray) Papers and Sir Arthur Willert Scrapbooks.
Public Record Office, London. Admiralty Papers (including Papers of the First Lord of the Admiralty, Sir Eric Geddes).
War Cabinet, Public Record Office, London.

PUBLISHED DOCUMENTS OF THE U.S. GOVERNMENT (LISTED CHRONOLOGICALLY)

U.S. Statutes at Large. Vol. 38, 1913–1915.
U.S. Navy Department. *Annual Reports of the Navy Department.* Washington, D.C.: Government Printing Office, fiscal years 1914, 1915, 1916.
U.S. Congress. House. Committee on Naval Affairs. *Hearings . . . on Estimates Submitted by the Secretary of the Navy.* 3 vols. 64th Cong., 1st sess., 1916.
U.S. Statutes at Large. Vol. 39, 1915–1917.
U.S. Congress. House. Committee on Naval Affairs. *Hearings on Naval Estimates for 1919.* 65th Cong., 3d sess., 1919.
Revised Organization Orders of the Office of Naval Operations (1 August 1919). Washington, D.C.: Government Printing Office, 1919.
U.S. Congress. House. Committee on Naval Affairs. *Hearings . . . on Estimates Submitted by the Secretary of the Navy.* 2 vols. 66th Cong., 2d sess., 1920.
U.S. Congress. Senate. *Naval Investigation: Hearings before the Subcommittee of the Committee on Naval Affairs, United States Senate.* 2 vols. 66th Cong., 2d sess., 1920. Sims-Daniels Investigation.
U.S. Office of Naval Records and Library. *Monographs.* Washington, D.C., 1920–1923.
   No. 1: *German Submarine Activities and the Atlantic Coast of the United States and Canada.* 1920.
   No. 7: *The American Naval Planning Section, London.* 1923.
U.S. Shipping Board. *Fourth Annual Report of the United States Shipping Board, Fiscal Year Ending June 30, 1920.* Washington, D.C.: Government Printing Office, 1921.
U.S. Shipping Board. *Fifth Annual Report of the United States Shipping Board, Fiscal Year Ending June 30, 1921.* Washington, D.C.: Government Printing Office, 1921.
U.S. Congress. House. *Hearings by the Select Committee of Inquiry into Operations of the United States Air Services.* 2 pts. 68th Cong., 1st sess., 1925.
U.S. Department of State. *Papers Relating to the Foreign Relations of the United States, 1917: The World War.* Supplement 2. 2 vols. Washington, D.C.: Government Printing Office, 1932.
U.S. Department of State. *Papers Relating to the Foreign Relations of the United States, 1919: The Paris Peace Conference.* 13 vols. Washington, D.C.: Government Printing Office, 1942–1947.
U.S. Congress. House. Committee on Appropriations. *Hearings before a Subcommittee: Department of Defense Appropriations for 1974.* Pt. 3. 93d Cong., 1st sess., 1974.
U.S. Naval Historical Division [now the Naval Historical Center], Department of the Navy. *Dictionary of American Naval Fighting Ships.* 8 vols. Ed. James L. Mooney, in association with Commander Richard T. Speer, USN (ret.). Washington, D.C.: Government Printing Office, 1981. See vol. 7, pp. 421–24, re *Utah.*

PUBLISHED DOCUMENTS OF GREAT BRITAIN

"Correspondence of the British Mission to South America, 1918." Presented to Parliament by Command of His Majesty, May 1919. London, 1919.
Parliamentary Debates (Commons), 5th ser., vol. 101 (1918).

AUTOBIOGRAPHIES, MEMOIRS, AND PUBLISHED PAPERS

Allard, Dean C., Jr. *Spencer Fullerton Baird and the U.S. Fish Commission: A Study in the History of American Science.* New York: Arno Press, 1978.
Baker, Ray Stannard. *Woodrow Wilson: Life and Letters.* 8 vols. Garden City, N.Y.: Doubleday, Doran, 1927–39.
Baker, Ray Stannard, and William E. Dodd, eds. *The Public Papers of Woodrow Wilson.* 6 vols. New York: Harper & Brothers, 1925–27.
Beaverbrook, Lord. *Men and Power, 1917–1918.* London: Hutchinson, 1956.
Coletta, Paolo E. *Admiral Bradley A. Fiske and the American Navy.* Lawrence: Regents Press of Kansas, 1979.
———, ed. *American Secretaries of the Navy.* 2 vols. Annapolis: Naval Institute Press, 1980.
Cronon, E. David, ed. *The Cabinet Diaries of Josephus Daniels, 1913–1921.* Lincoln: University of Nebraska Press, 1963.
Daniels, Jonathan. *The End of Innocence.* Philadelphia: J. B. Lippincott, 1954.
Daniels, Josephus. *The Wilson Era: Years of Peace, 1910–1917.* Chapel Hill: University of North Carolina Press, 1946.
———. *The Wilson Era: Years of War and After, 1917–1923.* Chapel Hill: University of North Carolina Press, 1946.
Davis, Burke. *The Billy Mitchell Affair.* New York: Random House, 1967.
Dawson, Francis Warrington, ed. *The War Memoirs of William Graves Sharp: American Ambassador to France, 1914–1919.* London: Constable, 1931.
Dewey, George. *Autobiography of George Dewey, Admiral of the Navy.* New York: Charles Scribner's Sons, 1913.
Fisher, Admiral of the Fleet Lord. *Memories and Records.* Vol. 2. London: Hodder & Stoughton, 1919.
Fiske, Bradley A. *From Midshipman to Rear Admiral.* New York: Century, 1919.
Foch, Marshal Ferdinand. *The Memoirs of Marshal Foch.* Garden City, N.Y.: Doubleday, Doran, 1931.
Freidel, Frank. *Franklin D. Roosevelt.* 3 vols. Boston: Little, Brown, 1952–56.
Hurley, Edward N. *The Bridge to France.* Philadelphia: J. B. Lippincott, 1927.
Lawrence, David. *The True Story of Woodrow Wilson.* New York: George Doran, 1924.
Lejeune, John Archer. *The Reminiscences of a Marine.* Philadelphia: Dorrance, 1930.
Lloyd George, David. *Memoirs of the Peace Conference.* 2 vols. New Haven: Yale University Press, 1939.
———. *War Memoirs of David Lloyd George.* 6 vols. London: Ivor Nicholson & Watson, 1933–36.
Morison, Elting E. *Admiral Sims and the Modern American Navy.* Boston: Houghton Mifflin, 1942.
Palmer, Frederick. *Newton D. Baker: America at War.* 2 vols. New York: Dodd, Mead, 1931.

————. *Bliss, Peacemaker: The Life and Letters of General Tasker Howard Bliss.* New York: Dodd, Mead, 1934.
Patterson, A. Temple, ed. *The Jellicoe Papers: Selection from the Private and Official Correspondence of Admiral of the Fleet Earl Jellicoe.* Vol. 2, 1916–1935. London: Naval Records Society, 1968.
Pershing, John J. *My Experiences in the World War.* 2 vols. New York: Frederick A. Stokes, 1931.
Seager, Robert II. *Alfred Thayer Mahan: The Man and His Letters.* Annapolis: Naval Institute Press, 1977.
Seymour, Charles. *The Intimate Papers of Colonel House.* 4 vols. London: Ernest Benn, 1926–28.
Sims, William Sowden, in collaboration with Burton J. Hendrick. *The Victory at Sea.* Garden City: Doubleday, Page, 1920. Reprint. Ed. David F. Trask. Annapolis: Naval Institute Press, 1984.
Spector, Ronald. *Admiral of the New Empire: The Life and Career of George Dewey.* Baton Rouge: Louisiana State University Press, 1974.
Stirling, Yates. *Sea Duty: The Memoirs of a Fighting Admiral.* New York: G. P. Putnam's Sons, 1939.
Wemyss, Lady Wester. *Life and Letters of Lord Wester Wemyss . . . Admiral of the Fleet.* London: Eyre and Spottiswoode, 1935.
Wheeler, Gerald E. *Admiral William Veazie Pratt, U.S. Navy: A Sailor's Life.* Washington, D.C.: Naval Historical Division, Department of the Navy, 1974.

SECONDARY WORKS

Albion, Robert Greenhalgh. *Makers of Naval Policy, 1798–1947.* Ed. Rowena Reed. Annapolis: Naval Institute Press, 1980.
Arthur, Reginald Wright. *Contact: Careers of U.S. Naval Aviators Assigned Numbers 1 to 2,000.* Washington, D.C.: Naval Aviators Register, 1967.
Bane, Suda Lorena, and Ralph Haswell Lutz, eds. *The Blockade of Germany after the Armistice, 1918–1919.* Stanford, Calif.: Stanford University Press, 1942.
Benson, William Shepherd. *The Merchant Marine: "A Necessity in Time of War; A Source of Independence and Strength in Time of Peace."* New York: Macmillan, 1923.
Braisted, William Reynolds. *The United States Navy in the Pacific, 1909–1922.* Austin: University of Texas Press, 1971.
Churchill, Winston S. *The World Crisis.* New York: Charles Scribner's Sons, 1923.
Clephane, Lewis P. *History of the Naval Overseas Transportation Service in World War I.* Washington, D.C.: Government Printing Office, 1961.
Fowler, Wilton B. *British-American Relations, 1917–1918: The Role of Sir William Wiseman.* Princeton, N.J.: Princeton University Press, 1969.
Frothingham, Thomas G. *The Naval History of the World War.* 3 vols. Vol. 3, *The United States in the War, 1917–1918.* Cambridge: Harvard University Press, 1926.
Gelfand, Lawrence E. *The Inquiry: American Preparations for Peace, 1917–1919.* New Haven: Yale University Press, 1963.
Hagan, Kenneth J., ed. *In Peace and War: Interpretations of American Naval History, 1775–1978.* Westport, Conn.: Greenwood Press, 1978.
Heinl, Robert Debs, Jr. *Soldiers of the Sea: The United States Marine Corps, 1775–1962.* Annapolis: Naval Institute Press, 1962.

Howeth, Linwood S. *History of Communications: Electronics in the United States.* Washington, D.C.: Government Printing Office, 1963.

Kittredge, Tracy Barrett. *Naval Lessons of the Great War.* Garden City, N.Y.: Doubleday, Page, 1921.

Levine, Isaac Don. *Mitchell, Pioneer of Air Power.* London: P. Davies, 1943.

Love, Robert William, Jr., ed. *The Chiefs of Naval Operations.* Annapolis: Naval Institute Press, 1980.

Luce, Stephen B. *Text-Book of Seamanship: The Equipping and Handling of Vessels under Sail for the Use of the United States Naval Academy.* Revised by Lieutenant W. S. Benson, USN. New York: D. Van Nostrand, 1898.

Marder, Arthur J. *From the Dreadnought to Scapa Flow.* 6 vols. Vol. 2, *The War Years: To the Eve of Jutland, 1914–1916.* Vol. 4, *1917: Year of Crisis.* London: Oxford University Press, 1966, 1969.

Payne, George Henry. *England: Her Treatment of America.* New York: Sears Publishing, 1931.

Roskill, Stephen. *Naval Policy between the Wars.* 2 vols. Vol. 1, *The Period of Anglo-American Antagonism, 1919–1929.* London: Collins, St. James's Place, 1968.

Rudin, Harry R. *Armistice, 1918.* New Haven: Yale University Press, 1944.

Safford, Jeffrey J. *Wilsonian Maritime Diplomacy, 1913–1921.* New Brunswick, N.J.: Rutgers University Press, 1978.

Smith, Darrell Hevenor, and Paul V. Bettors. *The United States Shipping Board: Its History, Activities, and Organization.* Washington, D.C.: Brookings Institute, 1931.

Times (of London). *The History of the Times.* 2 pts. Pt. 1, *1912–1920.* Pt. 2, *1921–1948.* London: Office of the *Times,* 1952.

Trask, David F. *Captains and Cabinets: Anglo-American Naval Relations, 1917–1918.* Columbia: University of Missouri Press, 1972.

————. *The United States in the Supreme War Council: American War Aims and Inter-Allied Strategy, 1917–1918.* Middletown, Conn.: Wesleyan University Press, 1961.

Tuchman, Barbara W. *The Zimmermann Telegram.* New York: Viking Press, 1958.

Turnbull, Archibald D., and Clifford L. Lord. *History of United States Naval Aviation.* New Haven: Yale University Press, 1949.

UNPUBLISHED DISSERTATIONS, AUTOBIOGRAPHIES, REMINISCENCES, AND MANUSCRIPTS

Costello, Daniel Joseph. "Planning for War: A History of the General Board of the Navy, 1900–1914." Ph.D. diss., Fletcher School of Law and Diplomacy, 1968. Copy in Naval Historical Center, Washington Navy Yard, Washington, D.C.

Klachko, Mary. "Anglo-American Naval Competition, 1918–1922." Ph.D. diss., Columbia University, 1962. Copy in Naval Historical Center, Washington Navy Yard, Washington, D.C.

Knight, Austin M., and William D. Puleston. "History of the United States Naval War College." 1916. Naval War College Archives, Newport, R.I. Mimeographed.

Pratt, William V. "Autobiography." Pratt Papers, Naval Historical Center, Washington Navy Yard, Washington, D.C.

"Reminiscences of Admiral Thomas C. Hart." Oral history, Columbia University. Copy in Naval Historical Center, Washington Navy Yard, Washington, D.C.

"Reminiscences of Rear Admiral Harold Cecil Train." Oral history, Columbia University. Copy in Naval Historical Center, Washington Navy Yard, Washington, D.C.

Socas, Roberto Enrique. "France, Naval Armaments, and Naval Disarmament: 1918–1922." Ph.D. diss., Columbia University, 1965. University Microfilms no. 65-568.

U.S. Naval War College. "Outline History of the United States Naval War College, 1884 to Date." Naval War College Archives, Newport, R.I.

ARTICLES IN NEWSPAPERS AND PERIODICALS

"Became Distinguished Admiral Despite Early Flunk in Math." *Evening Star* (Washington), 24 October 1922.

"Captain Benson Is Appointed Chief of Naval Operations." *Philadelphia Inquirer*, 29 April 1915.

Daniels, Josephus. "March of Events: Britain Demanded at Paris to Woodrow Wilson Curtail the U.S. Navy." *New York Journal American*, 23 January 1927.

———. "The Navy Transports Set Records to Carry Out Gigantic Task." *Evening Star* (Washington), 13 May 1921.

"Denies Pacific Rate War." *Washington Post*, 23 August 1920.

Duffy, Patric R., C.S.C. "A Great and Honorable Man." *Columbia*, April 1933.

"Facts and Comments." *Catholic Mirror*, June 1921.

"Fiske Says Navy Is Unprepared to Guard Coast." *New York Times*, 15 June 1915.

"Georgia Opponents Oppose Honor Benson." *Catholic Standard and Times*, 28 August 1920.

"The Giant *Utah* Shatters Speed Records of Navy: In Dash at Twenty-Two Knots Proves Herself Fastest of Battleships." *New York Herald*, 12 September 1911.

"The Merchant Marine." *Washington Post*, 5 July 1920.

Morrow, James B. "Who Should Run Our Ships?" *Nation's Business*, October 1920.

"New Destroyers." *Journal of the Royal United Service Institution* 62 (1917).

"New Navy Boss a Hard Worker: Rear Admiral Benson Takes Firm Hold as Chief of Naval Operations, Experienced by Long and Varied Service." *Public Ledger* (Philadelphia), 16 May 1915.

"Prepare for War to Assure Peace, Advice of Admiral Benson." *North American*, 6 June 1915.

"Scarcity of Fuel Bared by Benson." *World's Business*, 30 April 1920.

"Secret Document Reveals Britain's Darkest Hour: Lloyd George's Moving Appeal to America—the United States Gives Pledges and Redeems Them." *Current History* 22, no. 4 (July 1925).

"Ship Independence Is Aim of America." *Pittsburgh Dispatch*, 19 September 1920.

"U.S. German Ship Deal 100 Percent American, Admiral Benson Says." *Washington Herald*, 9 September 1920.

"Wants to Have the Fleet Quit New London for Good." *Telegram* (New London, Conn.), 5 July 1908.

SCHOLARLY ARTICLES

Allard, Dean C., Jr. "Admiral William S. Sims and United States Naval Policy in World War I." *American Neptune*, April 1975.

———. "Anglo-American Naval Differences during World War I." *Military Affairs*, April 1980.

Coletta, Paolo. "Josephus Daniels." In vol. 2 of *American Secretaries of the Navy*, ed. Paolo E. Coletta. 2 vols. Annapolis: Naval Institute Press, 1980.

Paullin, Charles Oscar. "A Half-Century of Naval Administration in America, 1861–1911." *U.S. Naval Institute Proceedings*, September 1913.

Symonds, Craig L. "William Veazie Pratt: 17 September 1930–30 June 1933." In *The Chiefs of Naval Operations*, ed. Robert William Love, Jr. Annapolis: Naval Institute Press, 1980.

Trask, David F. "The American Navy in a World at War, 1914–1919." In *In Peace and War: Interpretations of American Naval History, 1775–1978*, ed. Kenneth J. Hagan. Westport, Conn.: Greenwood Press, 1978.

———. "William Shepherd Benson: 11 May 1915–25 September 1919." In *The Chiefs of Naval Operations*, ed. Robert William Love, Jr. Annapolis: Naval Institute Press, 1980.

———. "Woodrow Wilson and International Statecraft: A Modern Assessment." *Naval War College Review*, March–April 1983.

INDEX

Benson, Adm. William Shepherd, *cont'd*:
naval building program, 142;
delivers memo on disposition of
German and Austrian fleets to
Wilson, arguing for naval parity
with Britain, 143; expresses concern
about the application of the principle
of the league to Germany, 144; seeks
to dissuade Daniels from supporting
distribution, 144; quarrels with
Wemyss, 144; in inter-Allied
meeting, expresses views on British
desire for naval supremacy, 145–46;
threatens Long with naval war, 147;
proposes that Daniels visit Rome
and not return to Paris, 148;
maintains inflexible position on
naval parity with Britain, 148;
opposes meeting between Daniels
and British naval leaders prior to
Daniels's meeting with president,
148; views of, on Anglo-American
relations, 149; makes arrangements
to bring *George Washington* to
Europe, 150; participation of, in
Paris negotiations, 153; retains
control of Navy Department while in
Paris, 154; informs Daniels of desire
to return to Washington from Paris
negotiations, 154–55; responds
decisively to perceived challenges to
his instructions to Navy Department,
155; demonstrates regard for Pratt,
155; reacts against unauthorized
initiative by Adm. Mayo, 155;
approves reassignment of Sims to
presidency of Naval War College,
156; works on naval building
program for 1919, 156; seeks to
reorganize fleet, creating Atlantic
Fleet and Pacific Fleet, 157; interests
himself in Destroyer Force, 157;
deals with lesser naval issues, 157–
58; opposes increase in size of Board
of Inspection and Survey, 158;
writes McKean in support of Adm.
Andrews's scheme to reduce
maritime disasters, 158; devotes
attention to naval communications,
158–59; writes Daniels in support
of government control of radio
communications, 159; states belief
that Wilson should threaten break
with Allies if necessary to assure
their support for League of Nations,
159; receives extension of term as
CNO by recess appointment, 159–
60; continues opposition to

distribution of German fleet, 160–
61; seeks to convince Wilson to
specify distribution of German fleet
in treaty of peace, 160–61; writes
Daniels about his fear of British
naval threat, 161; warns Wilson
about prospect of trade rivalry with
Britain, 161; returns to U.S. after
service in Paris, 161–63; seeks
arrangements to protect German
missionaries from losing property
and posts in former German
colonies, 162; receives decorations
for wartime services, 162; comments
on League of Nations and naval
aviation, 163; reorganizes Office of
Naval Operations, 163–65; puts
reorganization orders into effect,
165; supports expansion of naval
aviation, 166–67; opposes separate
department of aeronautics, 166–67;
continues support of naval building
and naval parity with Great Britain,
167; retires without permanent rank
of full admiral, 168; explains his
warning to Sims about British naval
policies, 170–71; describes Sims's
motives privately to Woodson, 171;
is recalled to active duty to prepare
testimony for Senate on Sims's
charges, 171; views of, on civilian
control of military, 172; refrains
from commenting publicly during
naval investigation, 172; is made
Knight of the Order of the Grand
Cross of St. Gregory the Great,
Military Class, 174; considers Sims's
testimony an outrage, 173; testifies
before Senate investigation, 174–78;
supports strengthened authority for
future CNOs in testimony before
Senate investigation, 177; expresses
view of Daniels, 177–78; explains
his statement to Sims about British
deception, 178; writes to Browning
about his testimony before Senate
investigation, 178; refutes Sims's
characterization of his testimony,
178–79; suffers at hands of scholars
and publicists, 179; fails to defend
himself in print, 179; is asked by
Wilson to become head of Shipping
Board, 180; accepts invitation to
join faculty of University of Notre
Dame, 181; is appointed chairman
of U.S. Shipping Board, 181;
assumes formidable task as chairman
of Shipping Board, 182; gives notice

Jellicoe, Adm. Sir John R., *cont'd*:
Benson, 82; indicates to Pratt his
wish for Benson to visit London, 87;
notes problems associated with
attacks on German naval bases, 93;
writes Beatty and criticizes Benson,
93; comments on strategy of Grand
Fleet in memo for War Cabinet, 94;
discusses formation of a naval
council, 97; is removed from office,
104; mentioned, 65, 82, 83, 88, 90,
98, 106
Joint Board of the Army and Navy, 42
Jones, Adm. Hilary, 36, 202
Jones, John Paul, 195
Jones, Sen. Wesley (D.-Wash.), 185
Jones Act. *See* Merchant Marine Act of
1920
Jupiter, USS (collier and aircraft
carrier), 166
Jutland, Battle of, 49, 90, 91

Kearsarge, USS (battleship), 14
Kiel Canal, 143
Kitchin, Rep. Claude (D.-N.C.), 49
Knapp, Rear Adm. Harry S., 161
Knight, Adm. Austin M., 106
Knox, Commander Dudley W., 29, 78,
95, 199
Krafft, Frederic, 199
Krafft, Herman, 199
Krafft, Mary Augusta Benson ("May"),
7, 136

Laning, Capt. Harris, 107
Lansing, Secretary of State Robert, 57,
112, 116, 131, 133, 134
Lasker, Albert D., 188, 192
Lawrence, David, 83
League of Nations, 54, 119, 120, 136,
138, 142, 144, 147, 148, 160, 163,
167, 202
League of Nations Commission, 151
Lejeune, Col. John A., 31
Leygues, Minister of Marine Georges,
63, 98, 141
Liberty airplane motor, 45
Light-House Board, 92
Lisle, R. Mason, 174
Lloyd George, Prime Minister David:
forces Admiralty to adopt convoy,
70; gives Geddes instructions
concerning Wilson and peace
initiatives, 119; informs House that
Britain cannot give up right of
blockade, 122; informs House that

Britain accepts the Fourteen Points
but reserves views on freedom of
seas, 123; offers compromise on
disposition of German fleet, 124;
debates naval terms with House,
124–25; successfully proposes
dismantling of German U-boats,
138; makes proposals intended to
avoid naval armaments race, 142;
links support for Monroe Doctrine
to American concessions on naval
construction, 150; supports
American position on Monroe
Doctrine, even without naval
agreement, 151; opposes specifying
disposition of German fleet in treaty
of peace with Germany, 160;
mentioned, 55, 66, 82, 96, 97, 131,
134, 137, 146, 148, 149, 161, 183
Lodge, Sen. Henry Cabot (R.-Mass.),
27, 138
London Naval Conference of 1930,
202
London Planning Section. *See* Planning
Section, London
Long, First Lord of the Admiralty
Walter, 146, 147, 148, 150, 189,
191
Long, Rear Adm. Andrew J., 134, 163
Long, Secretary of the Navy John D.,
12
Lord Commissioner of His Majesty's
Treasury, 133
Lord Commissioner of the Admiralty,
133
Lostende, Adm. Maurice Henry de, 63
Luce, Adm. Stephen B., 11
Lusitania, HMS, 46

McCandless, Lt. Byron, 33
McCloskey, John Cardinal, 7
McCormick, Vance, 158
McDougall, Capt. William D., 95
McGowan, Rear Adm. Samuel, 198,
203
McKean, Rear Adm. Josiah S.:
becomes assistant for materiel in
Navy Department, 39; summarizes
dilemma facing Navy Department,
84; replaces Pratt as assistant CNO,
155; defends Navy Department
against Sims's charges, 173;
mentioned, 158, 159, 179
Maclay, Sir Joseph P., 97
McNamee, Capt. Luke, 95, 143, 161,
163
Madison, Lt. Comdr. Zachariah H., 29